59372083278
D0337798

amity BLAmity

BOOK ONE

by mike white

SLG

Amity Blamity Book One is ™ & © 2011 by
Mike White. All rights reserved. No part of this
book may be reproduced, except for brief
excerpts for purposes of review, without the
expressed written permission of Mike White
and SLG Publishing.

Published by SLG Publishing
577 S. Market Street San Jose, CA 95113
www.slgcomic.com

ISBN 978-1-59362-209-1
Printed in Canada

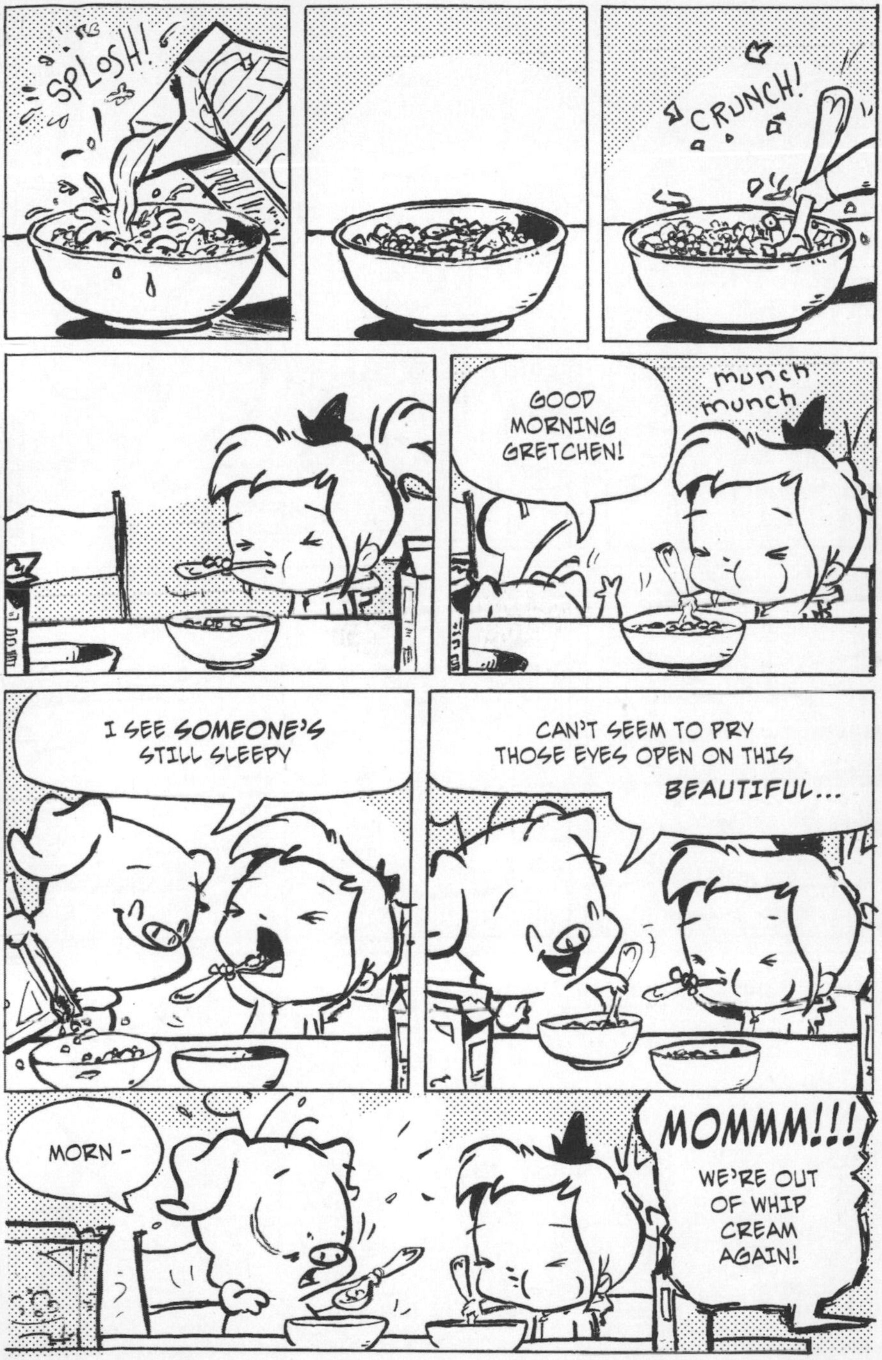
SPLOSH!
CRUNCH!
GOOD MORNING GRETCHEN!
munch munch
I SEE SOMEONE'S STILL SLEEPY
CAN'T SEEM TO PRY THOSE EYES OPEN ON THIS BEAUTIFUL...
MORN -
MOMMM!!!
WE'RE OUT OF WHIP CREAM AGAIN!

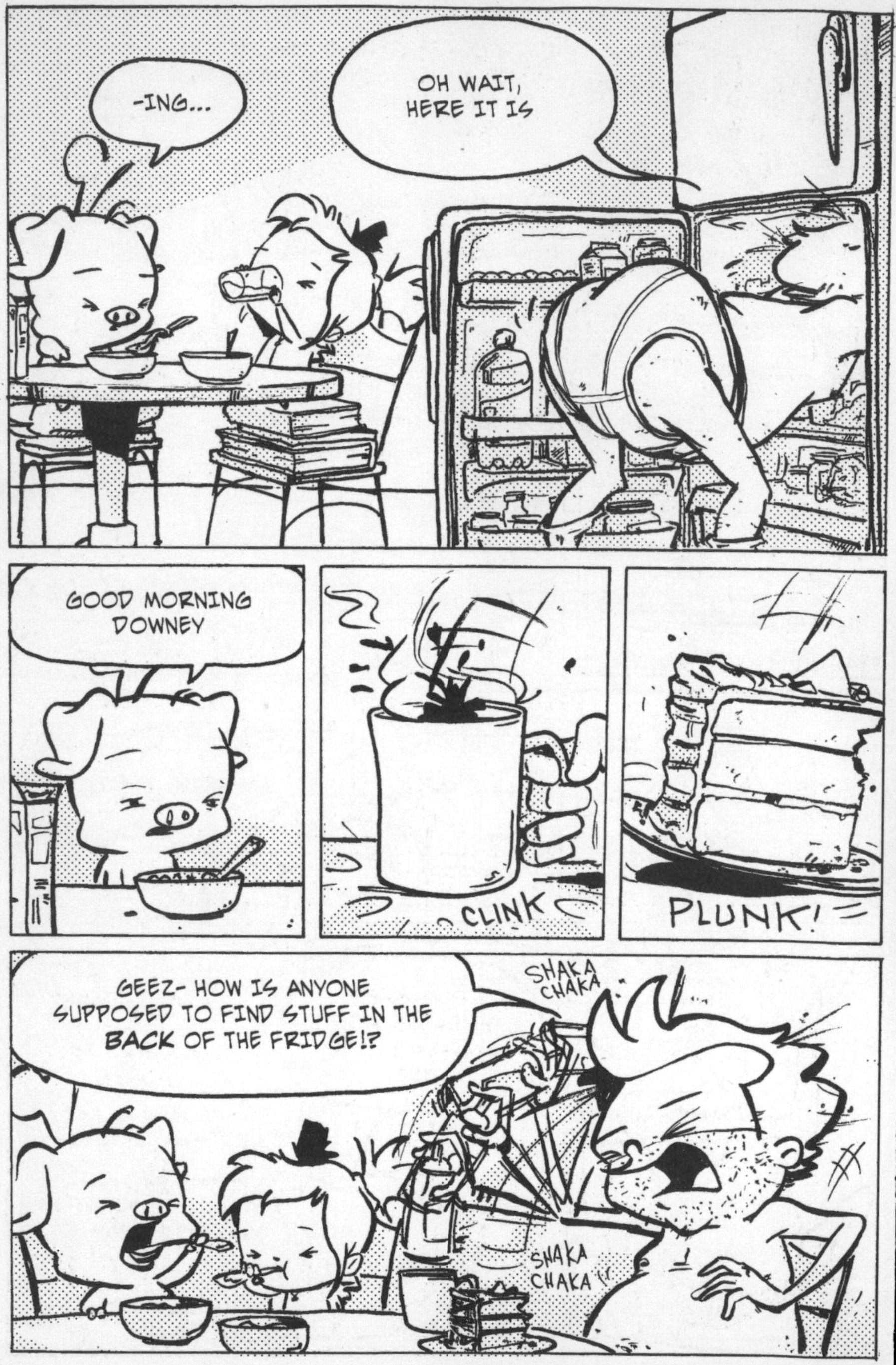
-ING...
OH WAIT, HERE IT IS
GOOD MORNING DOWNEY
CLINK
PLUNK!
GEEZ- HOW IS ANYONE SUPPOSED TO FIND STUFF IN THE BACK OF THE FRIDGE!?
SHAKA CHAKA
SHAKA CHAKA

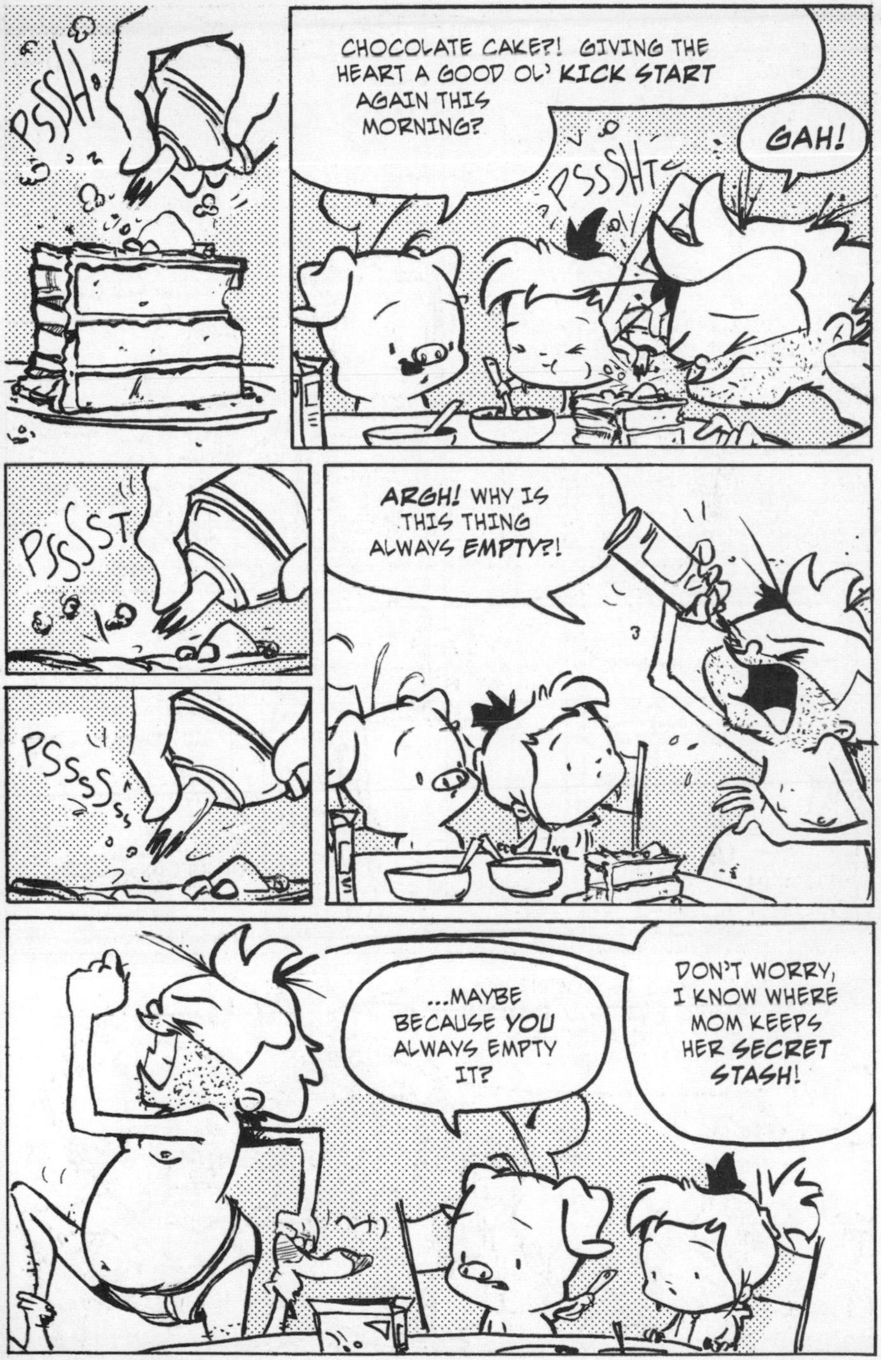
PSSH
CHOCOLATE CAKE?! GIVING THE HEART A GOOD OL' KICK START AGAIN THIS MORNING?
PSSSHT
GAH!
PSSST
PSSSS
ARGH! WHY IS THIS THING ALWAYS EMPTY?!
...MAYBE BECAUSE YOU ALWAYS EMPTY IT?
DON'T WORRY, I KNOW WHERE MOM KEEPS HER SECRET STASH!

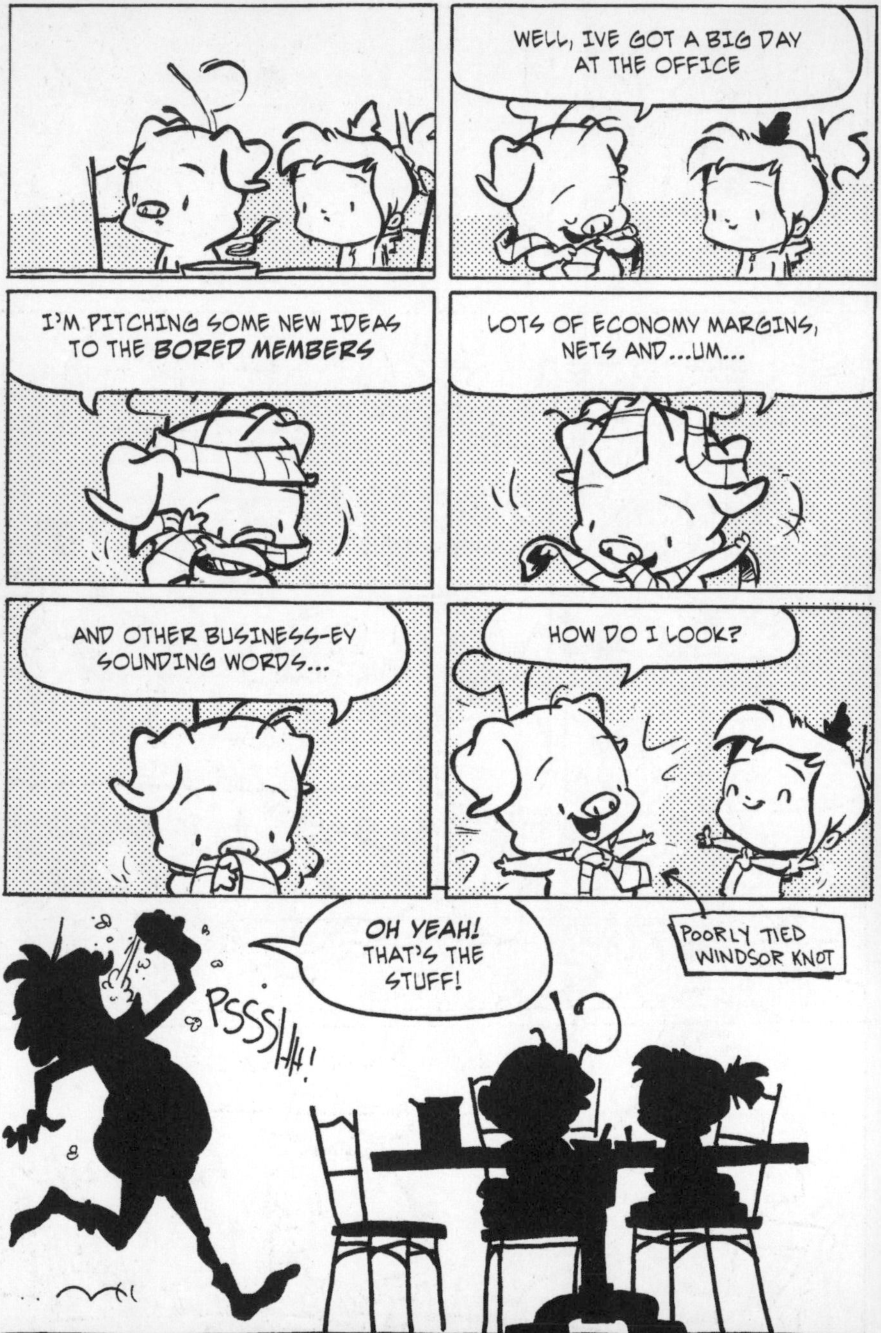
WELL, IVE GOT A BIG DAY AT THE OFFICE
I'M PITCHING SOME NEW IDEAS TO THE BORED MEMBERS
LOTS OF ECONOMY MARGINS, NETS AND...UM...
AND OTHER BUSINESS-EY SOUNDING WORDS...
HOW DO I LOOK?
POORLY TIED WINDSOR KNOT
OH YEAH! THAT'S THE STUFF!
PSSSHH!

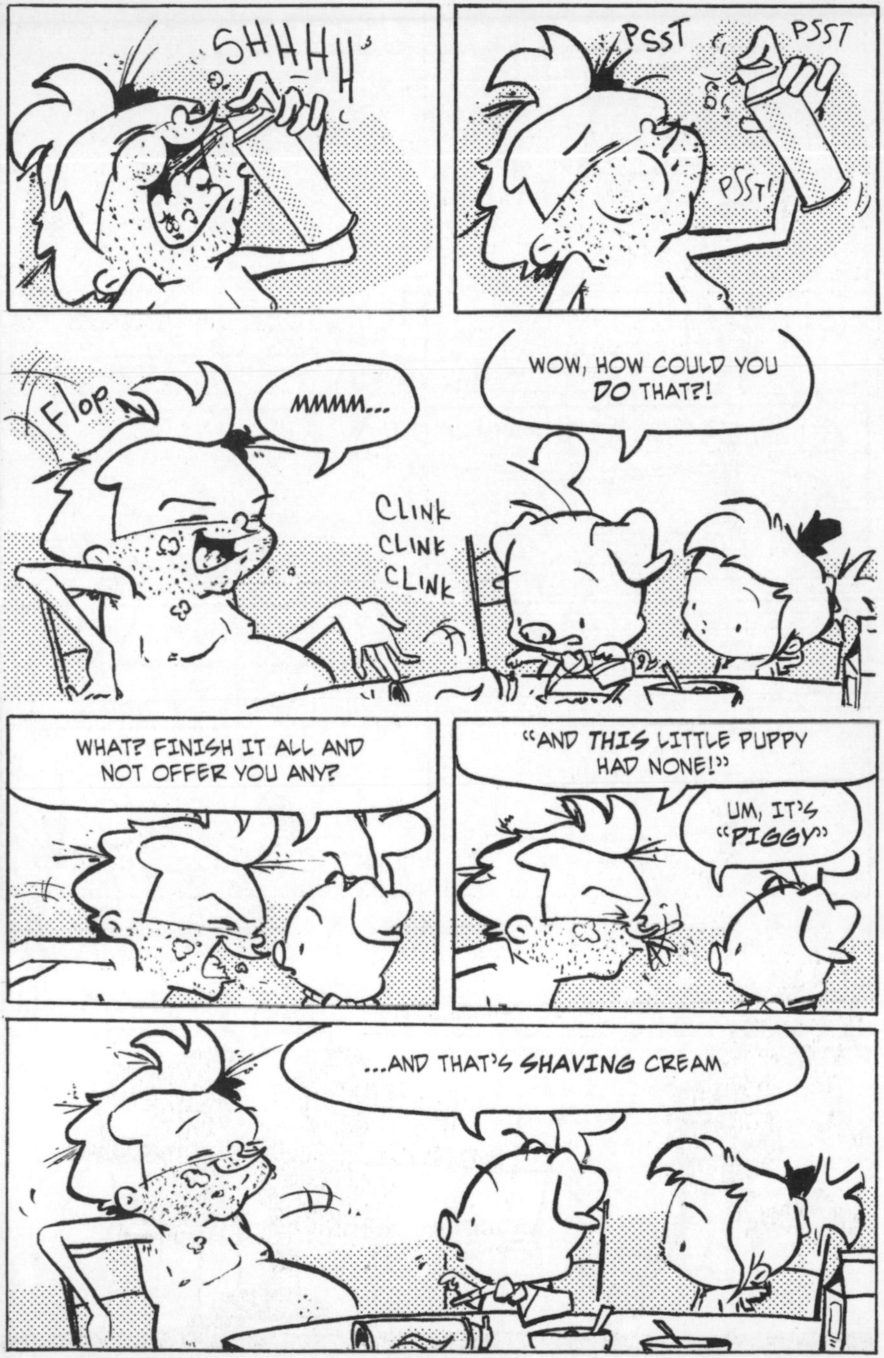
SHHHH
PSST
PSST
PSST!
Flop
MMMM...
WOW, HOW COULD YOU DO THAT?!
CLINK
CLINK
CLINK
WHAT? FINISH IT ALL AND NOT OFFER YOU ANY?
"AND THIS LITTLE PUPPY HAD NONE!"
UM, IT'S "PIGGY"
...AND THAT'S SHAVING CREAM

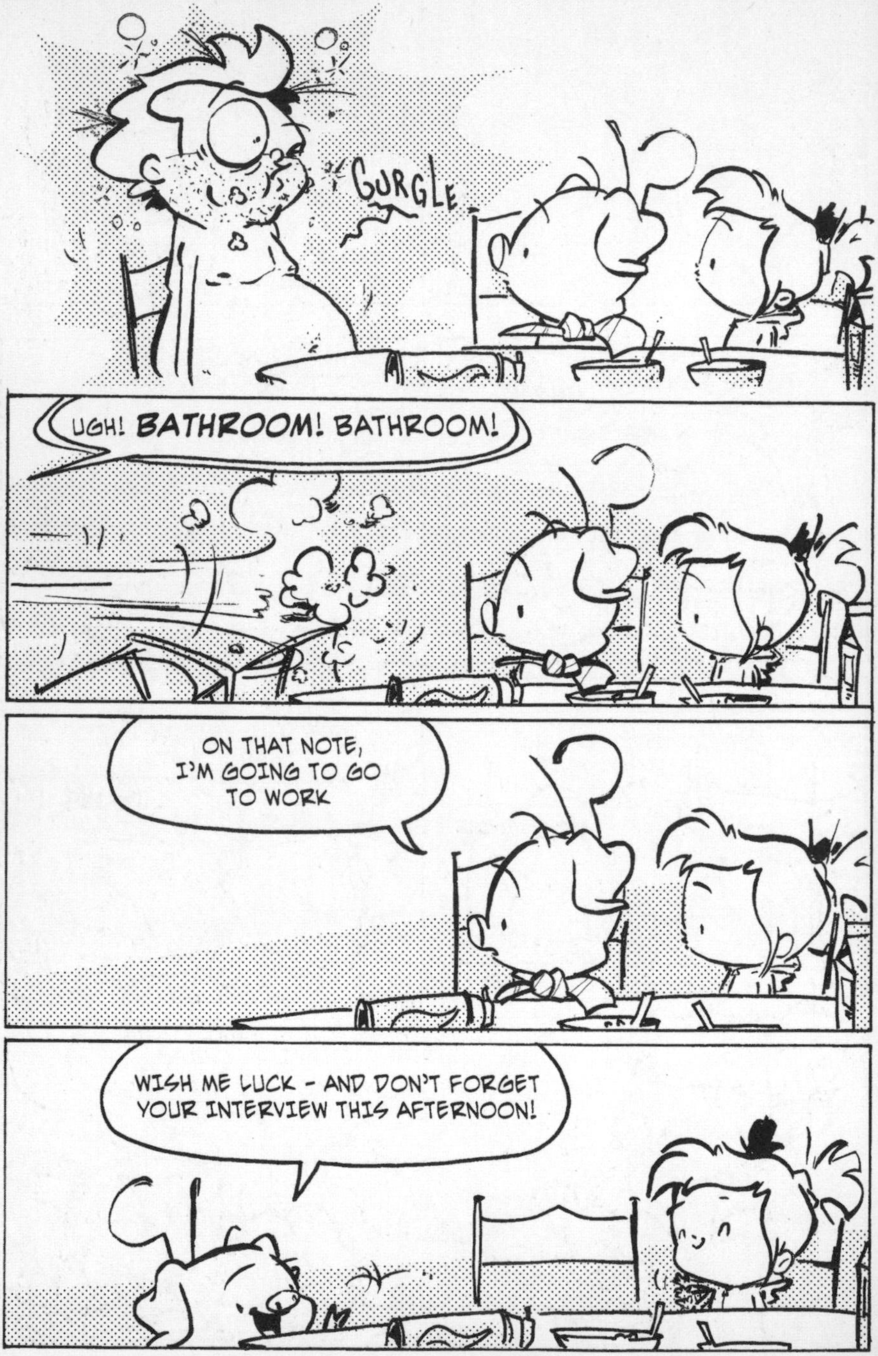
GURGLE
UGH! BATHROOM! BATHROOM!
ON THAT NOTE, I'M GOING TO GO TO WORK
WISH ME LUCK - AND DON'T FORGET YOUR INTERVIEW THIS AFTERNOON!

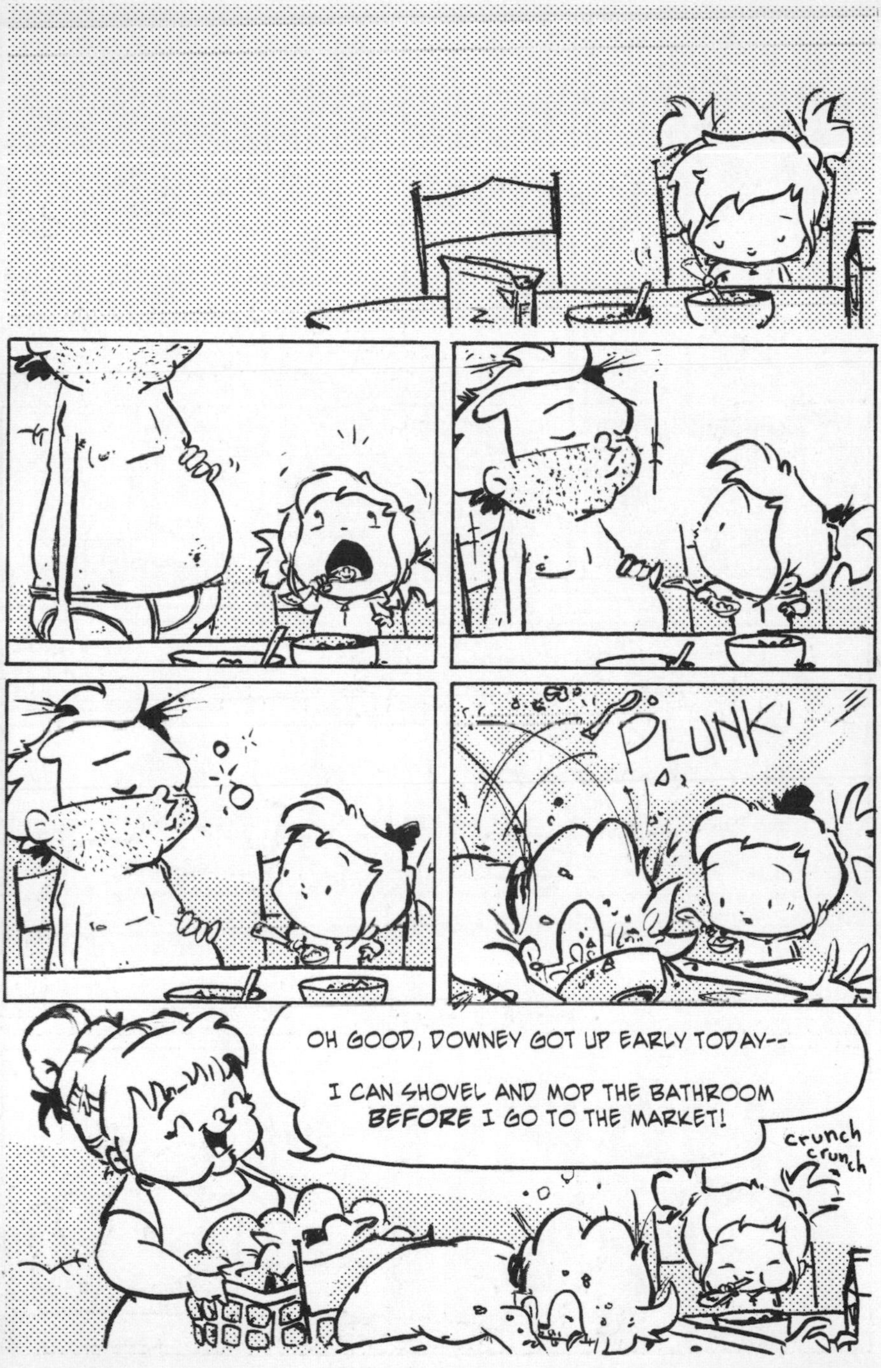
PLUNK!
OH GOOD, DOWNEY GOT UP EARLY TODAY--
I CAN SHOVEL AND MOP THE BATHROOM BEFORE I GO TO THE MARKET!
crunch crunch

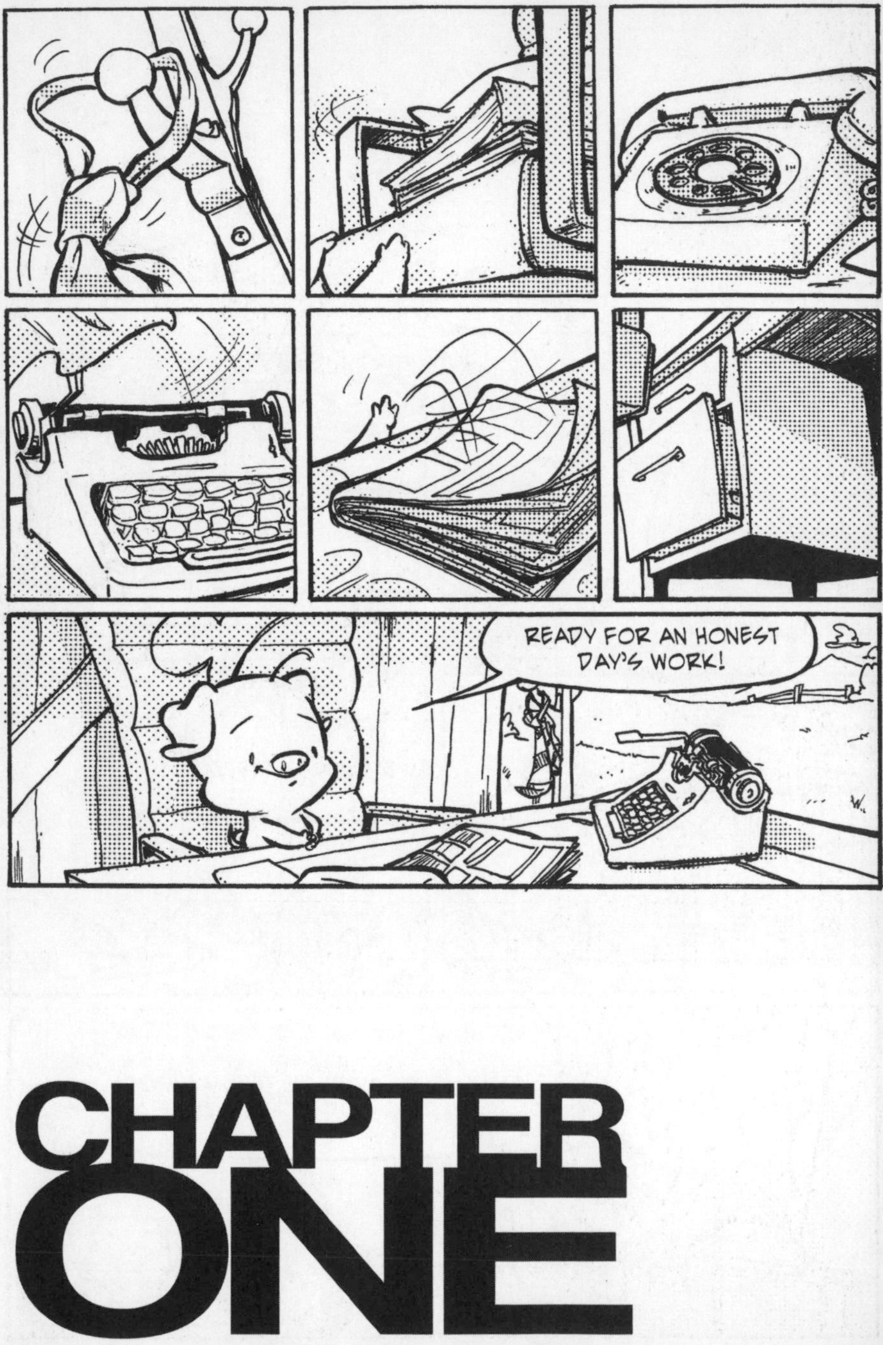
READY FOR AN HONEST DAY'S WORK!

CHAPTER ONE

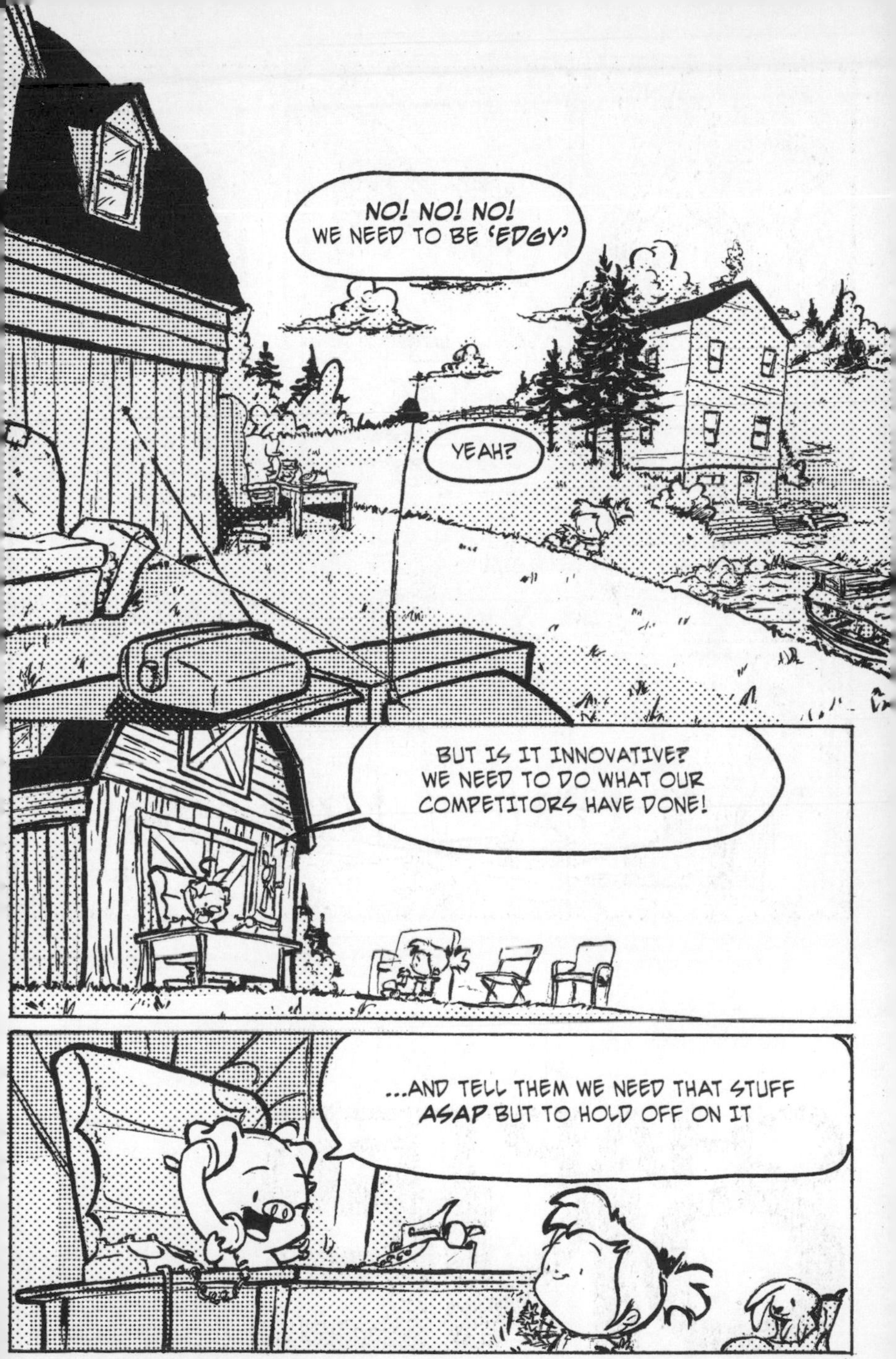
NO! NO! NO!
WE NEED TO BE 'EDGY'
YEAH?
BUT IS IT INNOVATIVE?
WE NEED TO DO WHAT OUR COMPETITORS HAVE DONE!
...AND TELL THEM WE NEED THAT STUFF ASAP BUT TO HOLD OFF ON IT

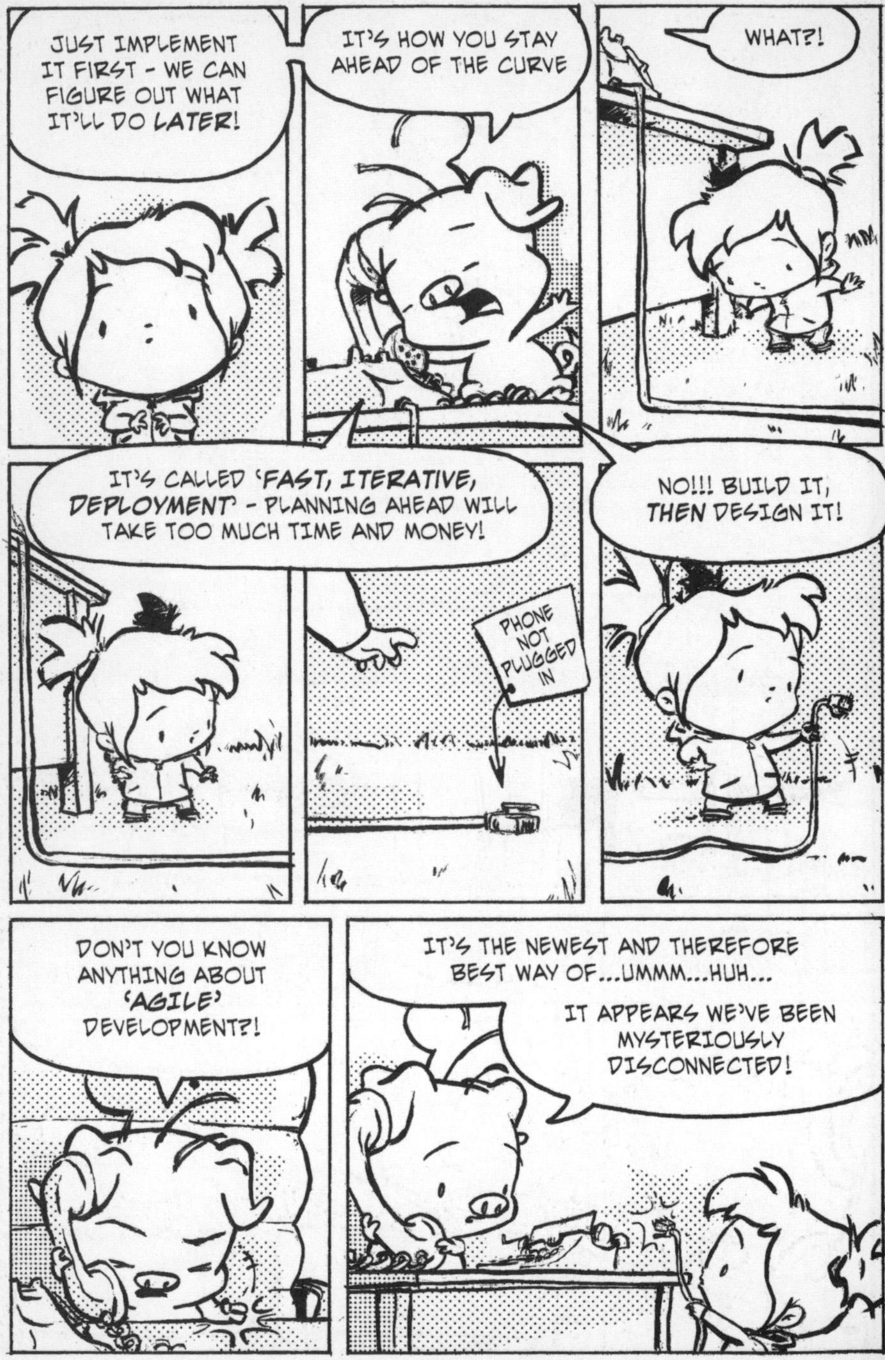
JUST IMPLEMENT IT FIRST - WE CAN FIGURE OUT WHAT IT'LL DO LATER!
IT'S HOW YOU STAY AHEAD OF THE CURVE
WHAT?!
IT'S CALLED 'FAST, ITERATIVE, DEPLOYMENT' - PLANNING AHEAD WILL TAKE TOO MUCH TIME AND MONEY!
PHONE NOT PLUGGED IN
NO!!! BUILD IT, THEN DESIGN IT!
DON'T YOU KNOW ANYTHING ABOUT 'AGILE' DEVELOPMENT?!
IT'S THE NEWEST AND THEREFORE BEST WAY OF...UMMM...HUH...
IT APPEARS WE'VE BEEN MYSTERIOUSLY DISCONNECTED!

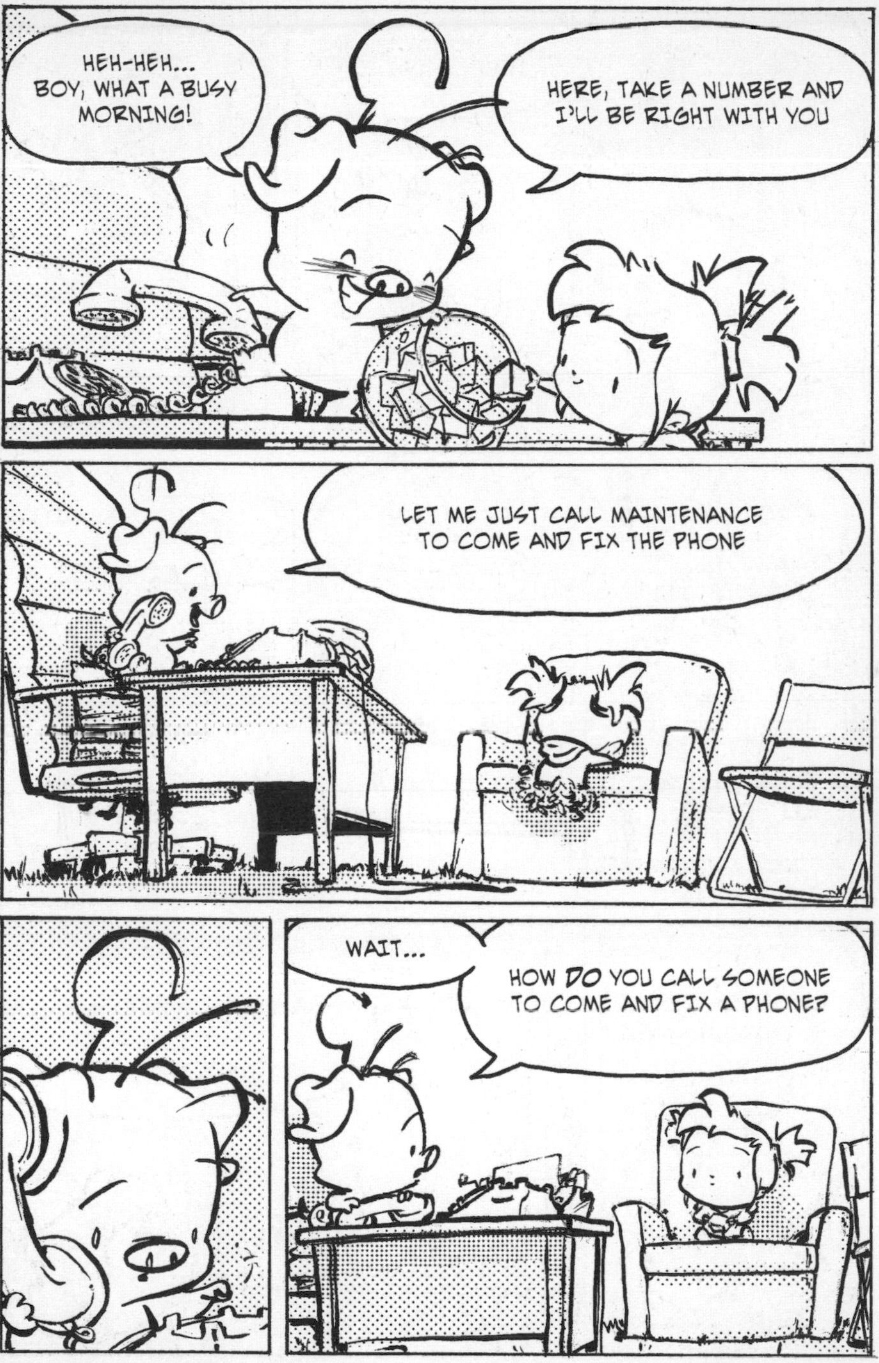
HEH-HEH...
BOY, WHAT A BUSY MORNING!
HERE, TAKE A NUMBER AND I'LL BE RIGHT WITH YOU
LET ME JUST CALL MAINTENANCE TO COME AND FIX THE PHONE
WAIT...
HOW DO YOU CALL SOMEONE TO COME AND FIX A PHONE?

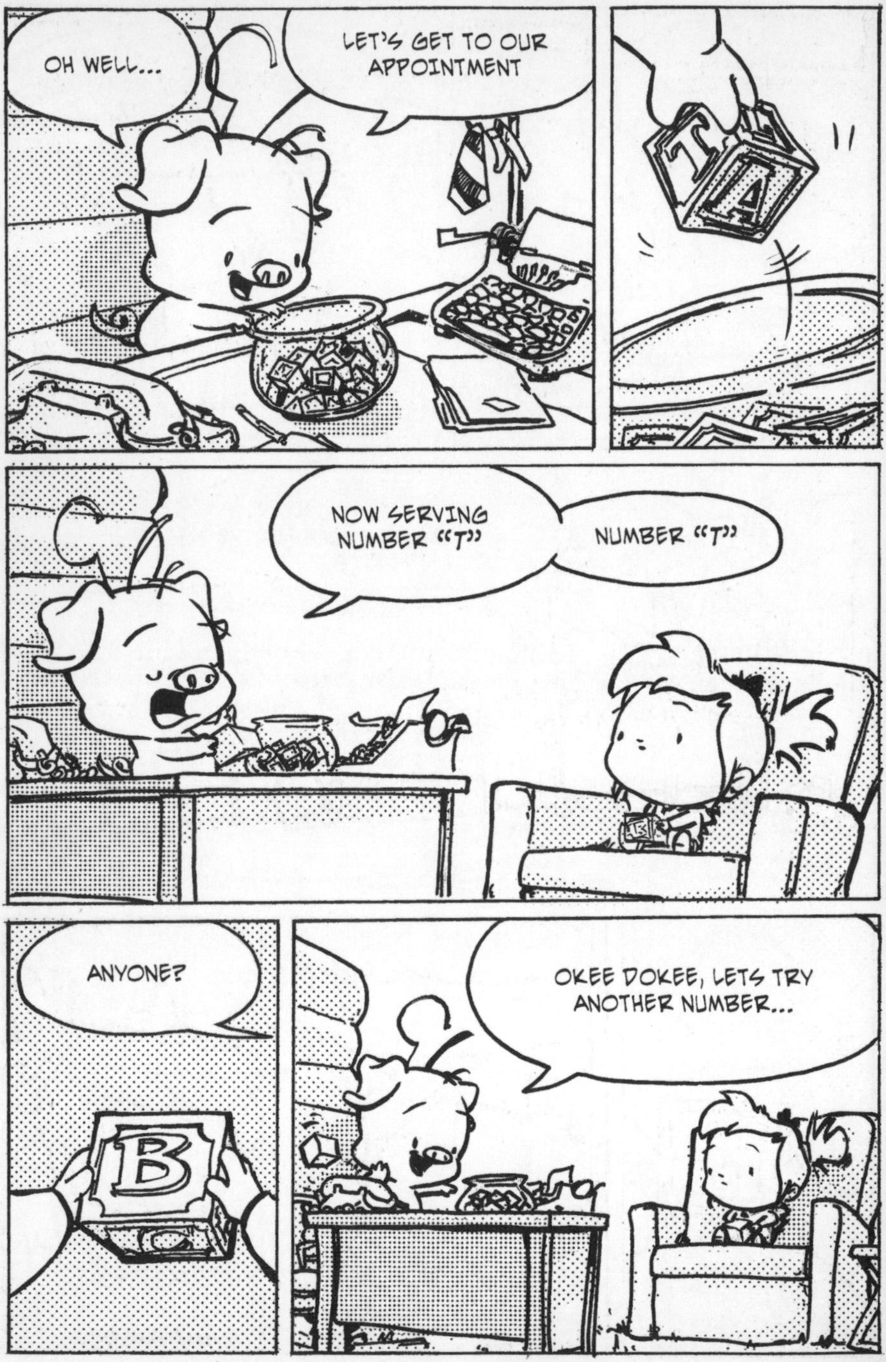
OH WELL...
LET'S GET TO OUR APPOINTMENT
NOW SERVING NUMBER "T"
NUMBER "T"
ANYONE?
OKEE DOKEE, LETS TRY ANOTHER NUMBER...

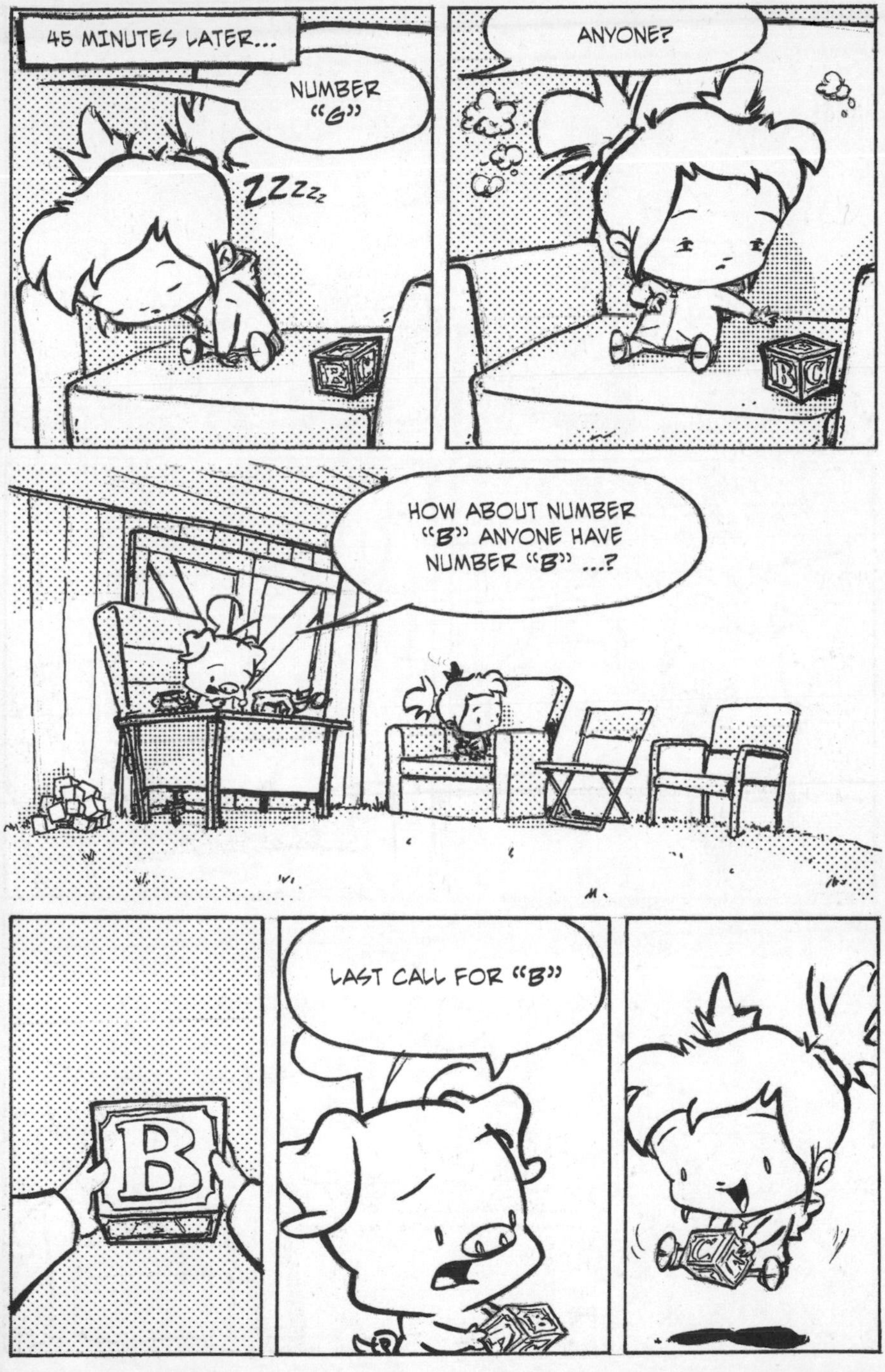
45 MINUTES LATER...
NUMBER "G"
ZZZzz
ANYONE?
HOW ABOUT NUMBER "B" ANYONE HAVE NUMBER "B" ...?
B
LAST CALL FOR "B"

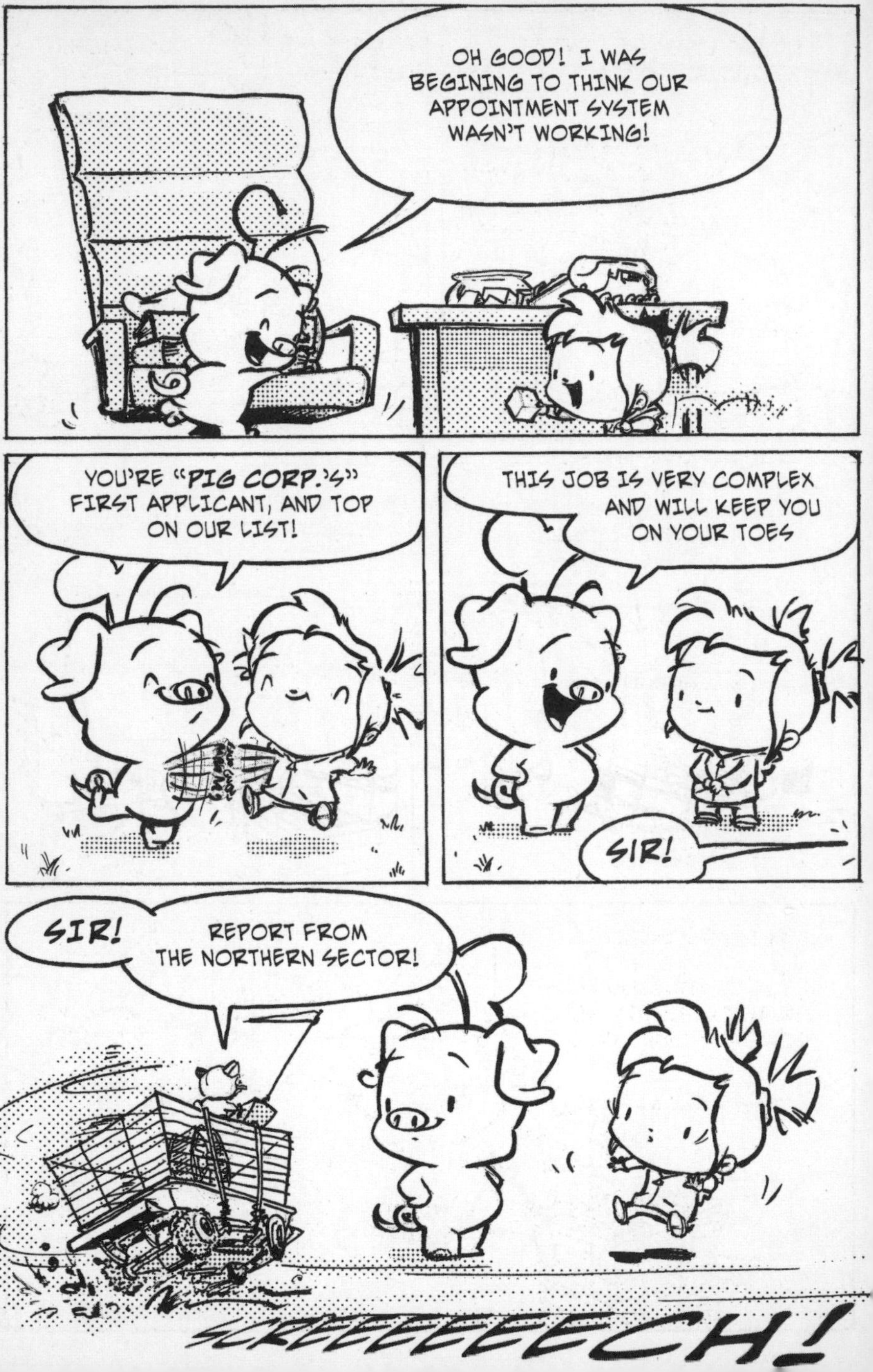
OH GOOD! I WAS BEGINING TO THINK OUR APPOINTMENT SYSTEM WASN'T WORKING!
YOU'RE "PIG CORP.'S" FIRST APPLICANT, AND TOP ON OUR LIST!
THIS JOB IS VERY COMPLEX AND WILL KEEP YOU ON YOUR TOES
SIR!
SIR!
REPORT FROM THE NORTHERN SECTOR!
SCREEEEEEEECH!

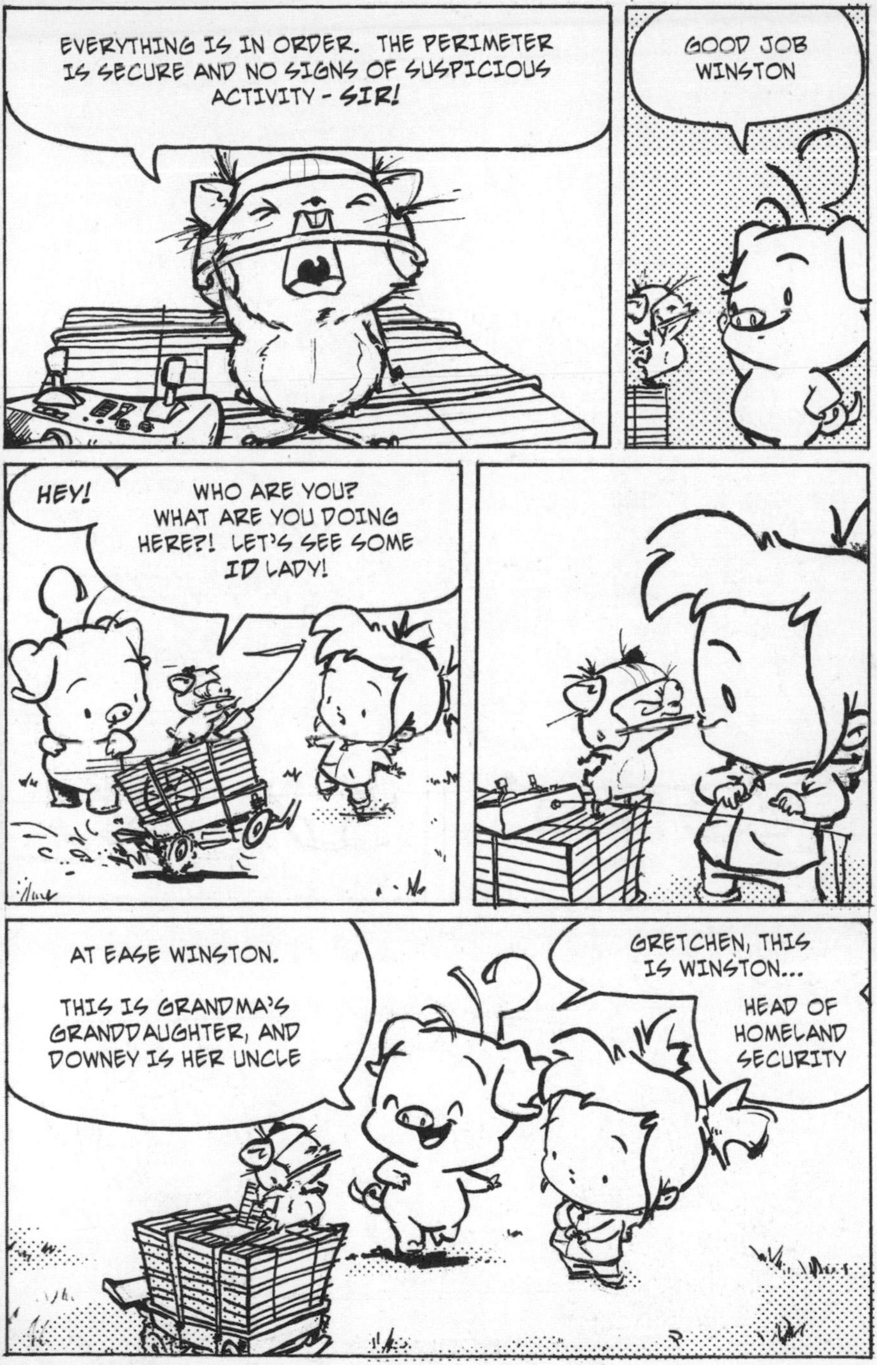
EVERYTHING IS IN ORDER. THE PERIMETER IS SECURE AND NO SIGNS OF SUSPICIOUS ACTIVITY - SIR!
GOOD JOB WINSTON
HEY!
WHO ARE YOU? WHAT ARE YOU DOING HERE?! LET'S SEE SOME ID LADY!
AT EASE WINSTON.
THIS IS GRANDMA'S GRANDDAUGHTER, AND DOWNEY IS HER UNCLE
GRETCHEN, THIS IS WINSTON...
HEAD OF HOMELAND SECURITY

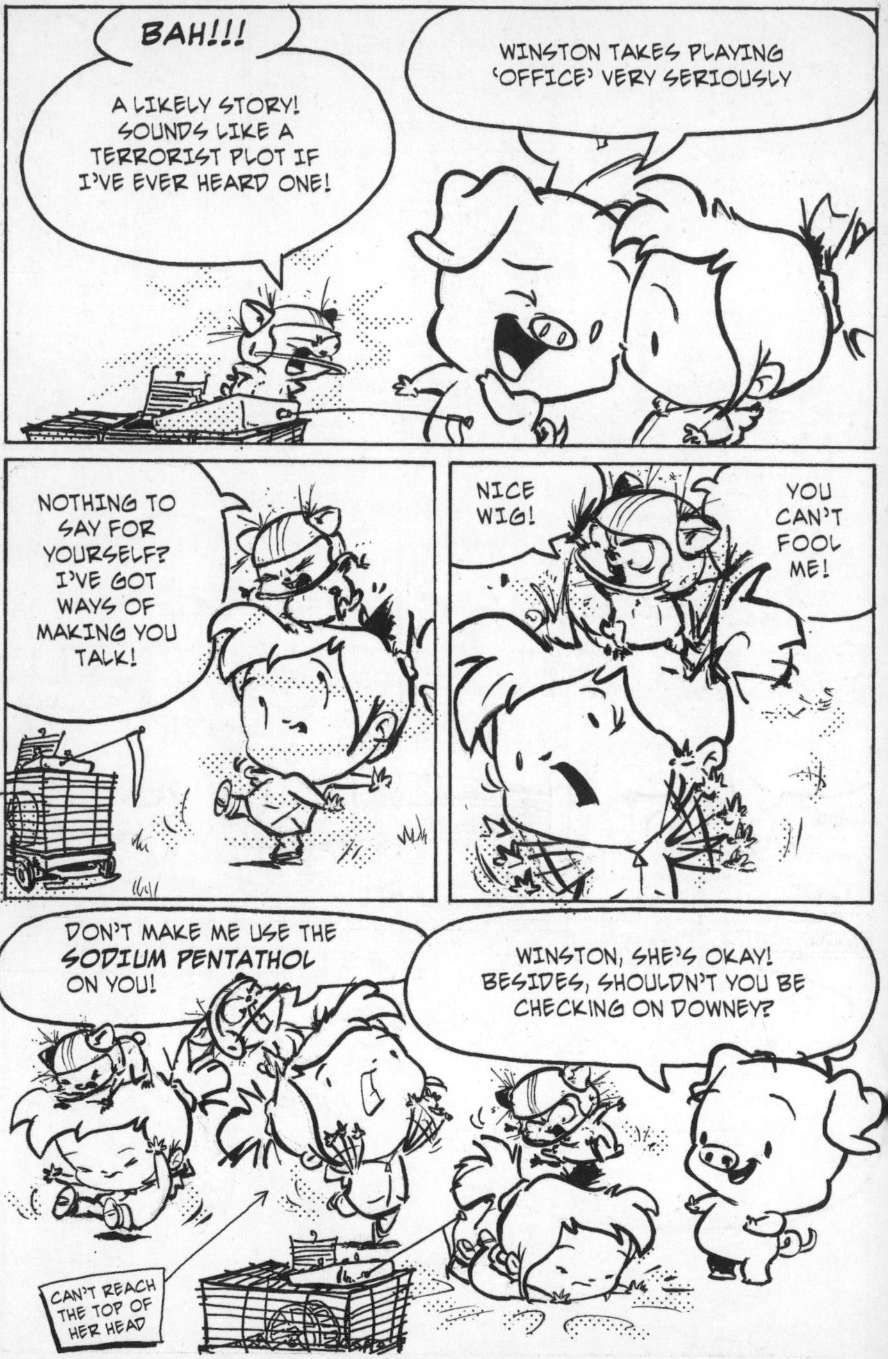
BAH!!!
A LIKELY STORY! SOUNDS LIKE A TERRORIST PLOT IF I'VE EVER HEARD ONE!
WINSTON TAKES PLAYING 'OFFICE' VERY SERIOUSLY
NOTHING TO SAY FOR YOURSELF? I'VE GOT WAYS OF MAKING YOU TALK!
NICE WIG!
YOU CAN'T FOOL ME!
DON'T MAKE ME USE THE SODIUM PENTATHOL ON YOU!
WINSTON, SHE'S OKAY! BESIDES, SHOULDN'T YOU BE CHECKING ON DOWNEY?
CAN'T REACH THE TOP OF HER HEAD

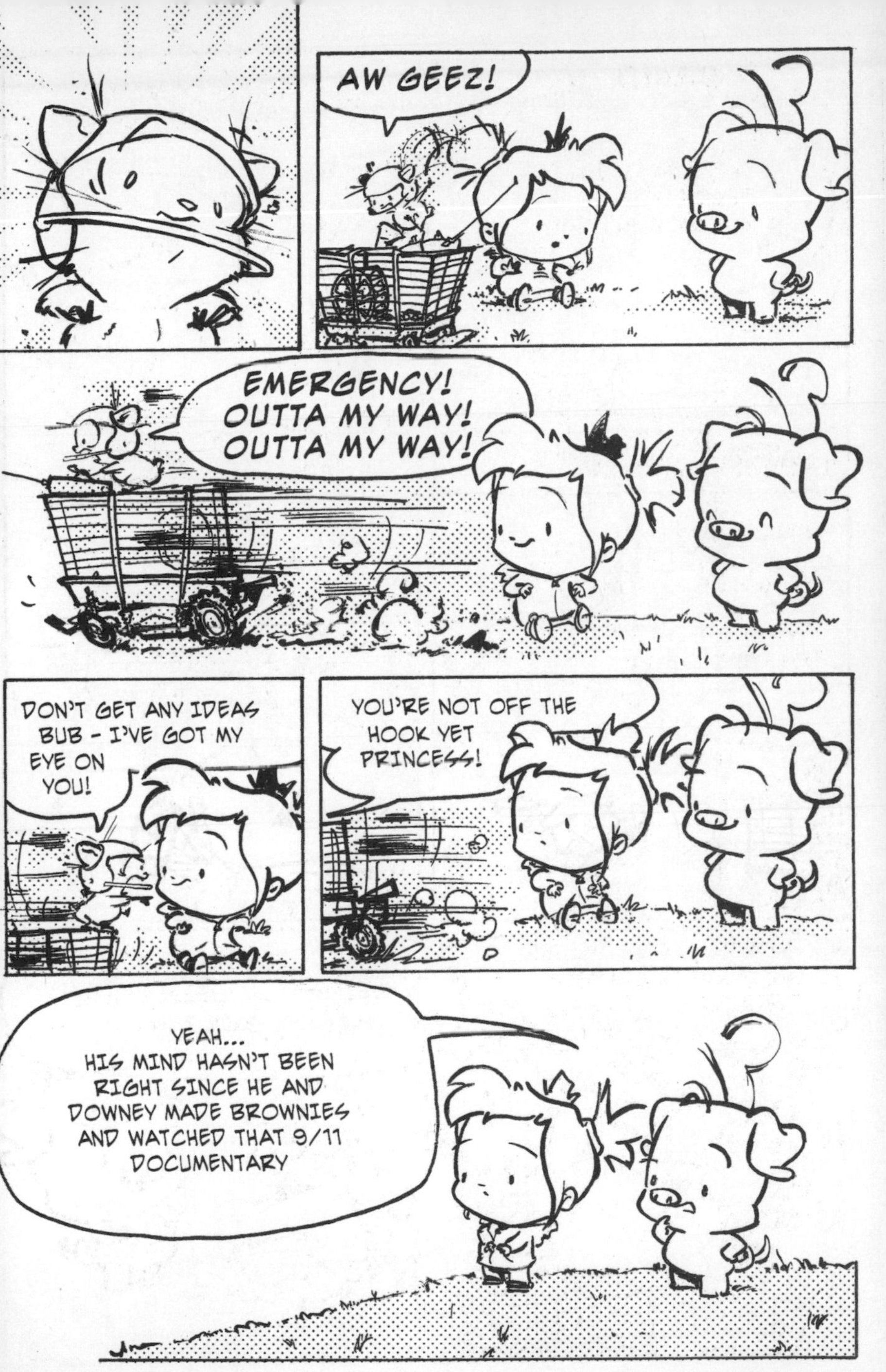
AW GEEZ!
EMERGENCY! OUTTA MY WAY! OUTTA MY WAY!
DON'T GET ANY IDEAS BUB - I'VE GOT MY EYE ON YOU!
YOU'RE NOT OFF THE HOOK YET PRINCESS!
YEAH... HIS MIND HASN'T BEEN RIGHT SINCE HE AND DOWNEY MADE BROWNIES AND WATCHED THAT 9/11 DOCUMENTARY

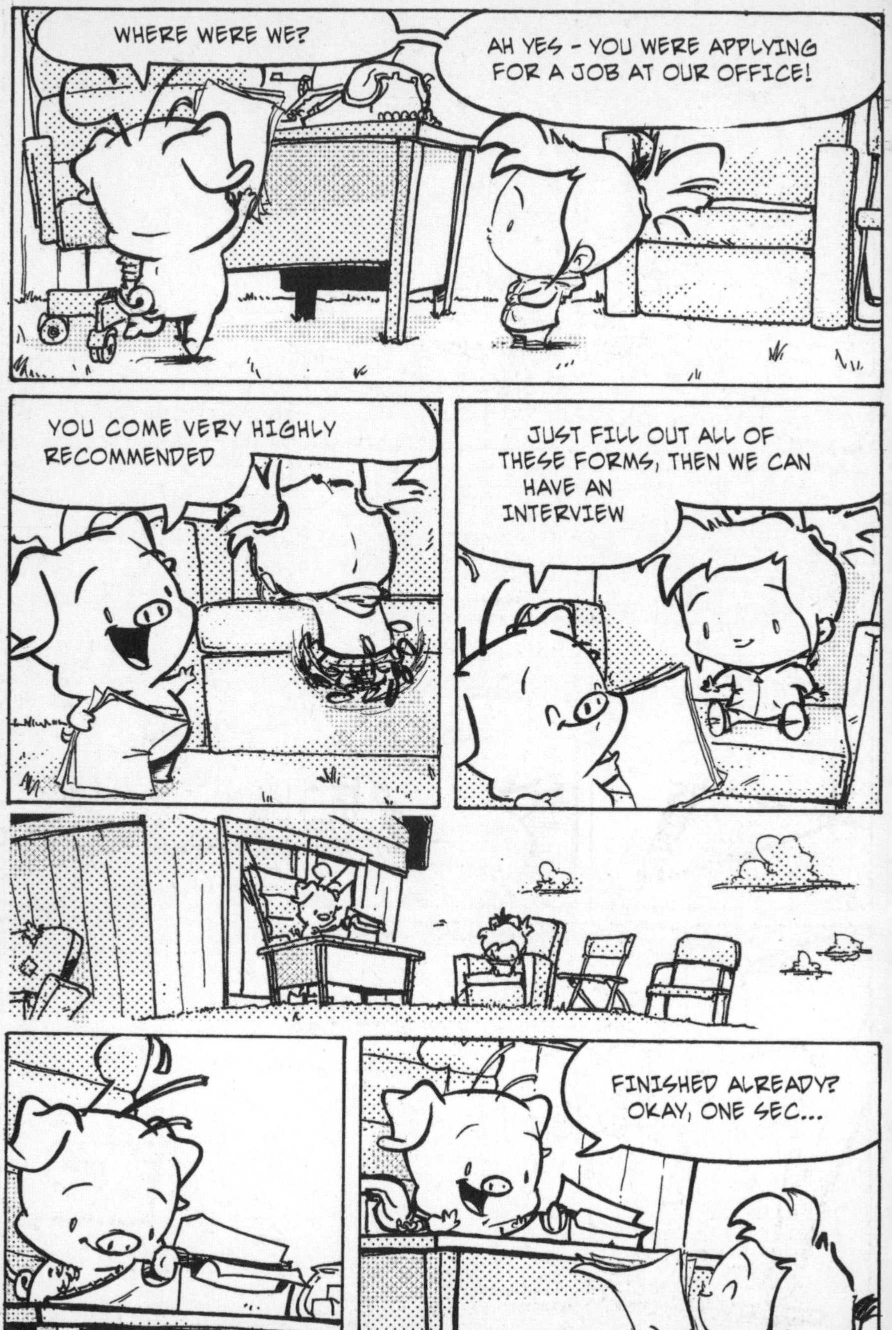
WHERE WERE WE?
AH YES - YOU WERE APPLYING FOR A JOB AT OUR OFFICE!
YOU COME VERY HIGHLY RECOMMENDED
JUST FILL OUT ALL OF THESE FORMS, THEN WE CAN HAVE AN INTERVIEW
FINISHED ALREADY? OKAY, ONE SEC...

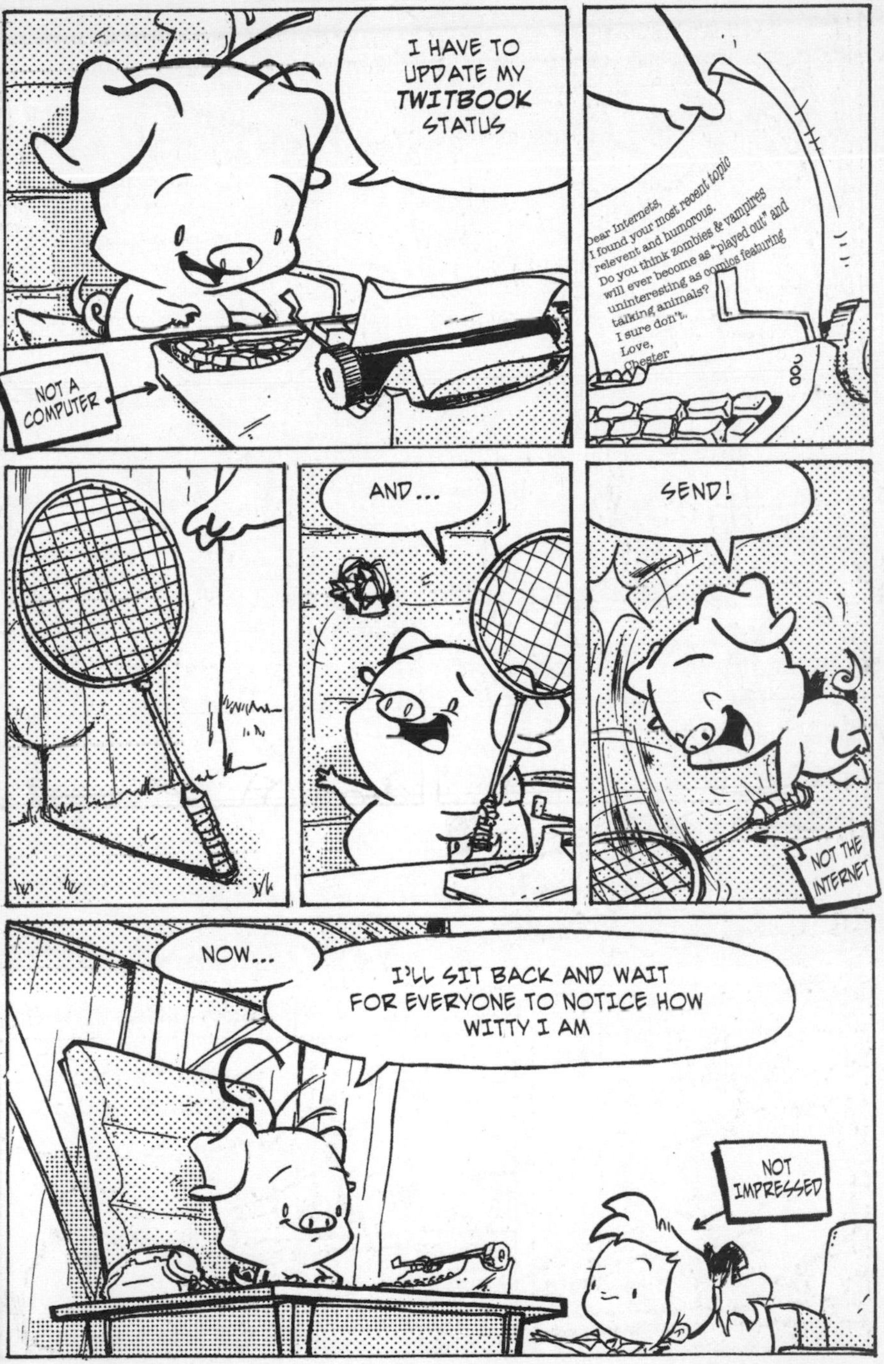
I HAVE TO UPDATE MY *TWITBOOK* STATUS
NOT A COMPUTER
Dear Internets,
I found your most recent topic relevent and humorous.
Do you think zombies & vampires will ever become as "played out" and uninteresting as comics featuring talking animals?
I sure don't.
Love,
Chester
AND...
SEND!
NOT THE INTERNET
NOW...
I'LL SIT BACK AND WAIT FOR EVERYONE TO NOTICE HOW WITTY I AM
NOT IMPRESSED

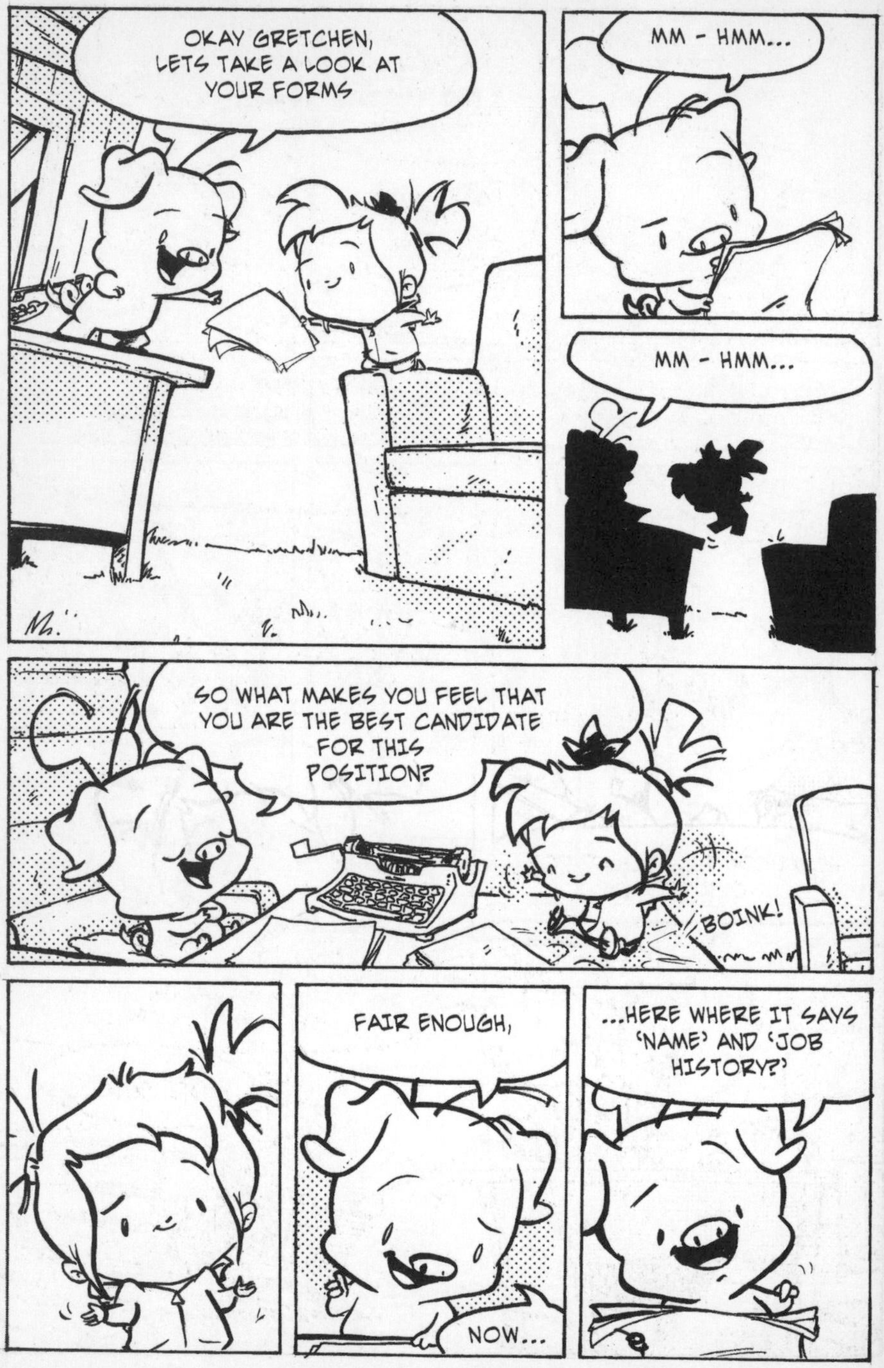
OKAY GRETCHEN, LETS TAKE A LOOK AT YOUR FORMS
MM - HMM...
MM - HMM...
SO WHAT MAKES YOU FEEL THAT YOU ARE THE BEST CANDIDATE FOR THIS POSITION?
BOINK!
FAIR ENOUGH,
NOW...
...HERE WHERE IT SAYS 'NAME' AND 'JOB HISTORY?'

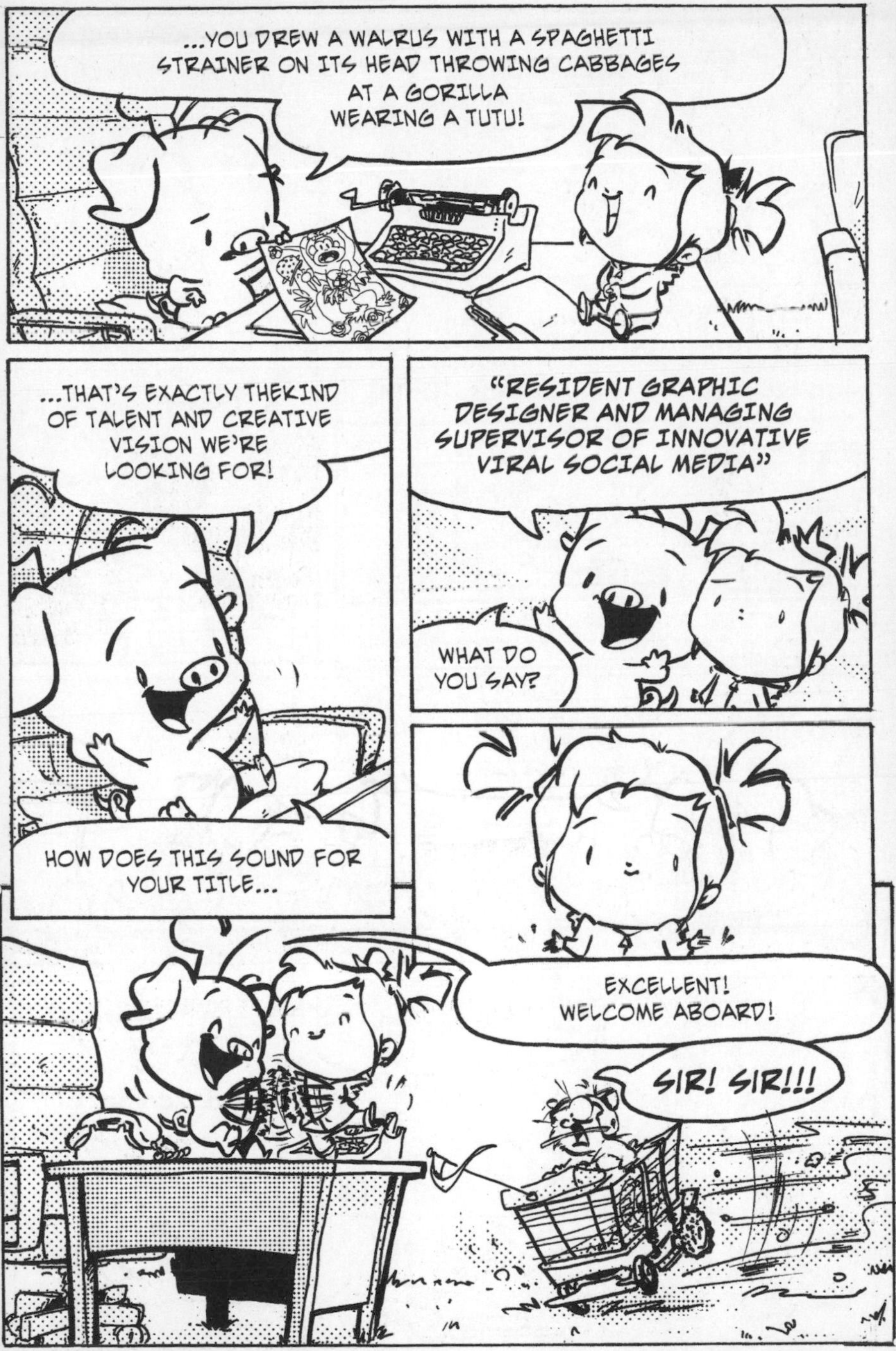
...YOU DREW A WALRUS WITH A SPAGHETTI STRAINER ON ITS HEAD THROWING CABBAGES AT A GORILLA WEARING A TUTU!
...THAT'S EXACTLY THEKIND OF TALENT AND CREATIVE VISION WE'RE LOOKING FOR!
HOW DOES THIS SOUND FOR YOUR TITLE...
"RESIDENT GRAPHIC DESIGNER AND MANAGING SUPERVISOR OF INNOVATIVE VIRAL SOCIAL MEDIA"
WHAT DO YOU SAY?
EXCELLENT! WELCOME ABOARD!
SIR! SIR!!!

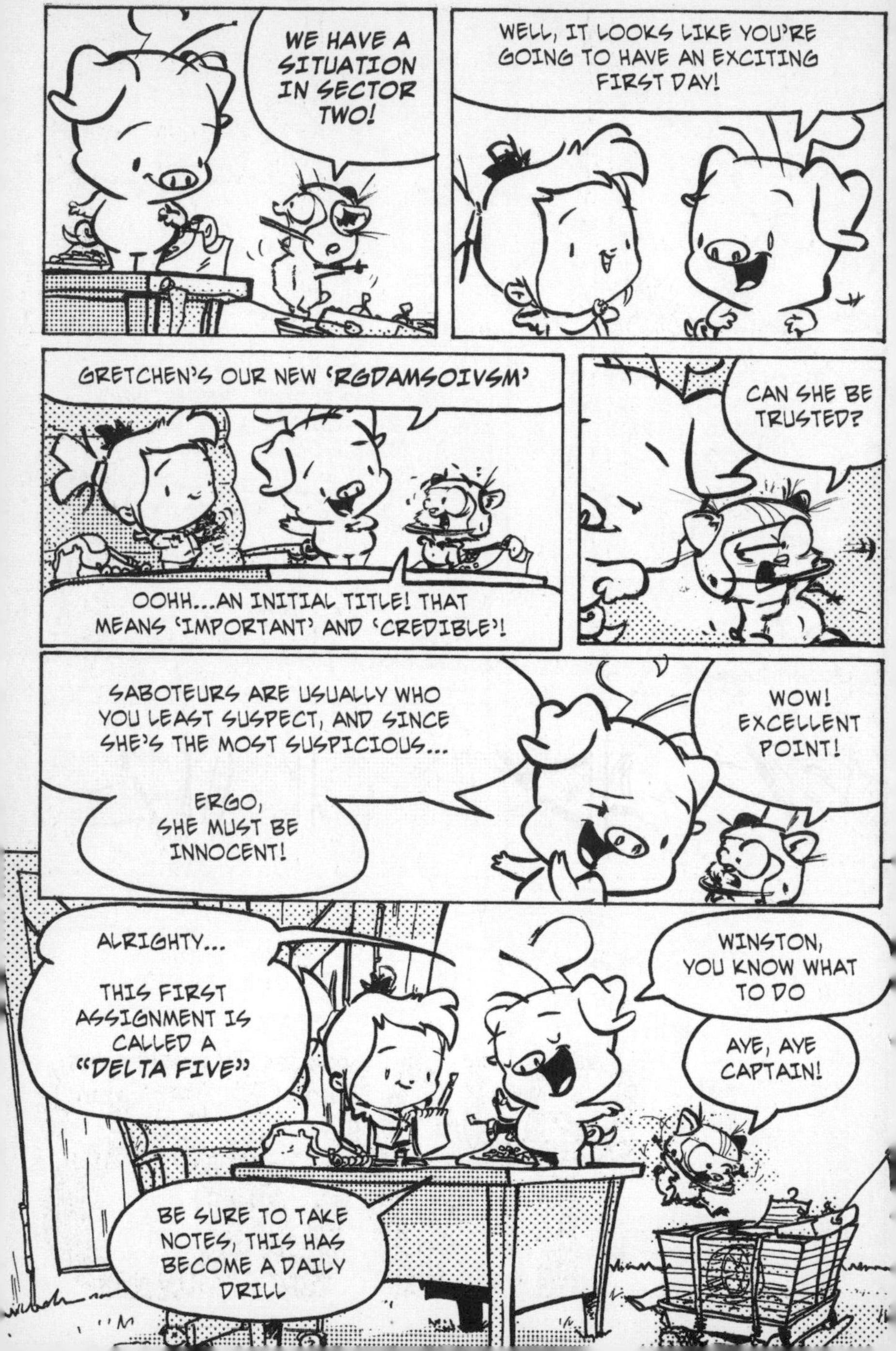
WE HAVE A SITUATION IN SECTOR TWO!
WELL, IT LOOKS LIKE YOU'RE GOING TO HAVE AN EXCITING FIRST DAY!
GRETCHEN'S OUR NEW 'RGDAMSOIVSM'
OOHH...AN INITIAL TITLE! THAT MEANS 'IMPORTANT' AND 'CREDIBLE'!
CAN SHE BE TRUSTED?
SABOTEURS ARE USUALLY WHO YOU LEAST SUSPECT, AND SINCE SHE'S THE MOST SUSPICIOUS...
ERGO, SHE MUST BE INNOCENT!
WOW! EXCELLENT POINT!
ALRIGHTY...
THIS FIRST ASSIGNMENT IS CALLED A "DELTA FIVE"
WINSTON, YOU KNOW WHAT TO DO
AYE, AYE CAPTAIN!
BE SURE TO TAKE NOTES, THIS HAS BECOME A DAILY DRILL

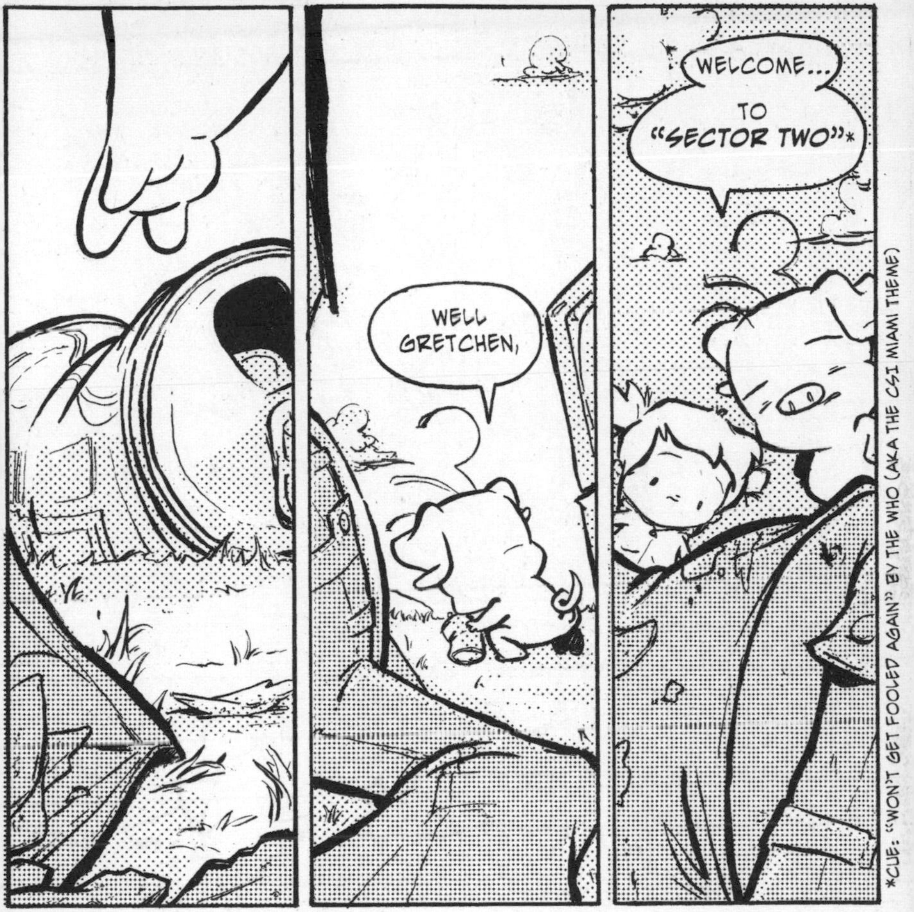
WELL GRETCHEN,
WELCOME...
TO "SECTOR TWO"*
*CUE: "WON'T GET FOOLED AGAIN" BY THE WHO (AKA THE CSI MIAMI THEME)

CHAPTER TWO

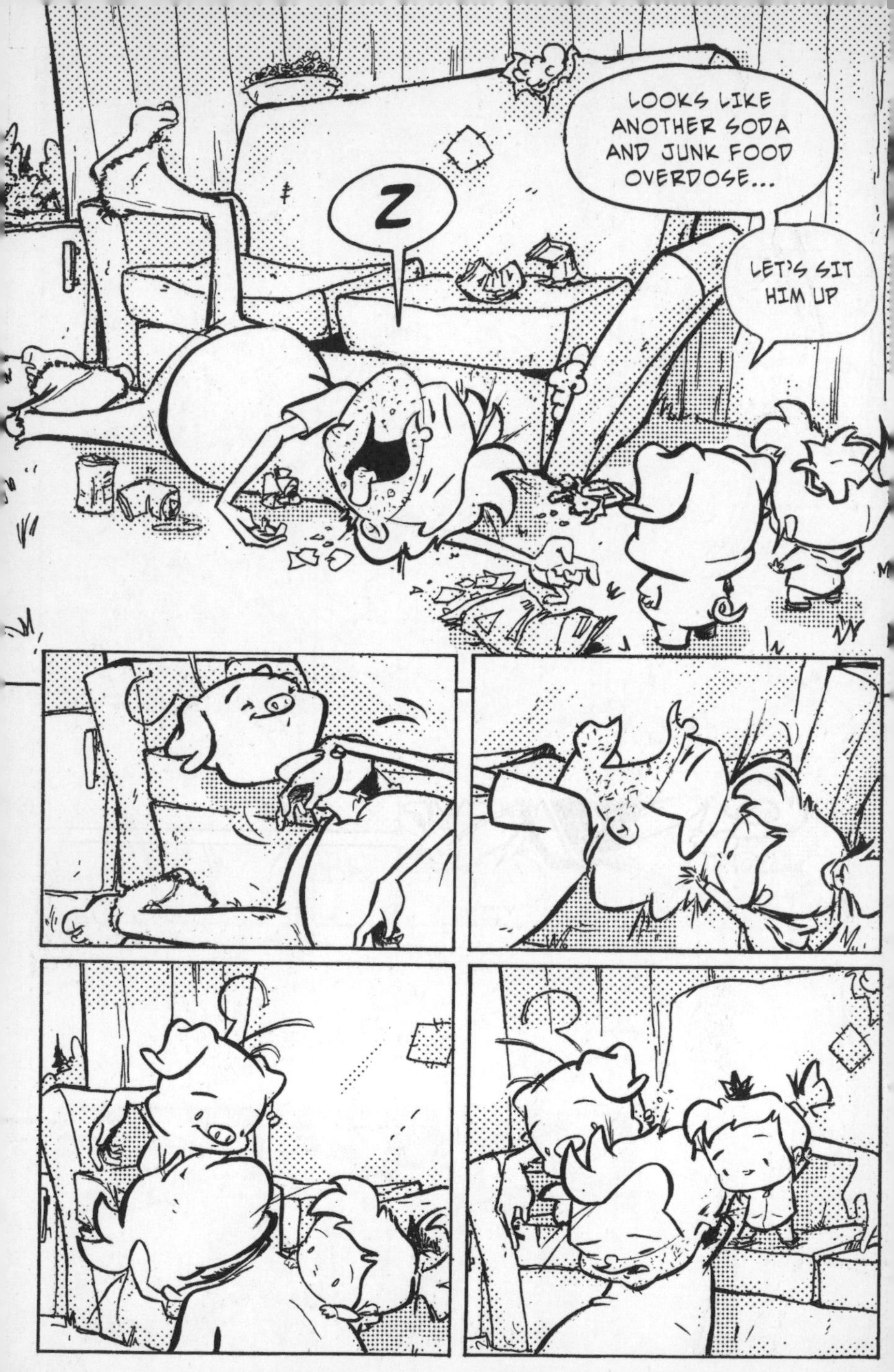
Z
LOOKS LIKE ANOTHER SODA AND JUNK FOOD OVERDOSE...
LET'S SIT HIM UP

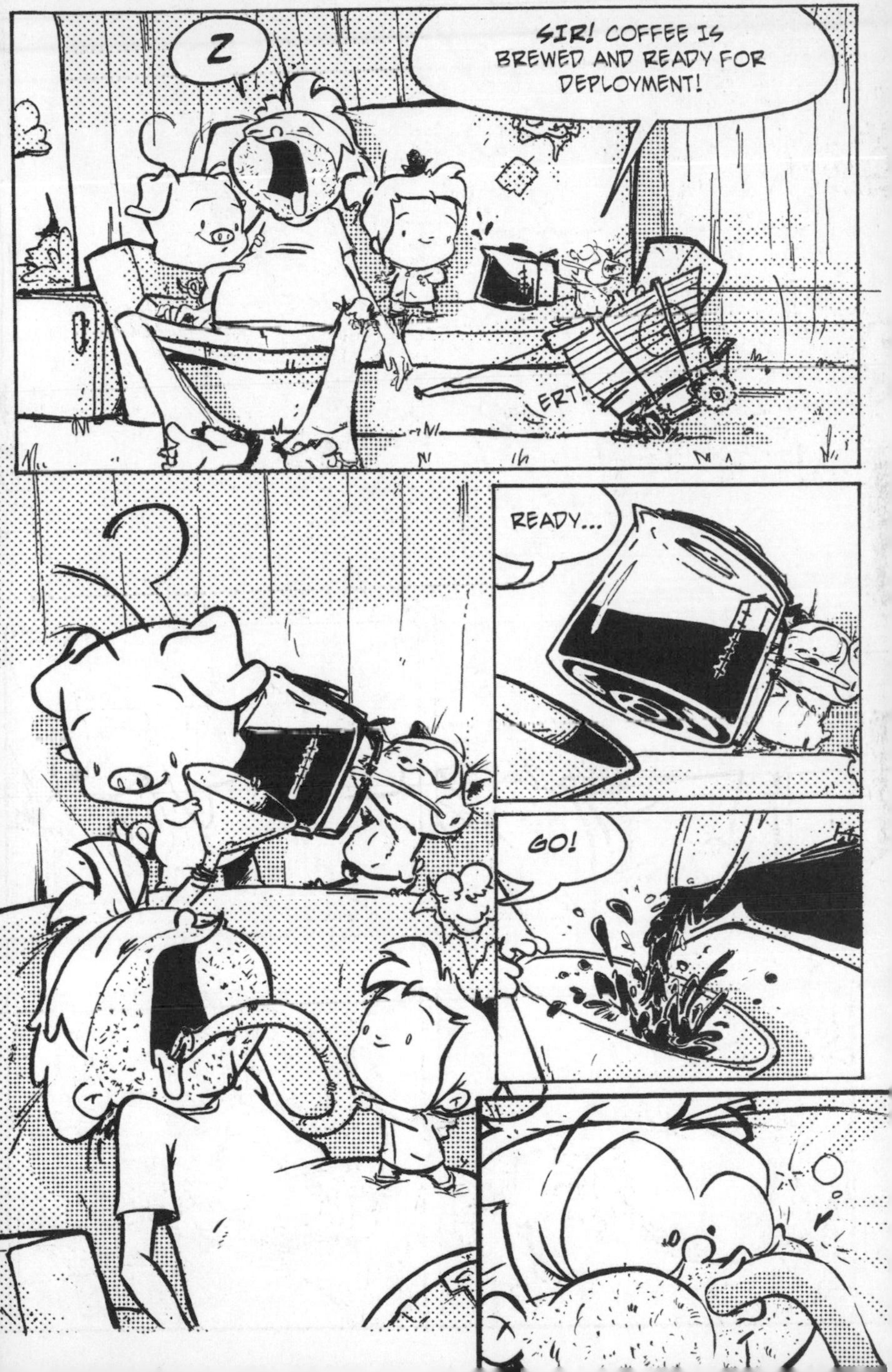
Z
SIR! COFFEE IS BREWED AND READY FOR DEPLOYMENT!
ERT!
READY...
GO!

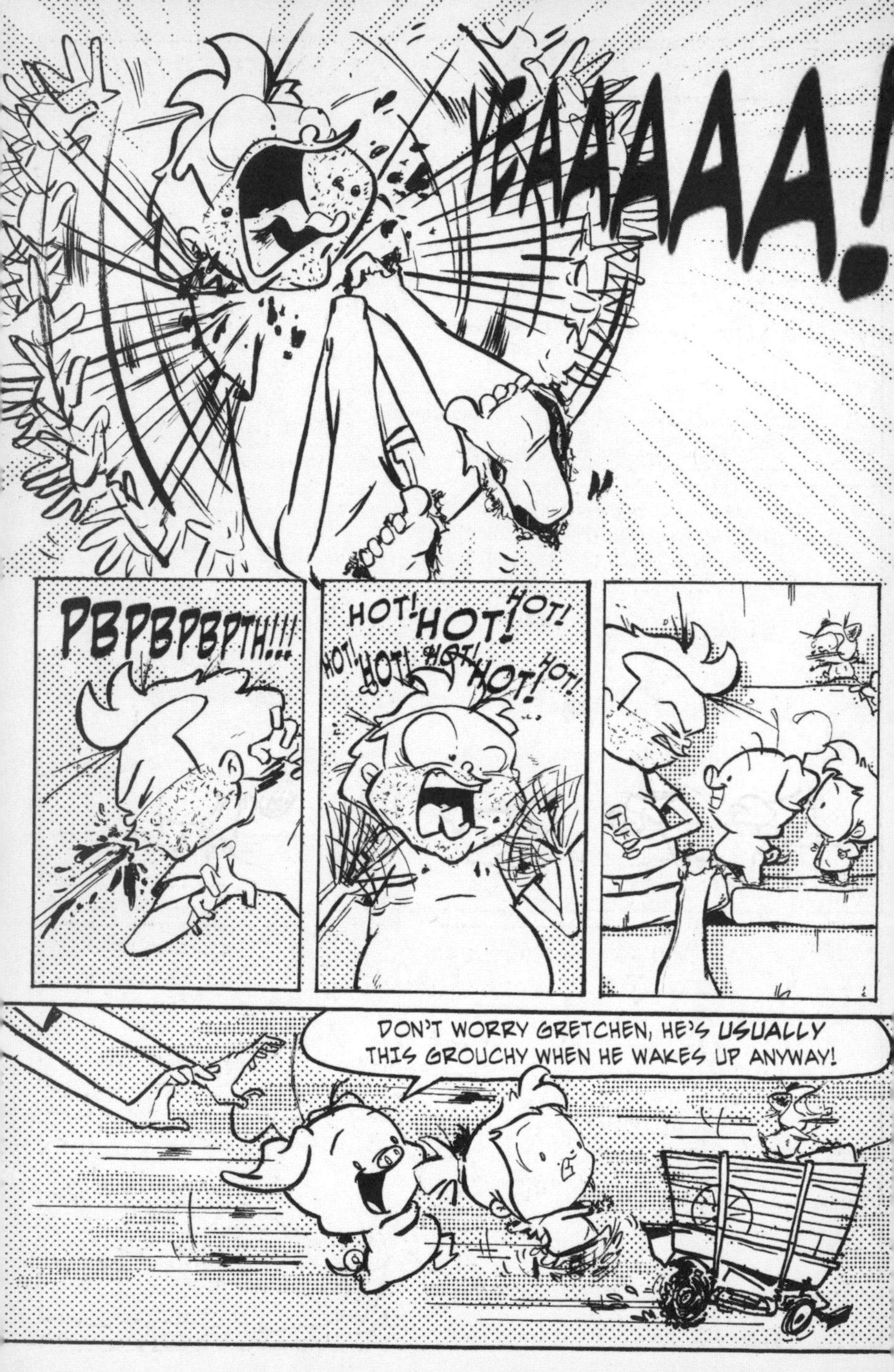
YEAAAAA!
PBPBPBPTH!!!
HOT! HOT! HOT! HOT! HOT! HOT! HOT! HOT!
DON'T WORRY GRETCHEN, HE'S USUALLY THIS GROUCHY WHEN HE WAKES UP ANYWAY!

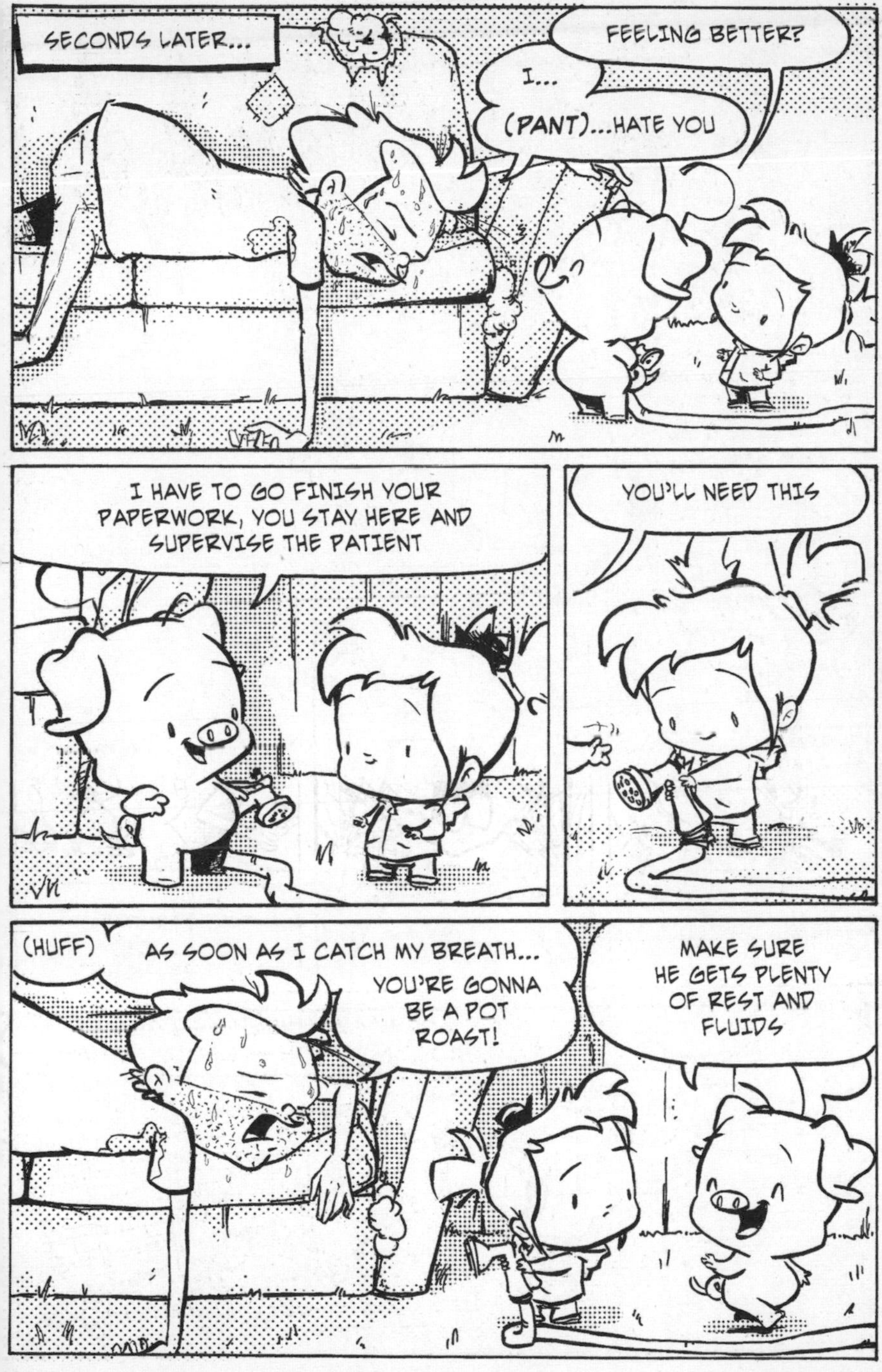
SECONDS LATER...
FEELING BETTER?
I...
(PANT)...HATE YOU
I HAVE TO GO FINISH YOUR PAPERWORK, YOU STAY HERE AND SUPERVISE THE PATIENT
YOU'LL NEED THIS
(HUFF)
AS SOON AS I CATCH MY BREATH...
YOU'RE GONNA BE A POT ROAST!
MAKE SURE HE GETS PLENTY OF REST AND FLUIDS

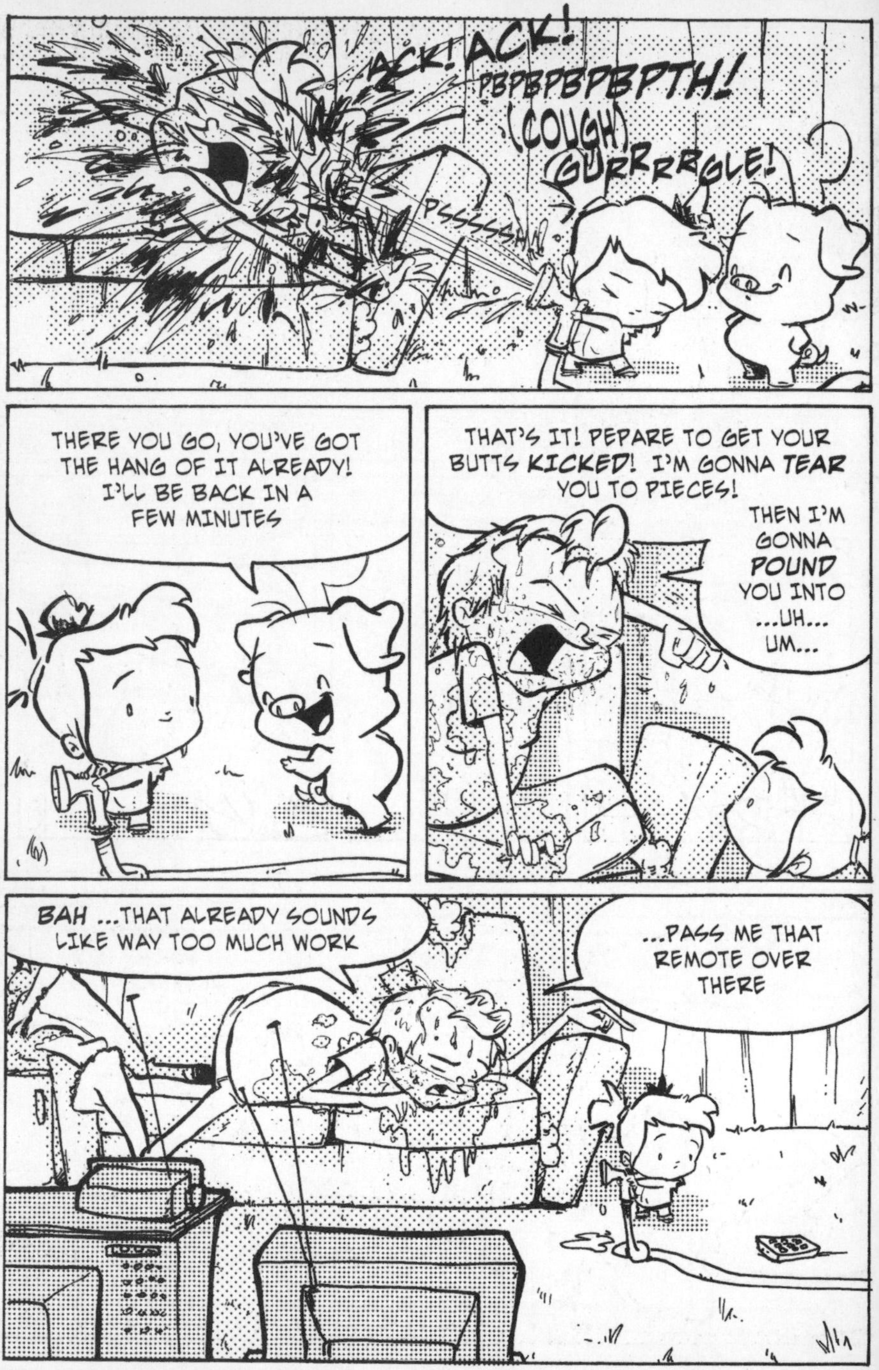
ACK! ACK!
PBPBPBPBPTH!
(COUGH)
GURRRRRGLE!
PSSSSSSHH
THERE YOU GO, YOU'VE GOT THE HANG OF IT ALREADY! I'LL BE BACK IN A FEW MINUTES
THAT'S IT! PEPARE TO GET YOUR BUTTS KICKED! I'M GONNA TEAR YOU TO PIECES!
THEN I'M GONNA POUND YOU INTO ...UH... UM...
BAH ...THAT ALREADY SOUNDS LIKE WAY TOO MUCH WORK
...PASS ME THAT REMOTE OVER THERE

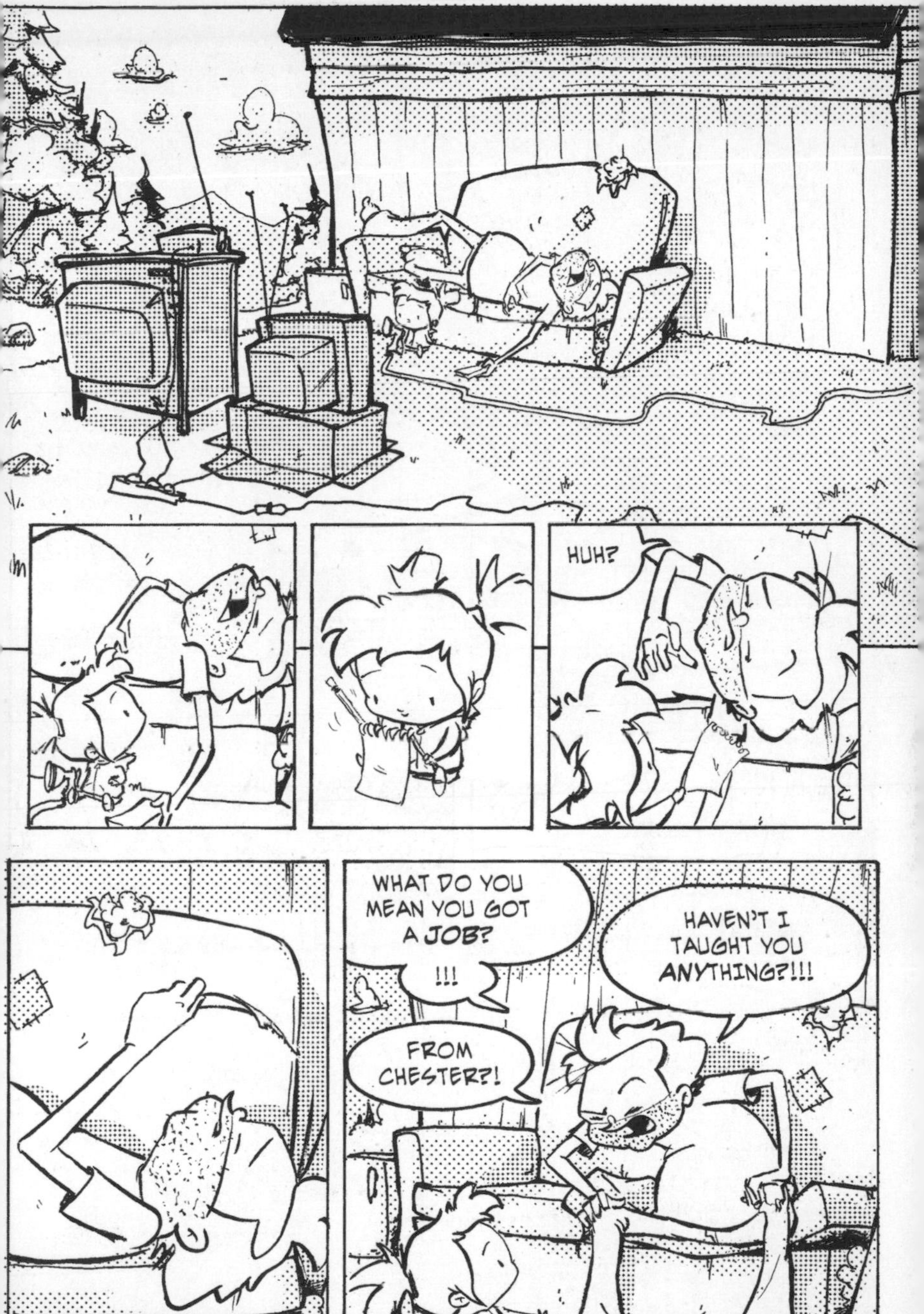
HUH?
WHAT DO YOU MEAN YOU GOT A JOB?
!!!
FROM CHESTER?!
HAVEN'T I TAUGHT YOU ANYTHING?!!!

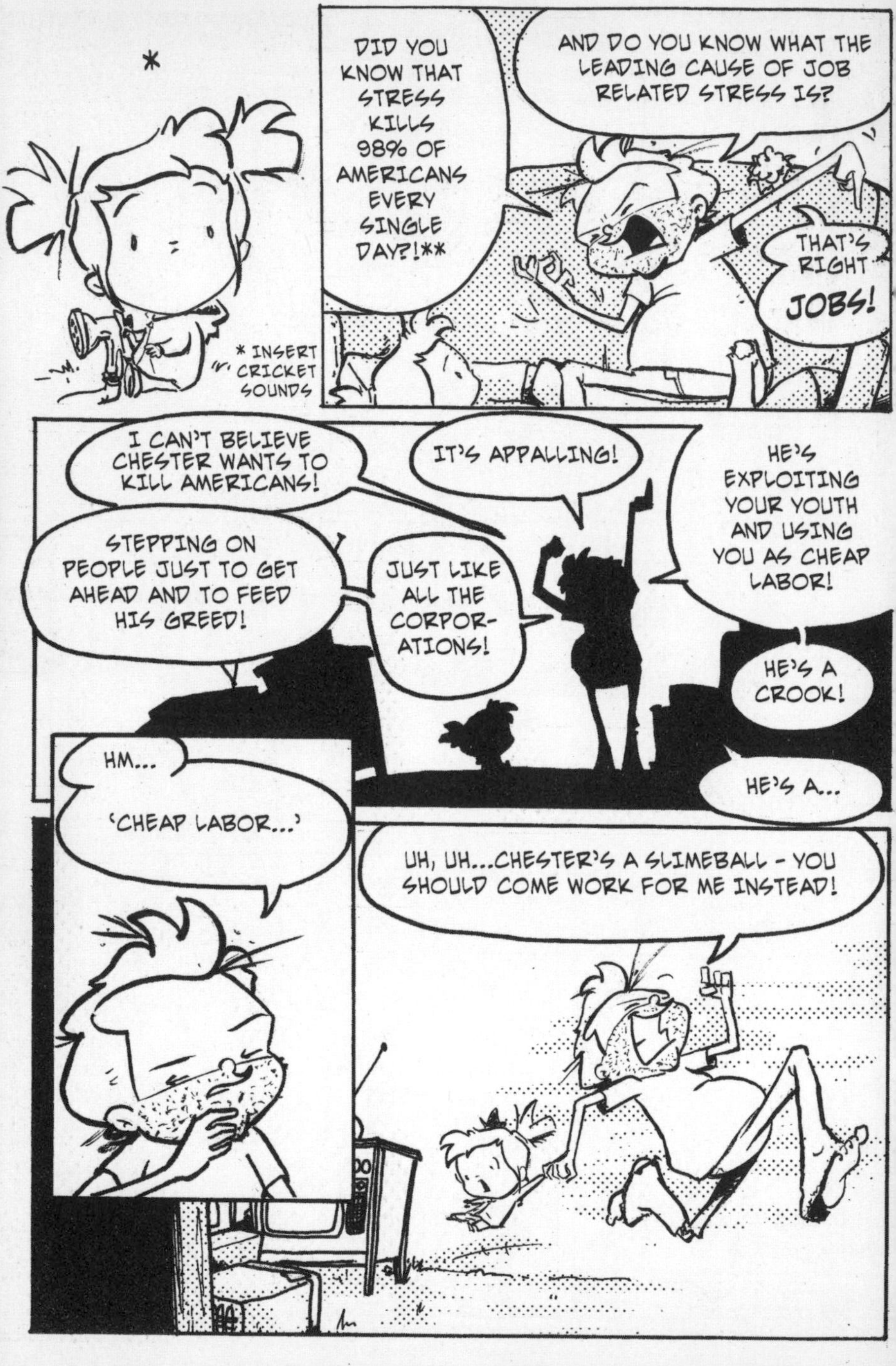
*
* INSERT CRICKET SOUNDS
DID YOU KNOW THAT STRESS KILLS 98% OF AMERICANS EVERY SINGLE DAY?!**
AND DO YOU KNOW WHAT THE LEADING CAUSE OF JOB RELATED STRESS IS?
THAT'S RIGHT JOBS!
I CAN'T BELIEVE CHESTER WANTS TO KILL AMERICANS!
IT'S APPALLING!
HE'S EXPLOITING YOUR YOUTH AND USING YOU AS CHEAP LABOR!
STEPPING ON PEOPLE JUST TO GET AHEAD AND TO FEED HIS GREED!
JUST LIKE ALL THE CORPOR-ATIONS!
HE'S A CROOK!
HE'S A...
HM...
'CHEAP LABOR...'
UH, UH...CHESTER'S A SLIMEBALL - YOU SHOULD COME WORK FOR ME INSTEAD!

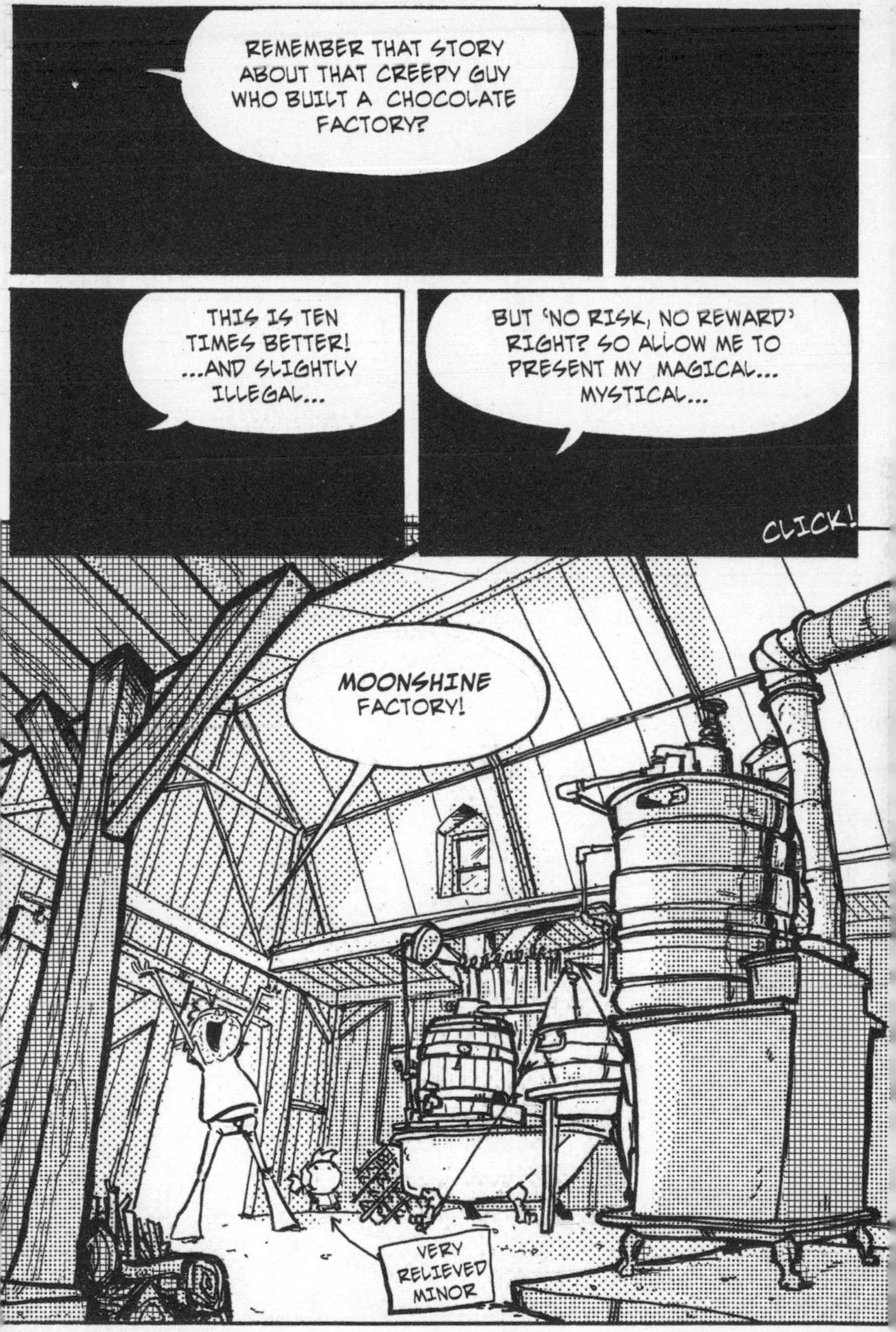
REMEMBER THAT STORY ABOUT THAT CREEPY GUY WHO BUILT A CHOCOLATE FACTORY?
THIS IS TEN TIMES BETTER! ...AND SLIGHTLY ILLEGAL...
BUT 'NO RISK, NO REWARD' RIGHT? SO ALLOW ME TO PRESENT MY MAGICAL... MYSTICAL...
CLICK!
MOONSHINE FACTORY!
VERY RELIEVED MINOR

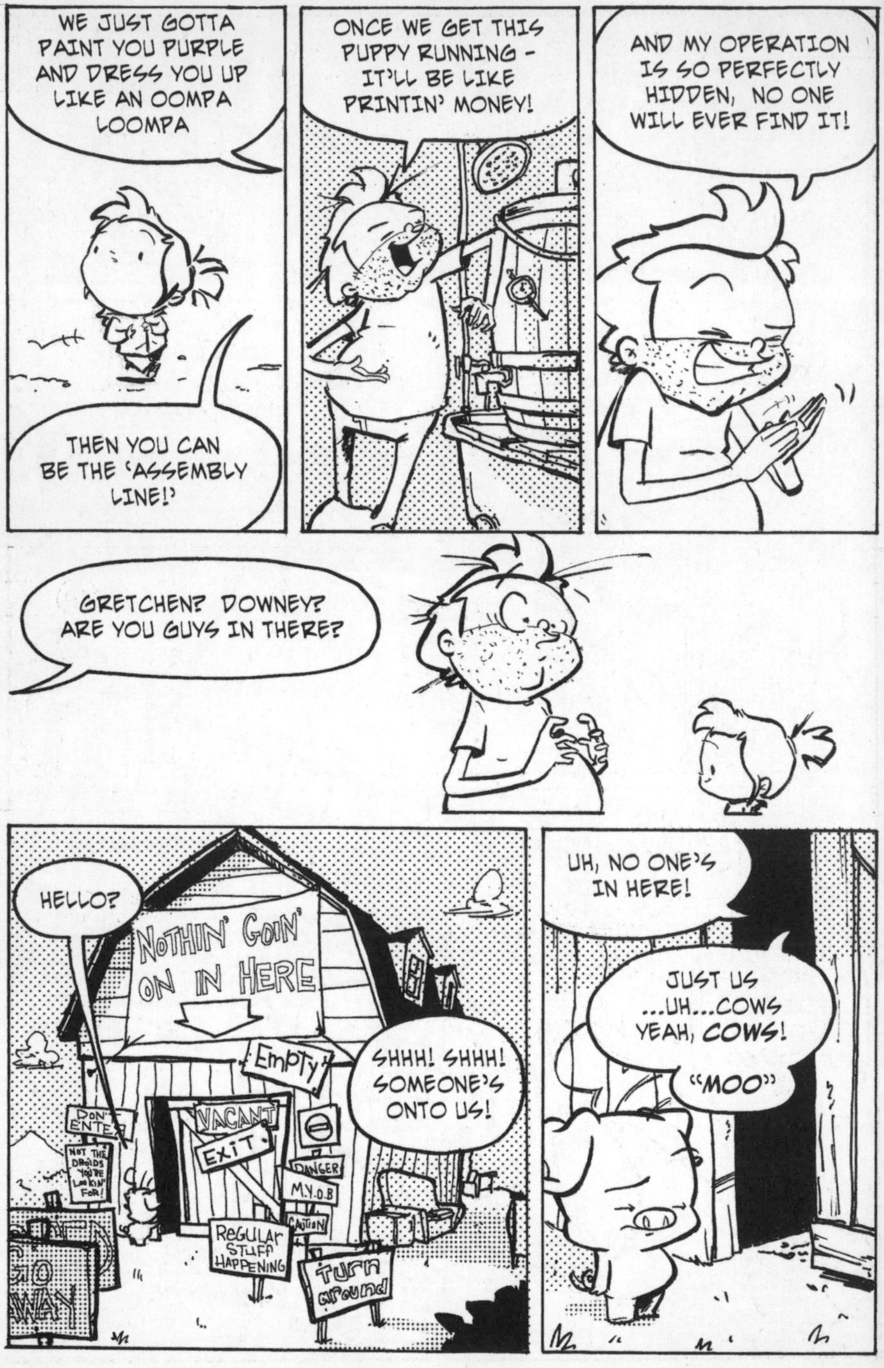

WE JUST GOTTA PAINT YOU PURPLE AND DRESS YOU UP LIKE AN OOMPA LOOMPA
THEN YOU CAN BE THE 'ASSEMBLY LINE!'
ONCE WE GET THIS PUPPY RUNNING - IT'LL BE LIKE PRINTIN' MONEY!
AND MY OPERATION IS SO PERFECTLY HIDDEN, NO ONE WILL EVER FIND IT!
GRETCHEN? DOWNEY? ARE YOU GUYS IN THERE?
HELLO?
NOTHIN' GOIN' ON IN HERE
EMPTY
DON'T ENTE
NOT THE DROIDS YOU'RE LOOKIN' FOR!
VACANT
EXIT
DANGER
M.Y.O.B
CAUTION
REGULAR STUFF HAPPENING
TURN AROUND
GO AWAY
SHHH! SHHH! SOMEONE'S ONTO US!
UH, NO ONE'S IN HERE!
JUST US ...UH...COWS YEAH, COWS!
"MOO"

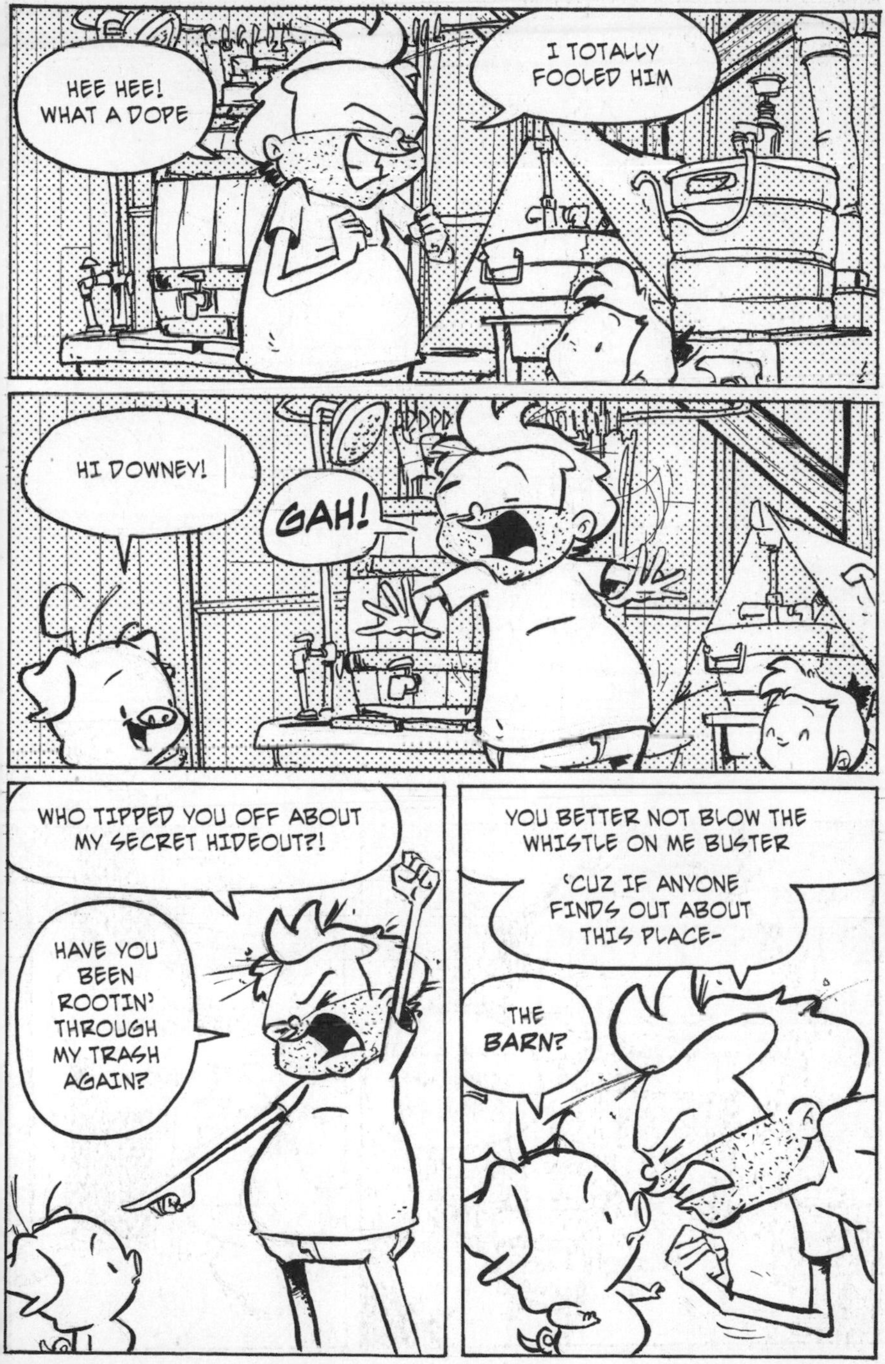
HEE HEE! WHAT A DOPE
I TOTALLY FOOLED HIM
HI DOWNEY!
GAH!
WHO TIPPED YOU OFF ABOUT MY SECRET HIDEOUT?!
HAVE YOU BEEN ROOTIN' THROUGH MY TRASH AGAIN?
YOU BETTER NOT BLOW THE WHISTLE ON ME BUSTER
'CUZ IF ANYONE FINDS OUT ABOUT THIS PLACE-
THE BARN?

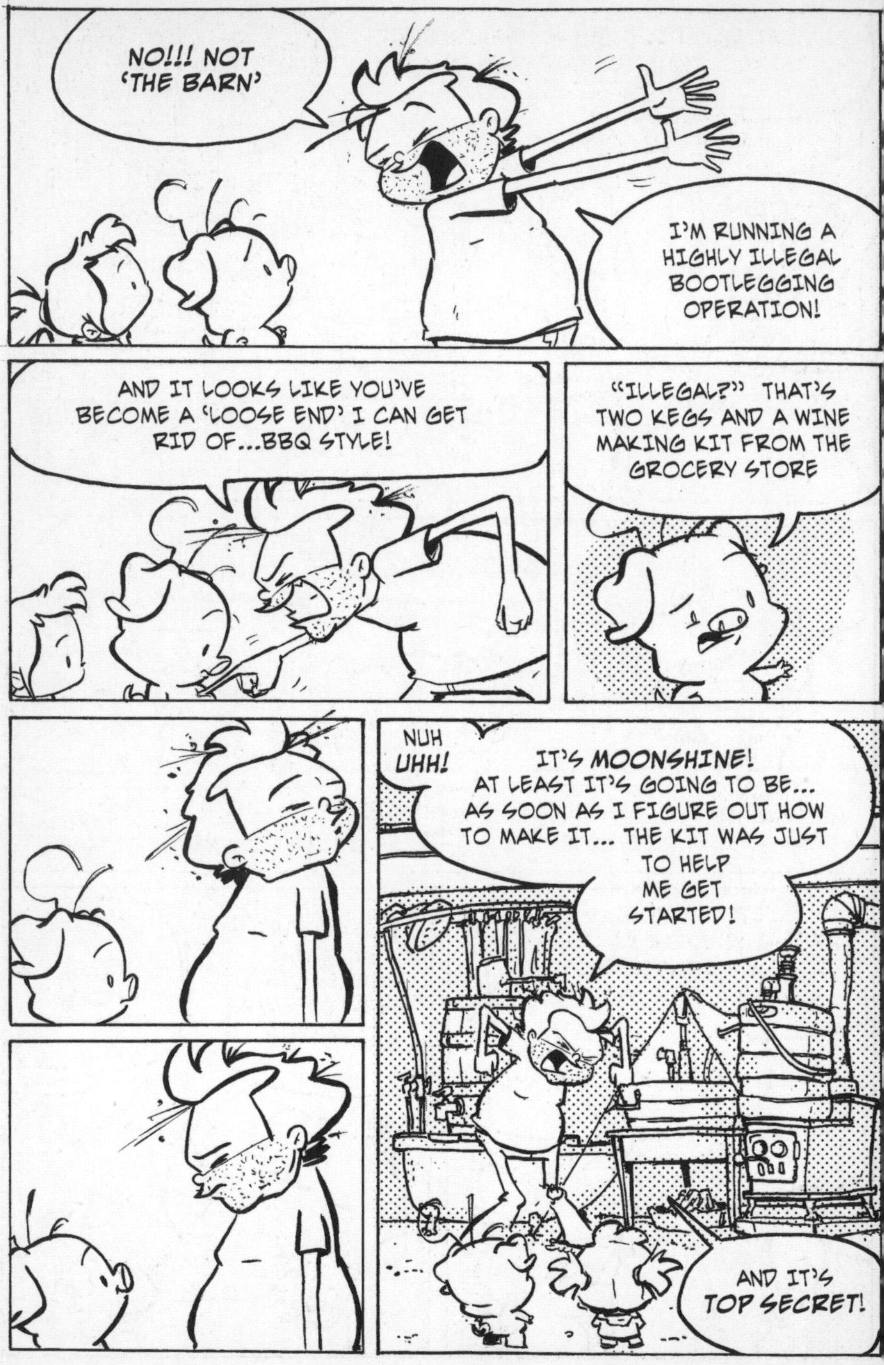
NO!!! NOT 'THE BARN'
I'M RUNNING A HIGHLY ILLEGAL BOOTLEGGING OPERATION!
AND IT LOOKS LIKE YOU'VE BECOME A 'LOOSE END' I CAN GET RID OF...BBQ STYLE!
"ILLEGAL?" THAT'S TWO KEGS AND A WINE MAKING KIT FROM THE GROCERY STORE
NUH UHH!
IT'S MOONSHINE! AT LEAST IT'S GOING TO BE... AS SOON AS I FIGURE OUT HOW TO MAKE IT... THE KIT WAS JUST TO HELP ME GET STARTED!
AND IT'S TOP SECRET!

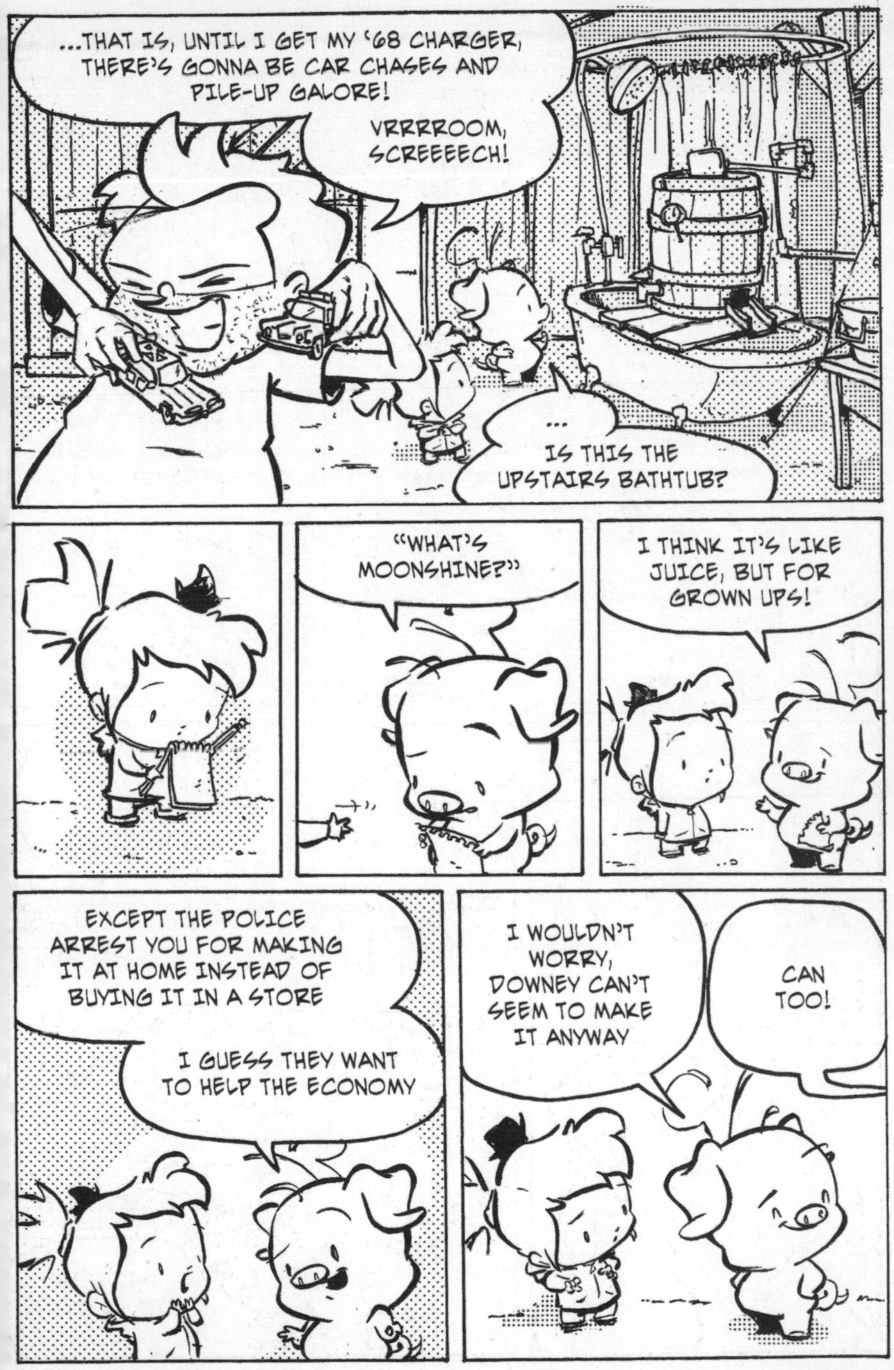
...THAT IS, UNTIL I GET MY '68 CHARGER, THERE'S GONNA BE CAR CHASES AND PILE-UP GALORE!
VRRRROOM, SCREEEECH!
... IS THIS THE UPSTAIRS BATHTUB?
"WHAT'S MOONSHINE?"
I THINK IT'S LIKE JUICE, BUT FOR GROWN UPS!
EXCEPT THE POLICE ARREST YOU FOR MAKING IT AT HOME INSTEAD OF BUYING IT IN A STORE
I GUESS THEY WANT TO HELP THE ECONOMY
I WOULDN'T WORRY, DOWNEY CAN'T SEEM TO MAKE IT ANYWAY
CAN TOO!

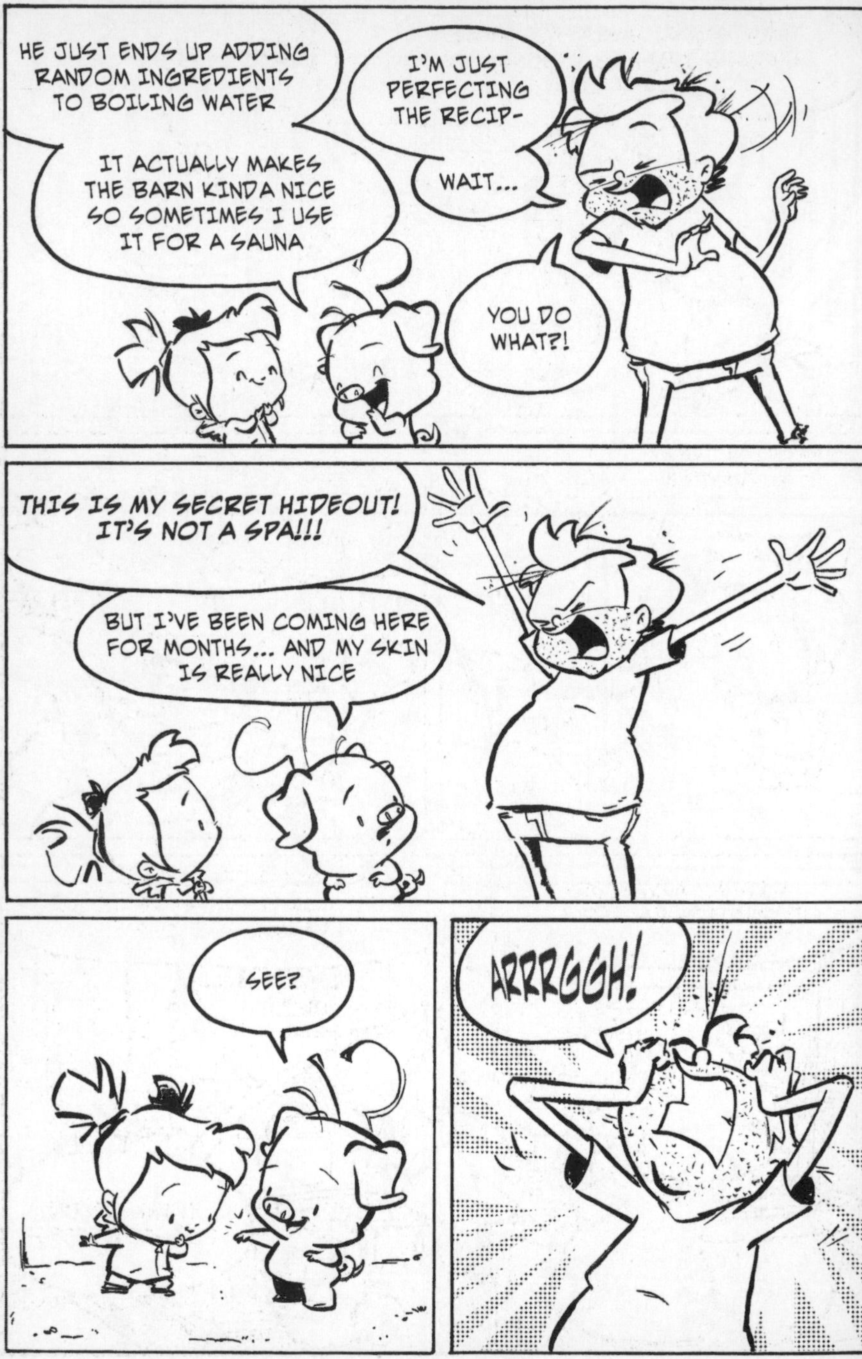
HE JUST ENDS UP ADDING RANDOM INGREDIENTS TO BOILING WATER
I'M JUST PERFECTING THE RECIP-
WAIT...
IT ACTUALLY MAKES THE BARN KINDA NICE SO SOMETIMES I USE IT FOR A SAUNA
YOU DO WHAT?!
THIS IS MY SECRET HIDEOUT! IT'S NOT A SPA!!!
BUT I'VE BEEN COMING HERE FOR MONTHS... AND MY SKIN IS REALLY NICE
SEE?
ARRRGGH!

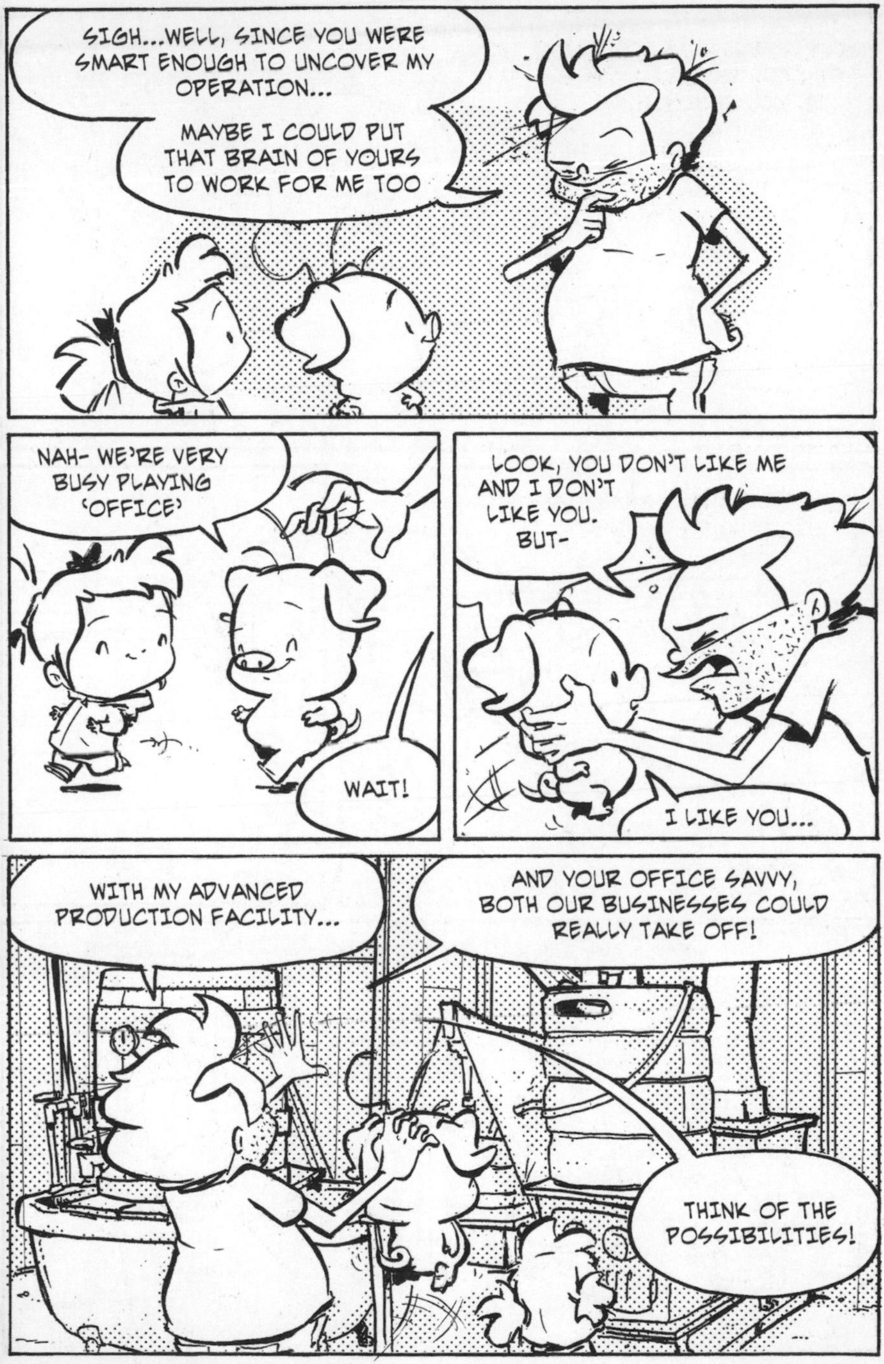
SIGH...WELL, SINCE YOU WERE SMART ENOUGH TO UNCOVER MY OPERATION...
MAYBE I COULD PUT THAT BRAIN OF YOURS TO WORK FOR ME TOO
NAH- WE'RE VERY BUSY PLAYING 'OFFICE'
WAIT!
LOOK, YOU DON'T LIKE ME AND I DON'T LIKE YOU. BUT-
I LIKE YOU...
WITH MY ADVANCED PRODUCTION FACILITY...
AND YOUR OFFICE SAVVY, BOTH OUR BUSINESSES COULD REALLY TAKE OFF!
THINK OF THE POSSIBILITIES!

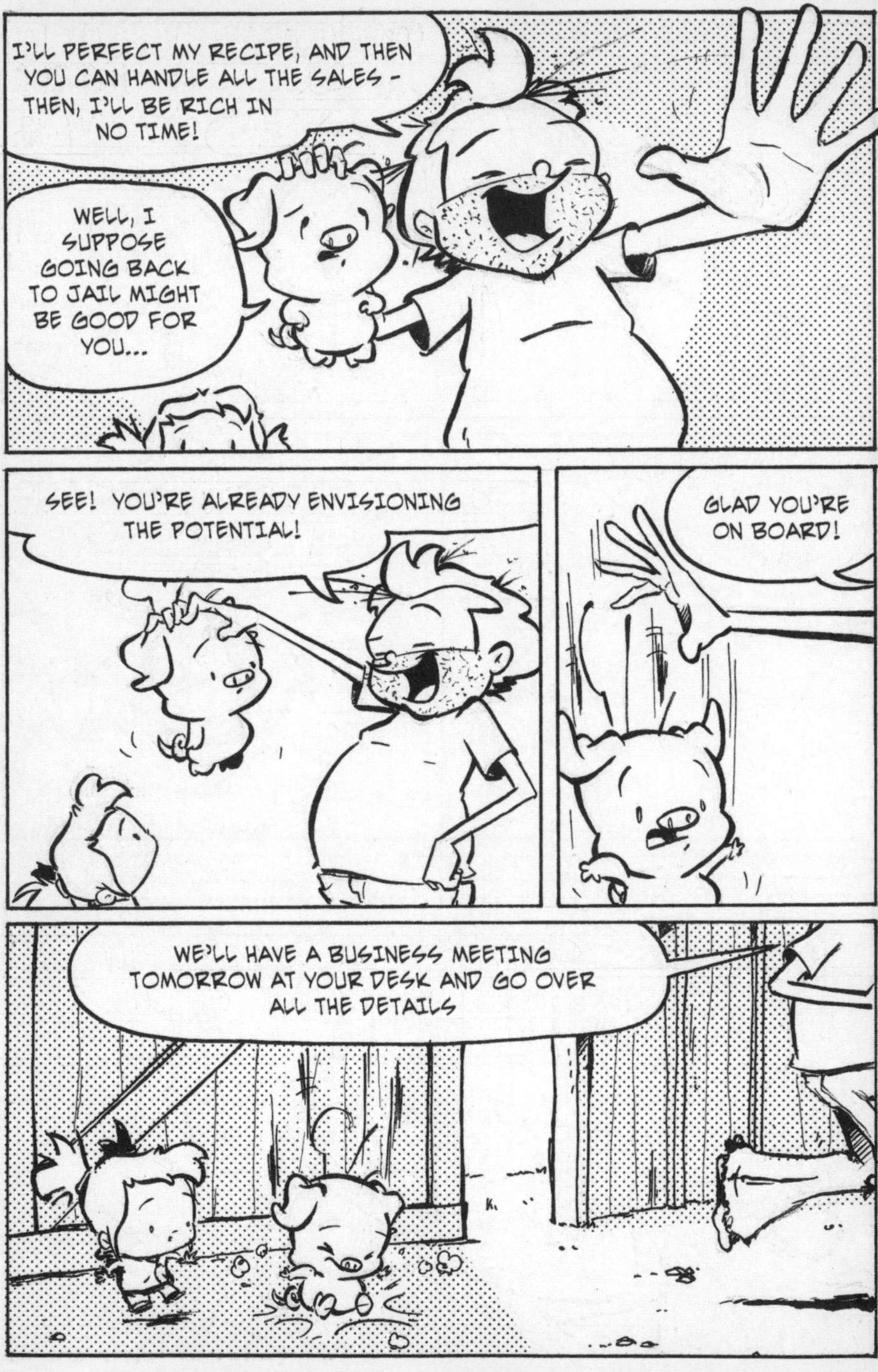
I'LL PERFECT MY RECIPE, AND THEN YOU CAN HANDLE ALL THE SALES - THEN, I'LL BE RICH IN NO TIME!
WELL, I SUPPOSE GOING BACK TO JAIL MIGHT BE GOOD FOR YOU...
SEE! YOU'RE ALREADY ENVISIONING THE POTENTIAL!
GLAD YOU'RE ON BOARD!
WE'LL HAVE A BUSINESS MEETING TOMORROW AT YOUR DESK AND GO OVER ALL THE DETAILS

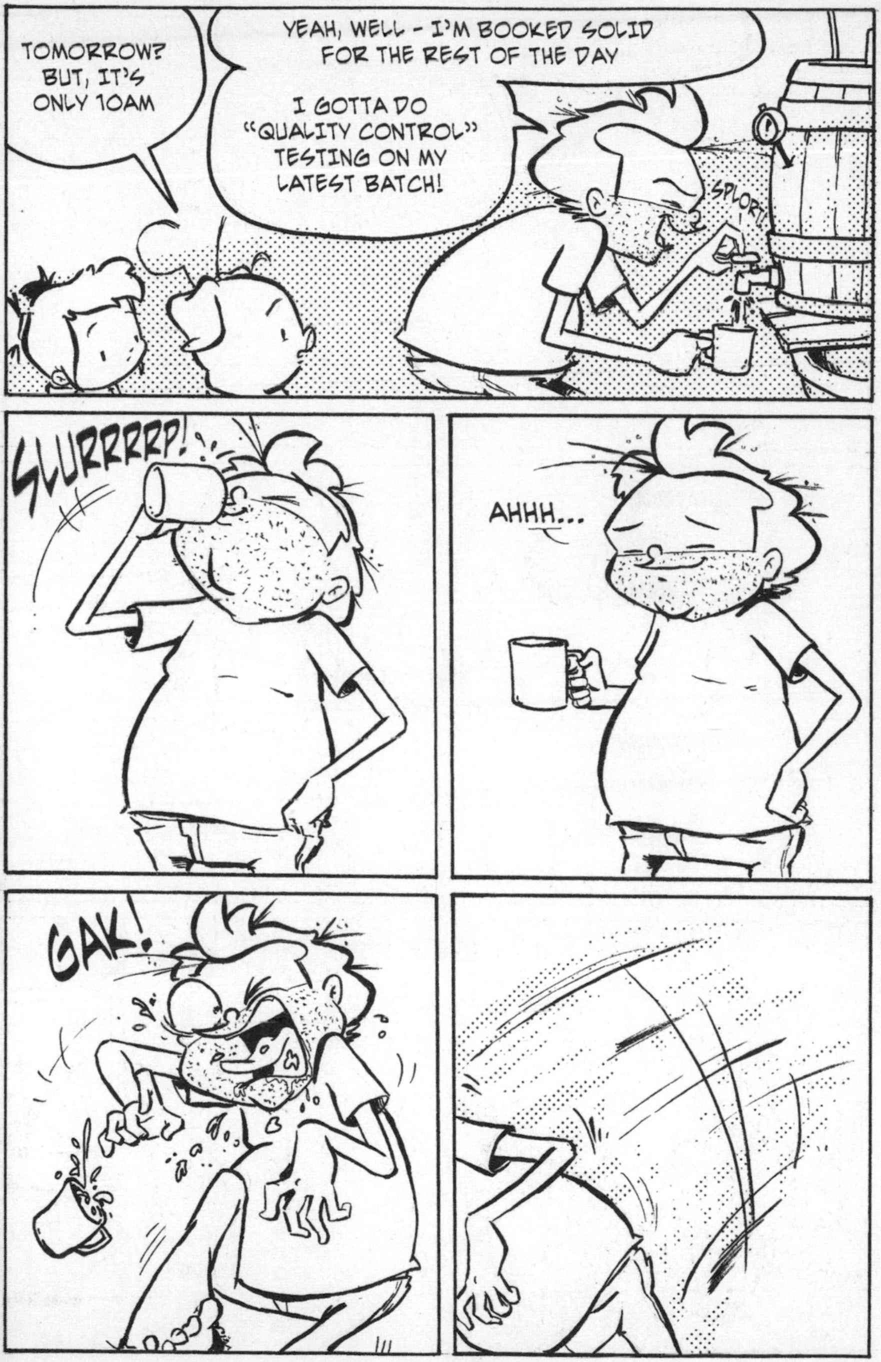
TOMORROW? BUT, IT'S ONLY 10AM
YEAH, WELL - I'M BOOKED SOLID FOR THE REST OF THE DAY
I GOTTA DO "QUALITY CONTROL" TESTING ON MY LATEST BATCH!
SPLORT!
SLURRRRP!
AHHH...
GAK!

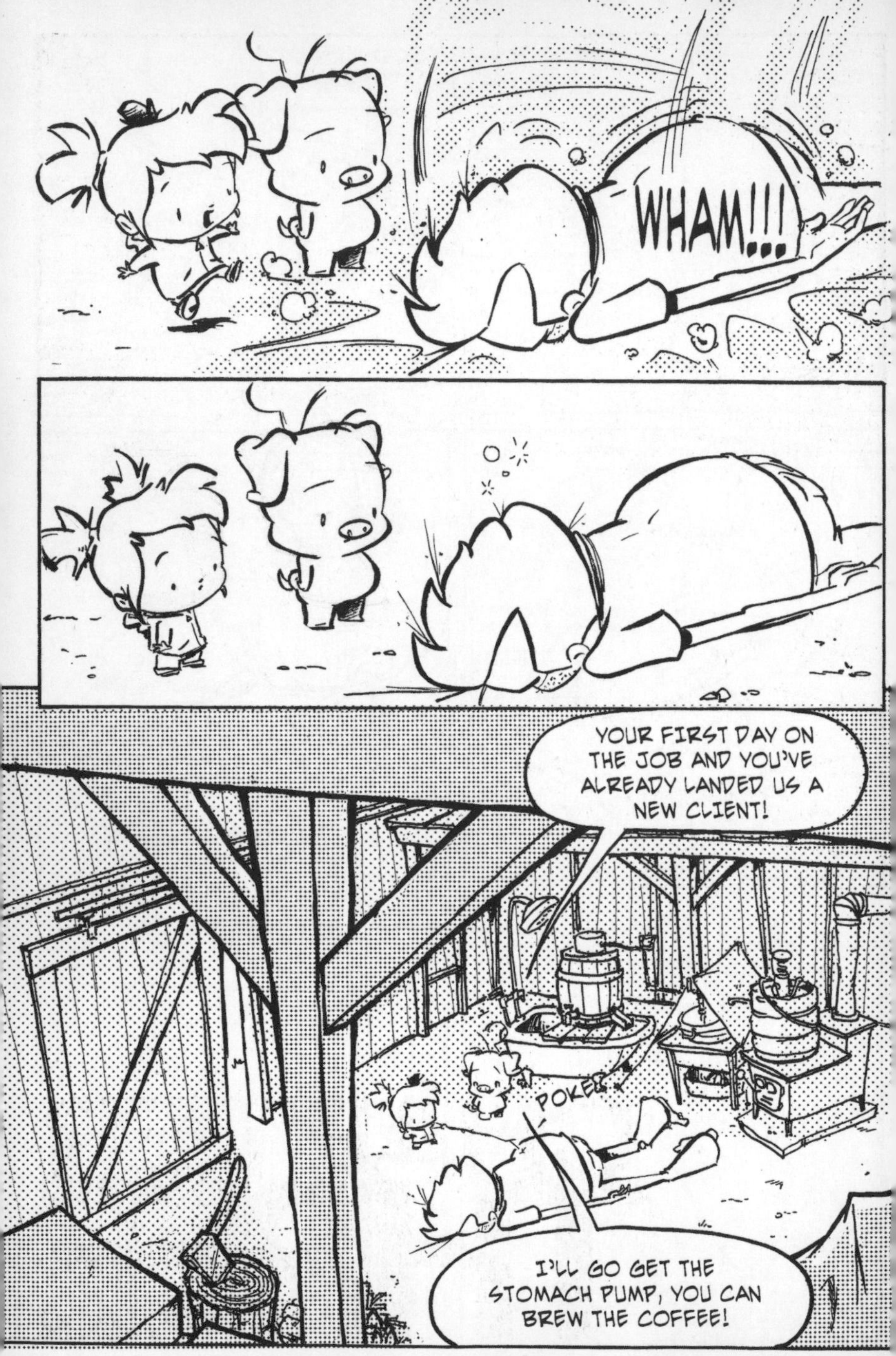
WHAM!!!
YOUR FIRST DAY ON THE JOB AND YOU'VE ALREADY LANDED US A NEW CLIENT!
POKE
I'LL GO GET THE STOMACH PUMP, YOU CAN BREW THE COFFEE!

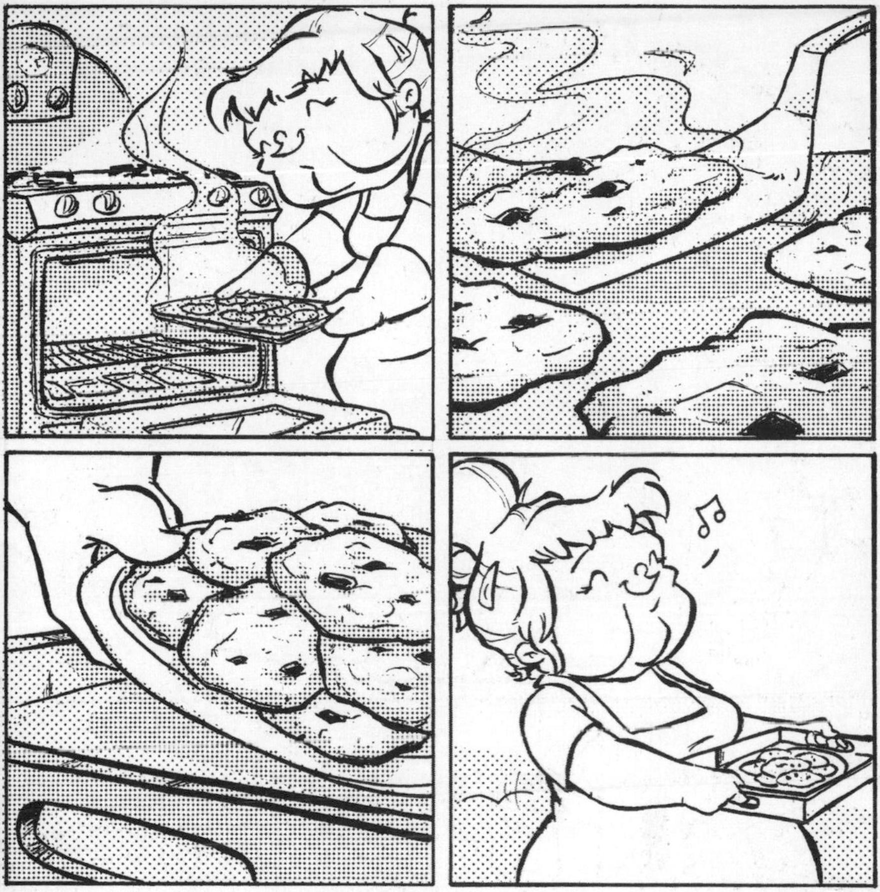

CHAPTER THREE

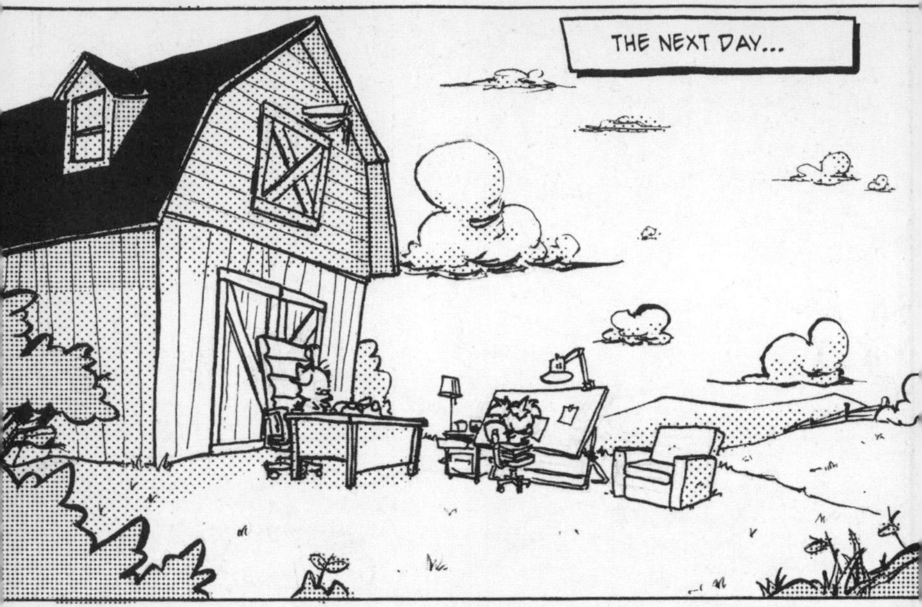
THE NEXT DAY...

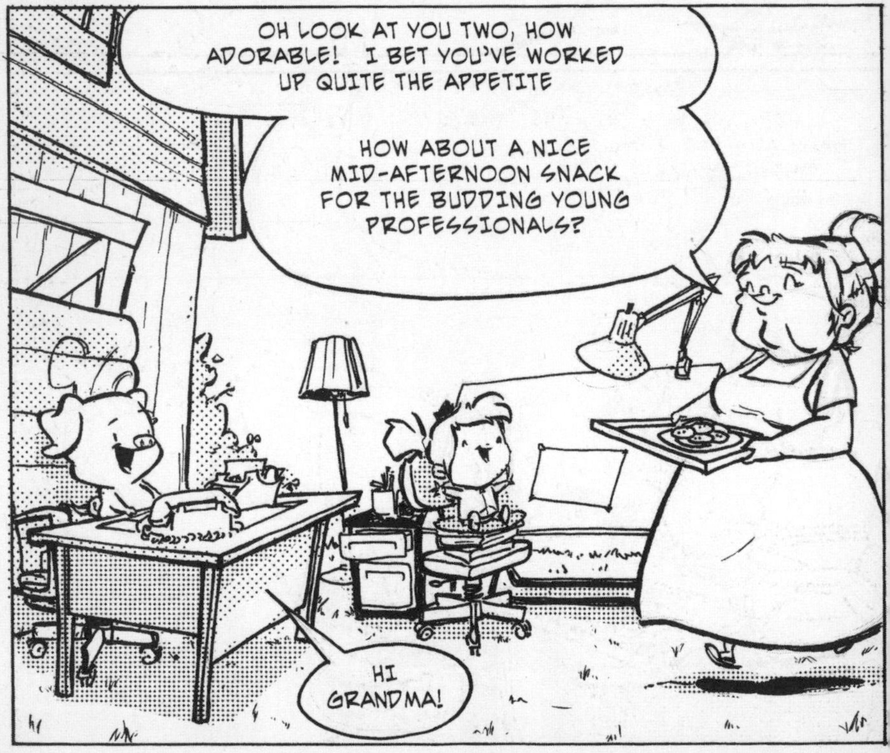
OH LOOK AT YOU TWO, HOW ADORABLE! I BET YOU'VE WORKED UP QUITE THE APPETITE
HOW ABOUT A NICE MID-AFTERNOON SNACK FOR THE BUDDING YOUNG PROFESSIONALS?
HI GRANDMA!

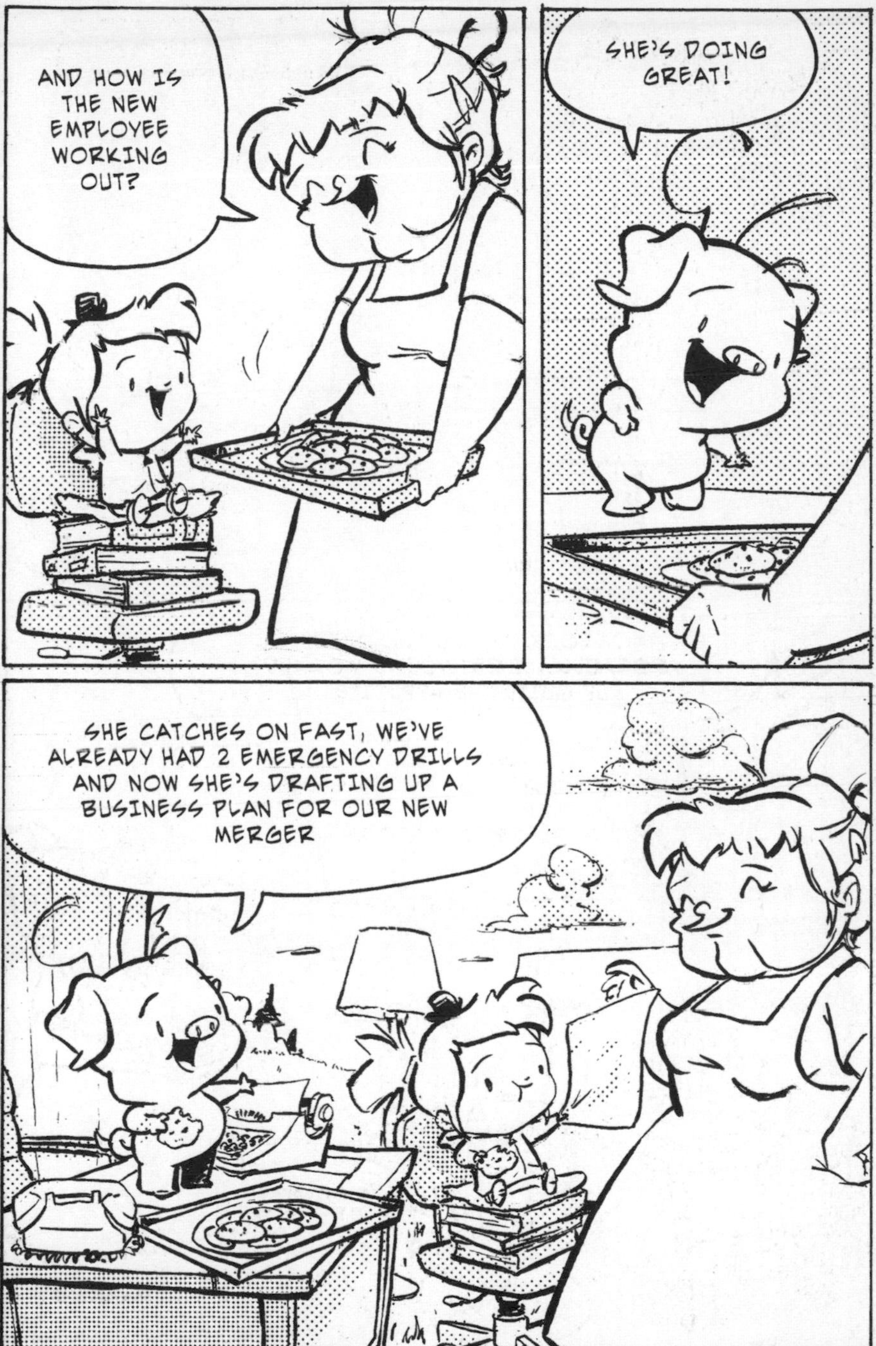
AND HOW IS THE NEW EMPLOYEE WORKING OUT?
SHE'S DOING GREAT!
SHE CATCHES ON FAST, WE'VE ALREADY HAD 2 EMERGENCY DRILLS AND NOW SHE'S DRAFTING UP A BUSINESS PLAN FOR OUR NEW MERGER

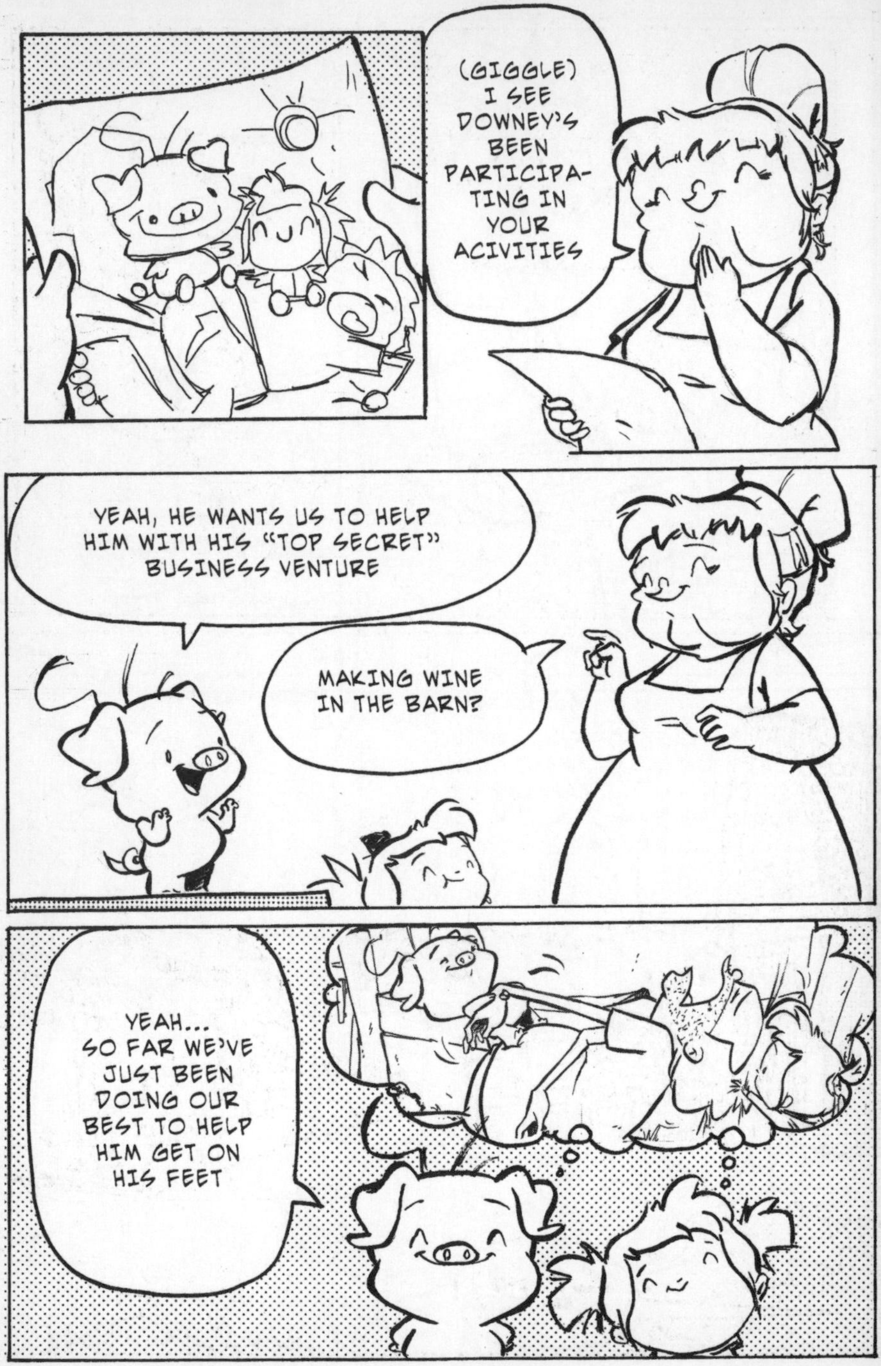
(GIGGLE) I SEE DOWNEY'S BEEN PARTICIPA-TING IN YOUR ACIVITIES
YEAH, HE WANTS US TO HELP HIM WITH HIS "TOP SECRET" BUSINESS VENTURE
MAKING WINE IN THE BARN?
YEAH... SO FAR WE'VE JUST BEEN DOING OUR BEST TO HELP HIM GET ON HIS FEET

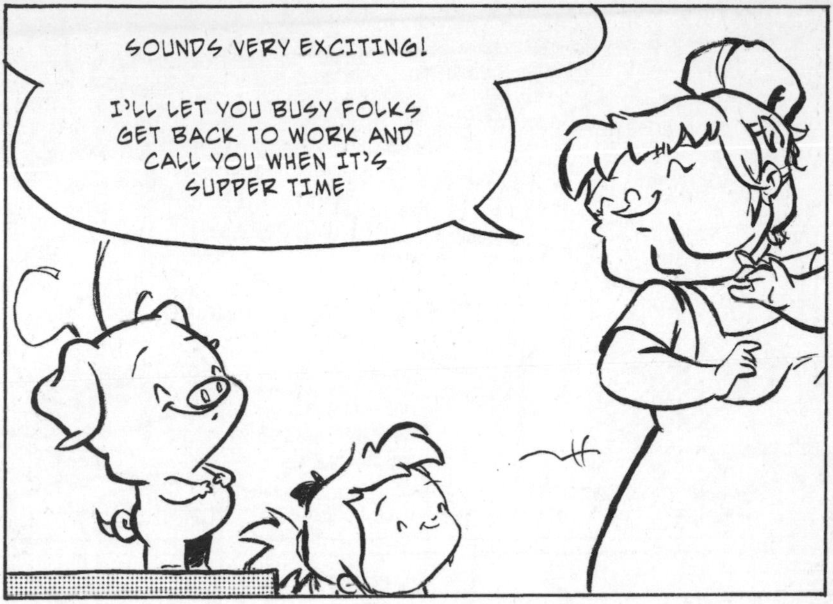
SOUNDS VERY EXCITING!
I'LL LET YOU BUSY FOLKS GET BACK TO WORK AND CALL YOU WHEN IT'S SUPPER TIME

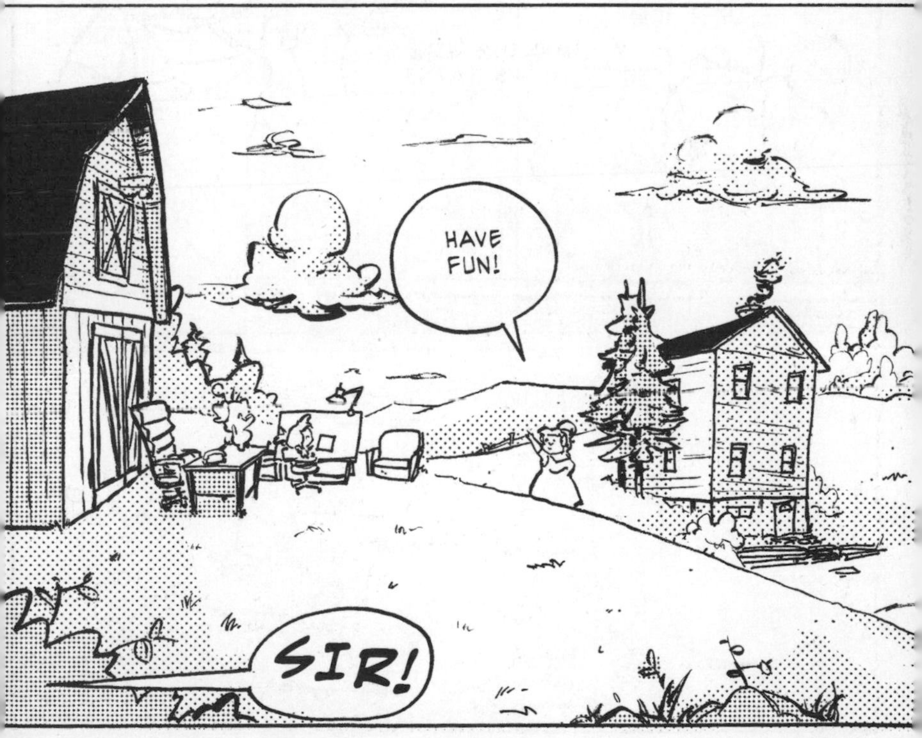
HAVE FUN!
SIR!

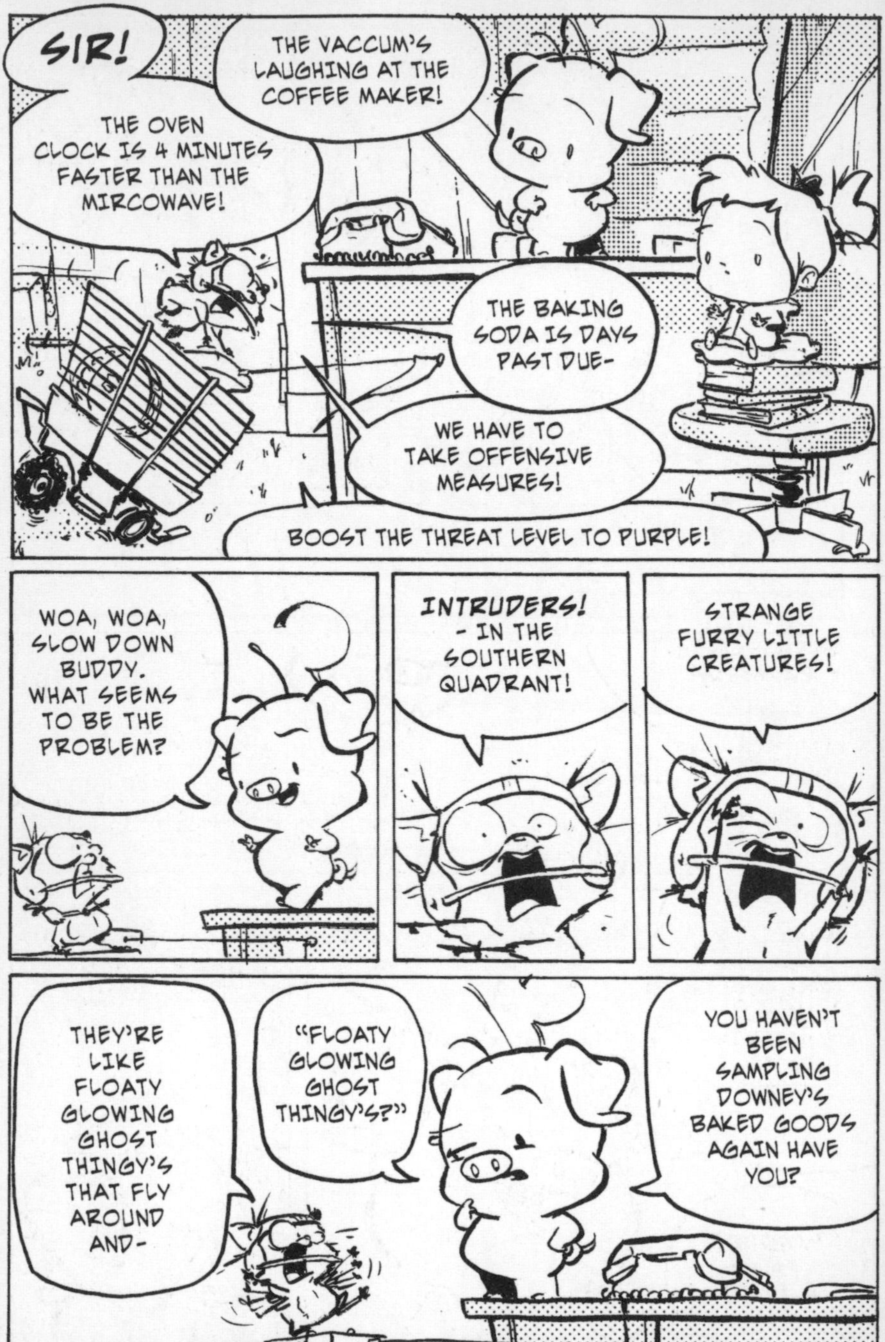
SIR!
THE VACCUM'S LAUGHING AT THE COFFEE MAKER!
THE OVEN CLOCK IS 4 MINUTES FASTER THAN THE MIRCOWAVE!
THE BAKING SODA IS DAYS PAST DUE-
WE HAVE TO TAKE OFFENSIVE MEASURES!
BOOST THE THREAT LEVEL TO PURPLE!
WOA, WOA, SLOW DOWN BUDDY. WHAT SEEMS TO BE THE PROBLEM?
INTRUDERS! - IN THE SOUTHERN QUADRANT!
STRANGE FURRY LITTLE CREATURES!
THEY'RE LIKE FLOATY GLOWING GHOST THINGY'S THAT FLY AROUND AND-
"FLOATY GLOWING GHOST THINGY'S?"
YOU HAVEN'T BEEN SAMPLING DOWNEY'S BAKED GOODS AGAIN HAVE YOU?

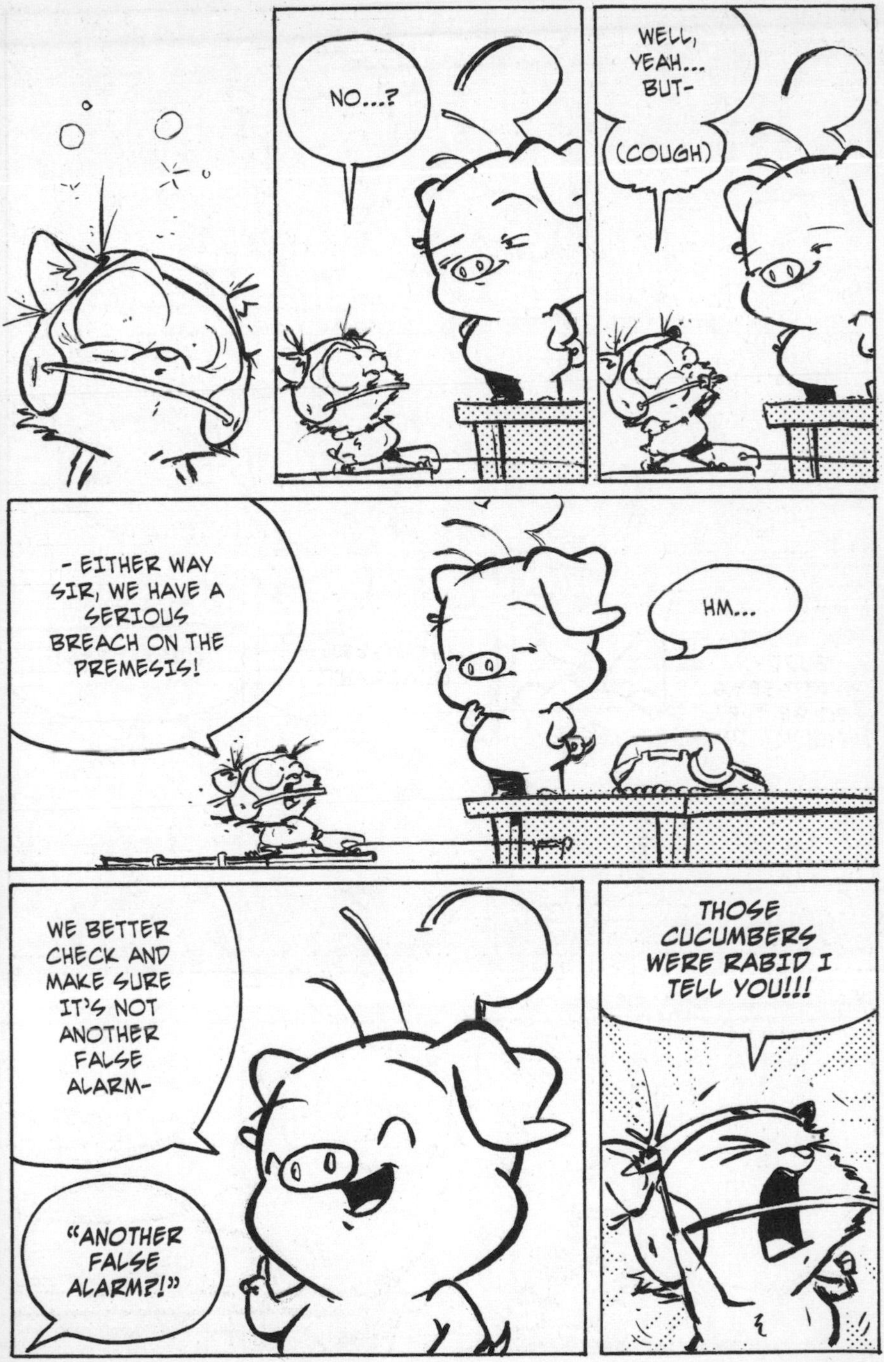
NO...?
WELL, YEAH... BUT-
(COUGH)
- EITHER WAY SIR, WE HAVE A SERIOUS BREACH ON THE PREMESIS!
HM...
WE BETTER CHECK AND MAKE SURE IT'S NOT ANOTHER FALSE ALARM-
"ANOTHER FALSE ALARM?!"
THOSE CUCUMBERS WERE RABID I TELL YOU!!!

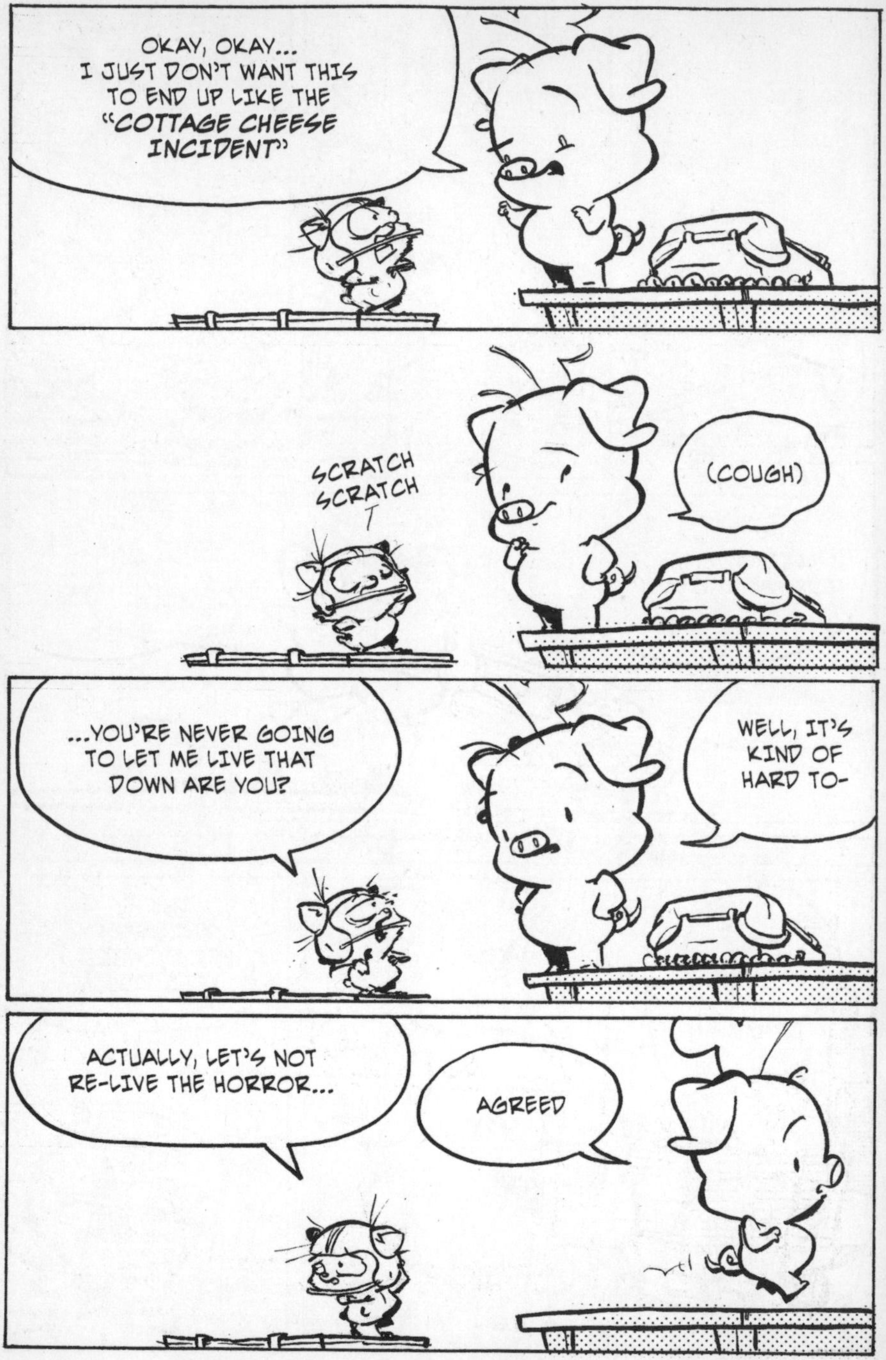
OKAY, OKAY... I JUST DON'T WANT THIS TO END UP LIKE THE "COTTAGE CHEESE INCIDENT"
SCRATCH SCRATCH
(COUGH)
...YOU'RE NEVER GOING TO LET ME LIVE THAT DOWN ARE YOU?
WELL, IT'S KIND OF HARD TO-
ACTUALLY, LET'S NOT RE-LIVE THE HORROR...
AGREED

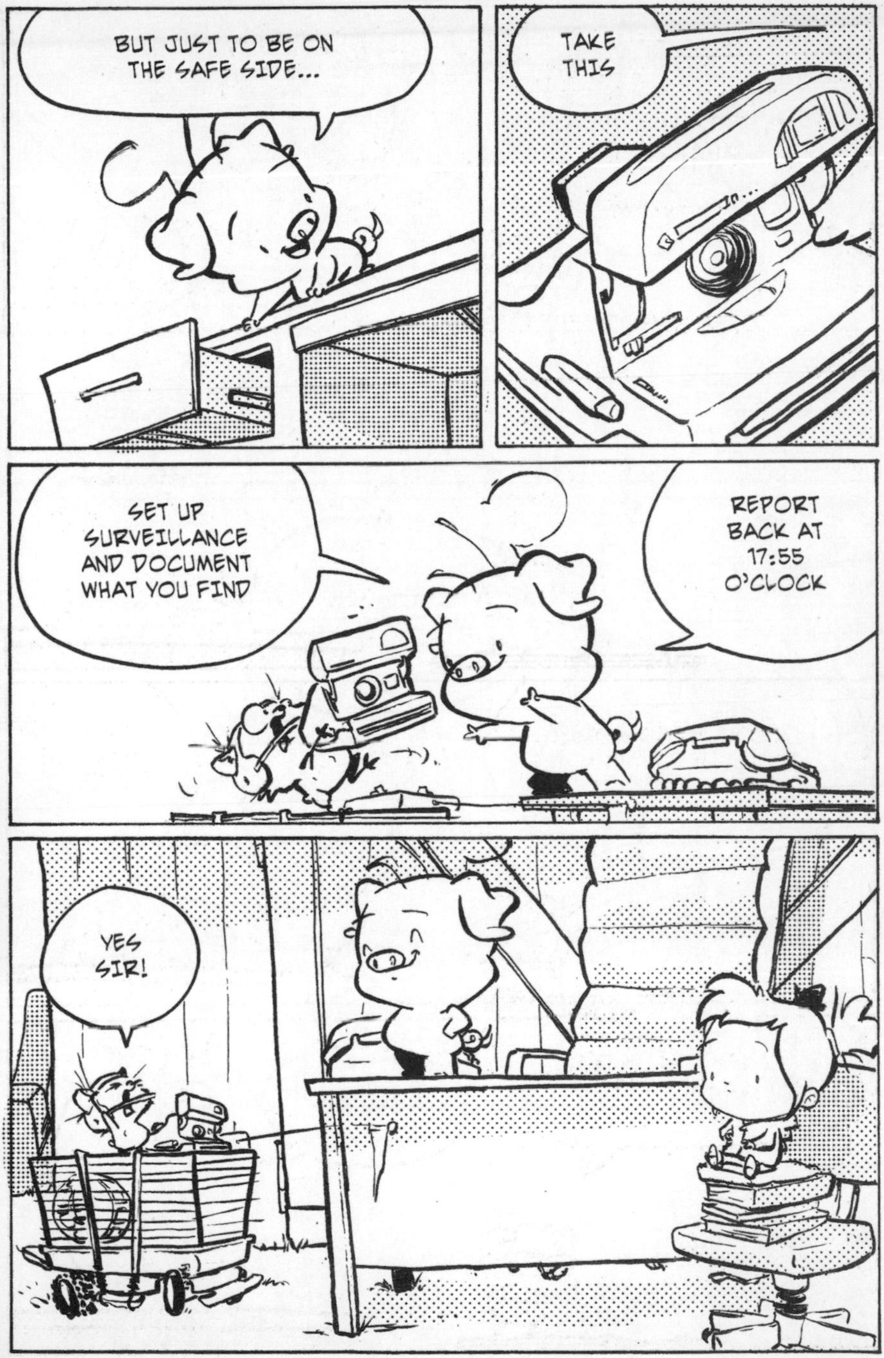
BUT JUST TO BE ON THE SAFE SIDE...
TAKE THIS
SET UP SURVEILLANCE AND DOCUMENT WHAT YOU FIND
REPORT BACK AT 17:55 O'CLOCK
YES SIR!

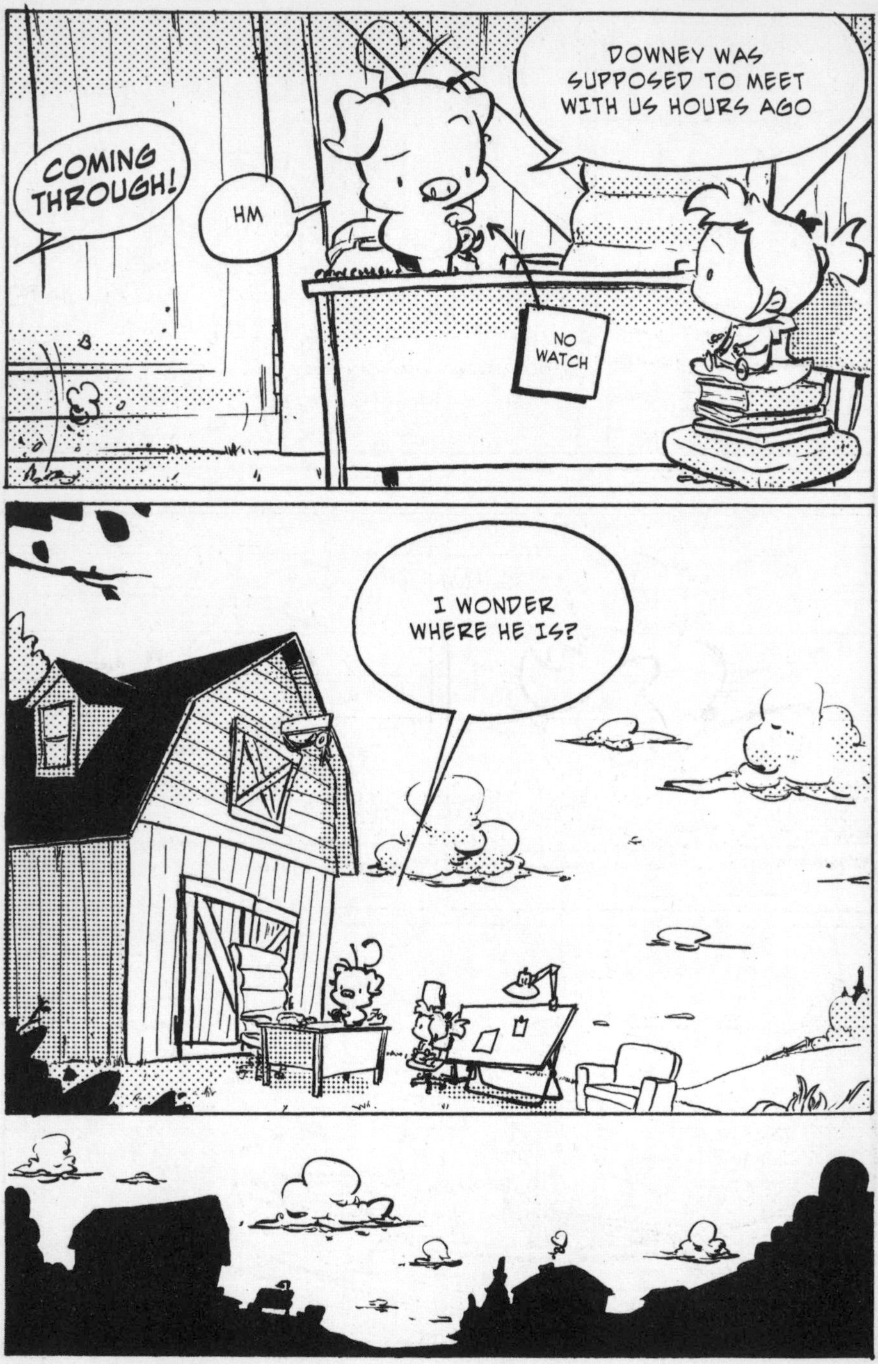
DOWNEY WAS SUPPOSED TO MEET WITH US HOURS AGO
HM
COMING THROUGH!
NO WATCH
I WONDER WHERE HE IS?

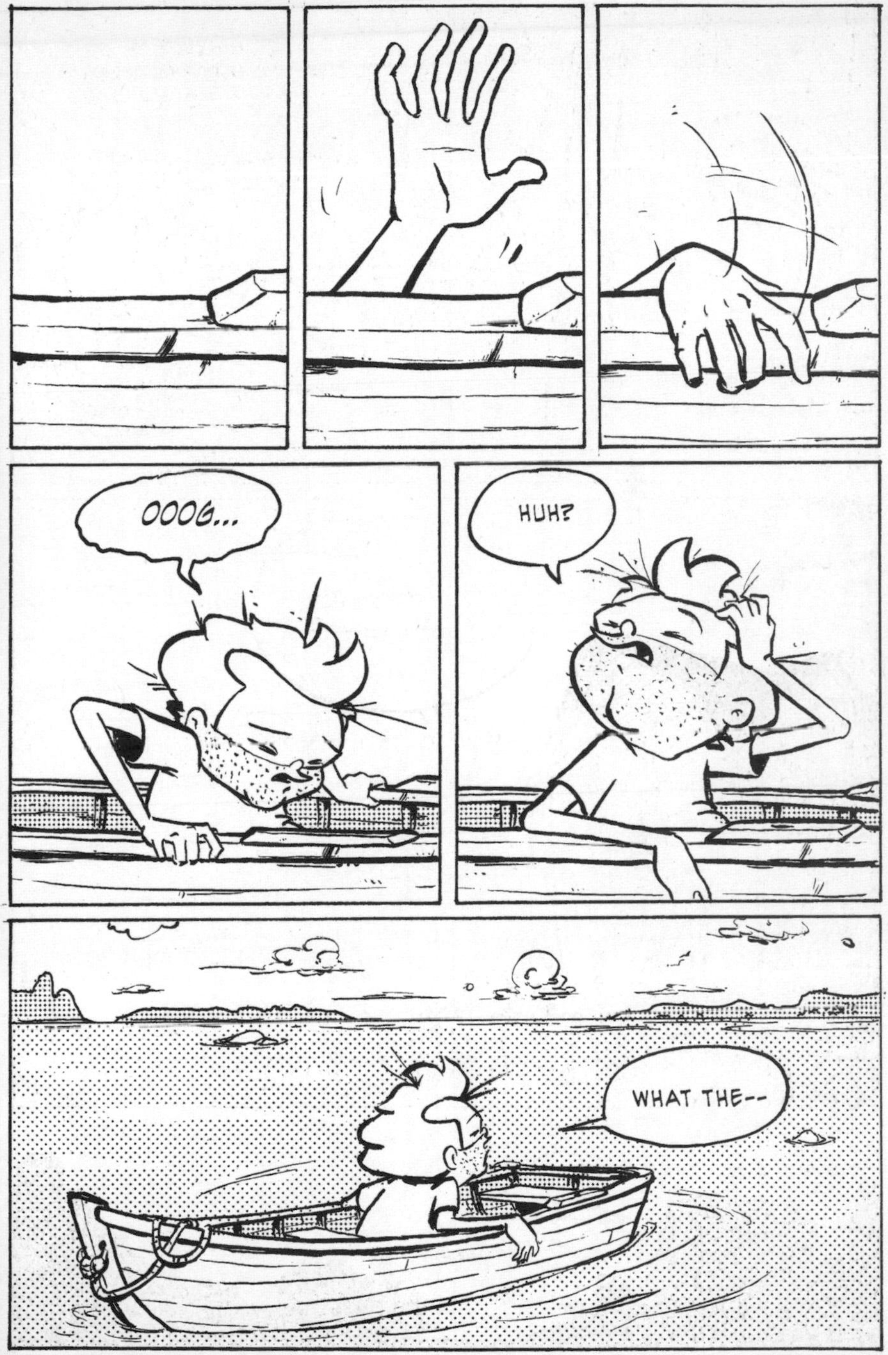
OOOG...
HUH?
WHAT THE--

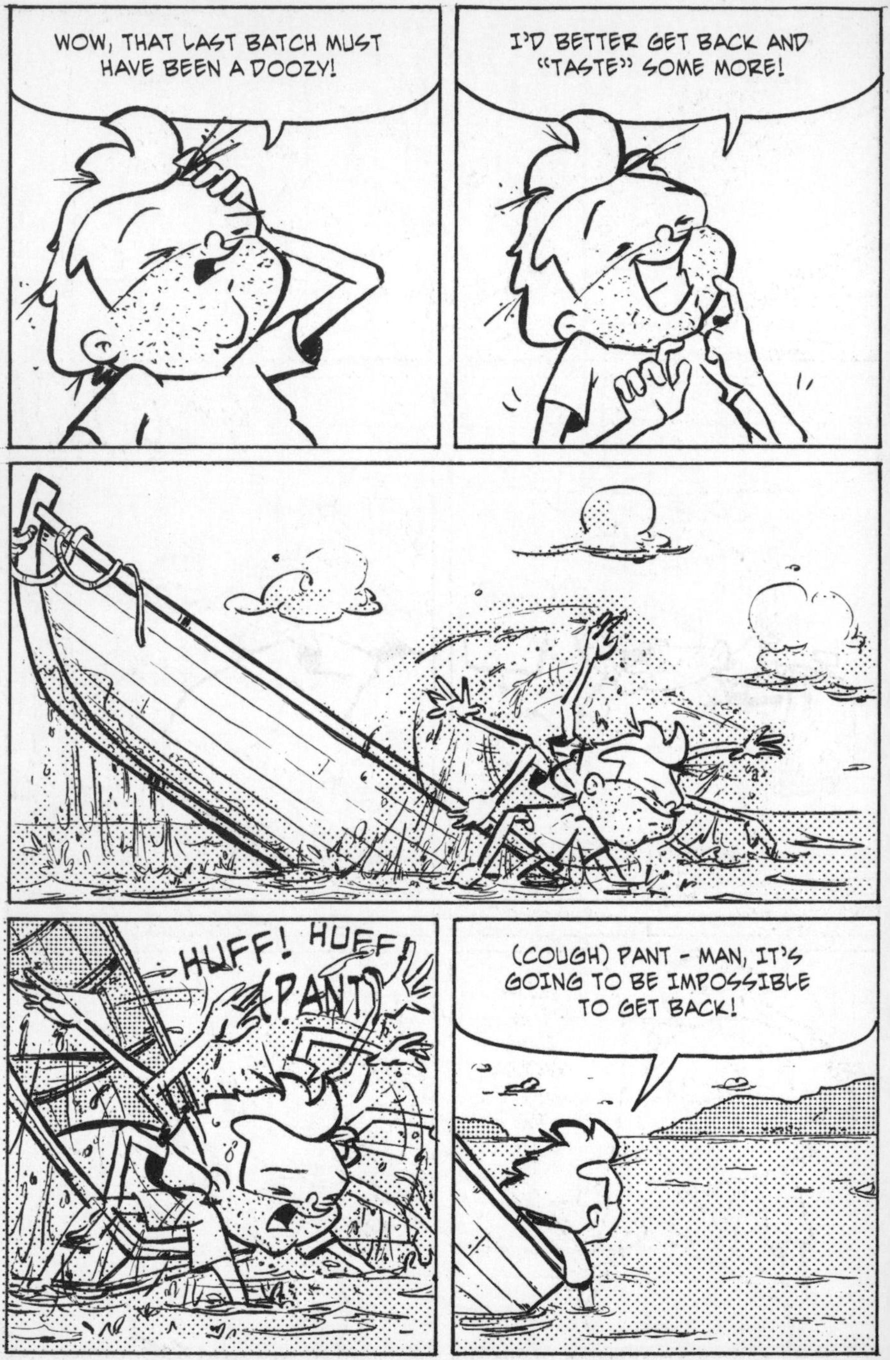
WOW, THAT LAST BATCH MUST HAVE BEEN A DOOZY!
I'D BETTER GET BACK AND "TASTE" SOME MORE!
HUFF! HUFF!
(PANT)
(COUGH) PANT - MAN, IT'S GOING TO BE IMPOSSIBLE TO GET BACK!

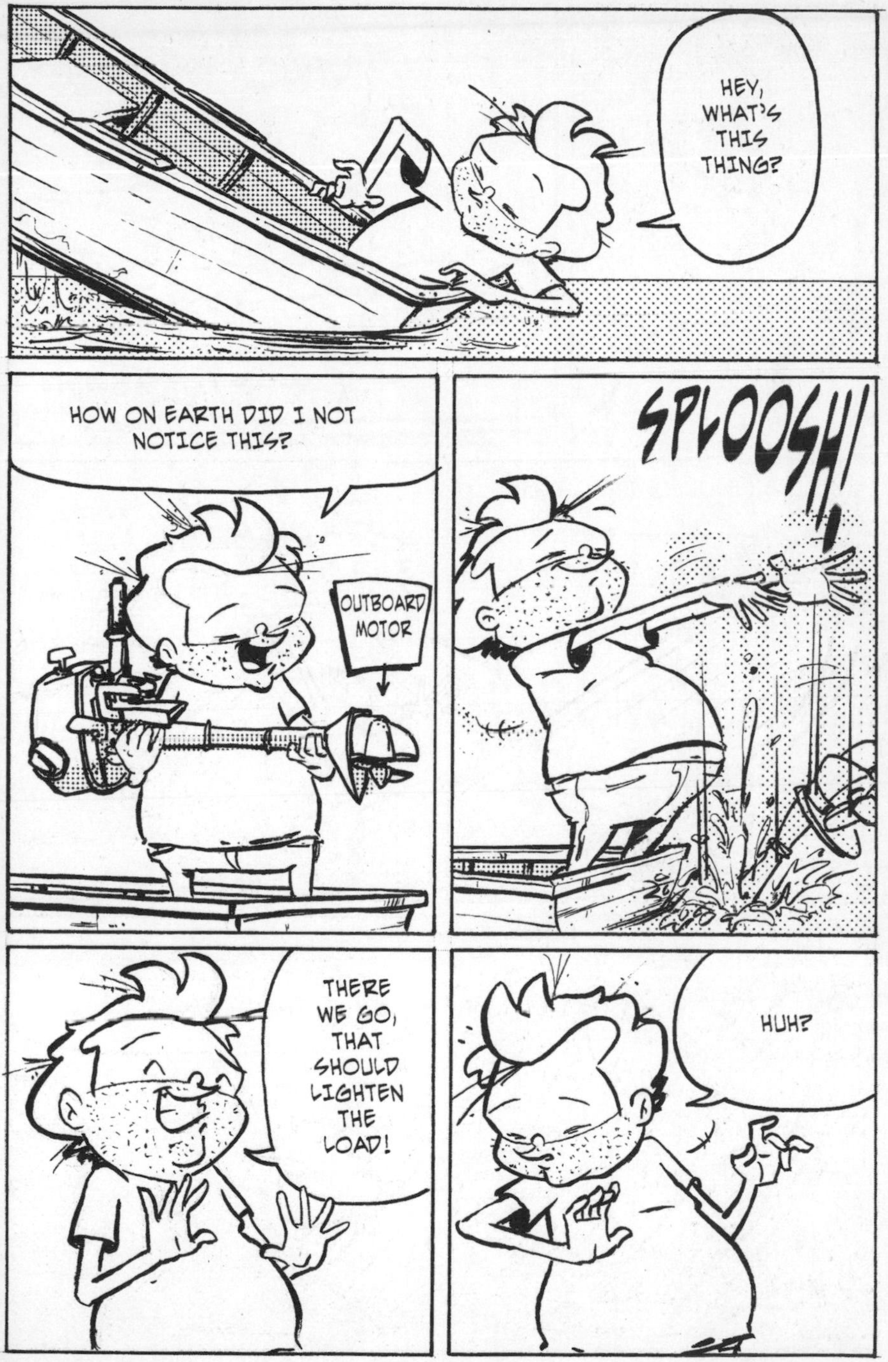
HEY, WHAT'S THIS THING?
HOW ON EARTH DID I NOT NOTICE THIS?
OUTBOARD MOTOR
SPLOOSH!
THERE WE GO, THAT SHOULD LIGHTEN THE LOAD!
HUH?

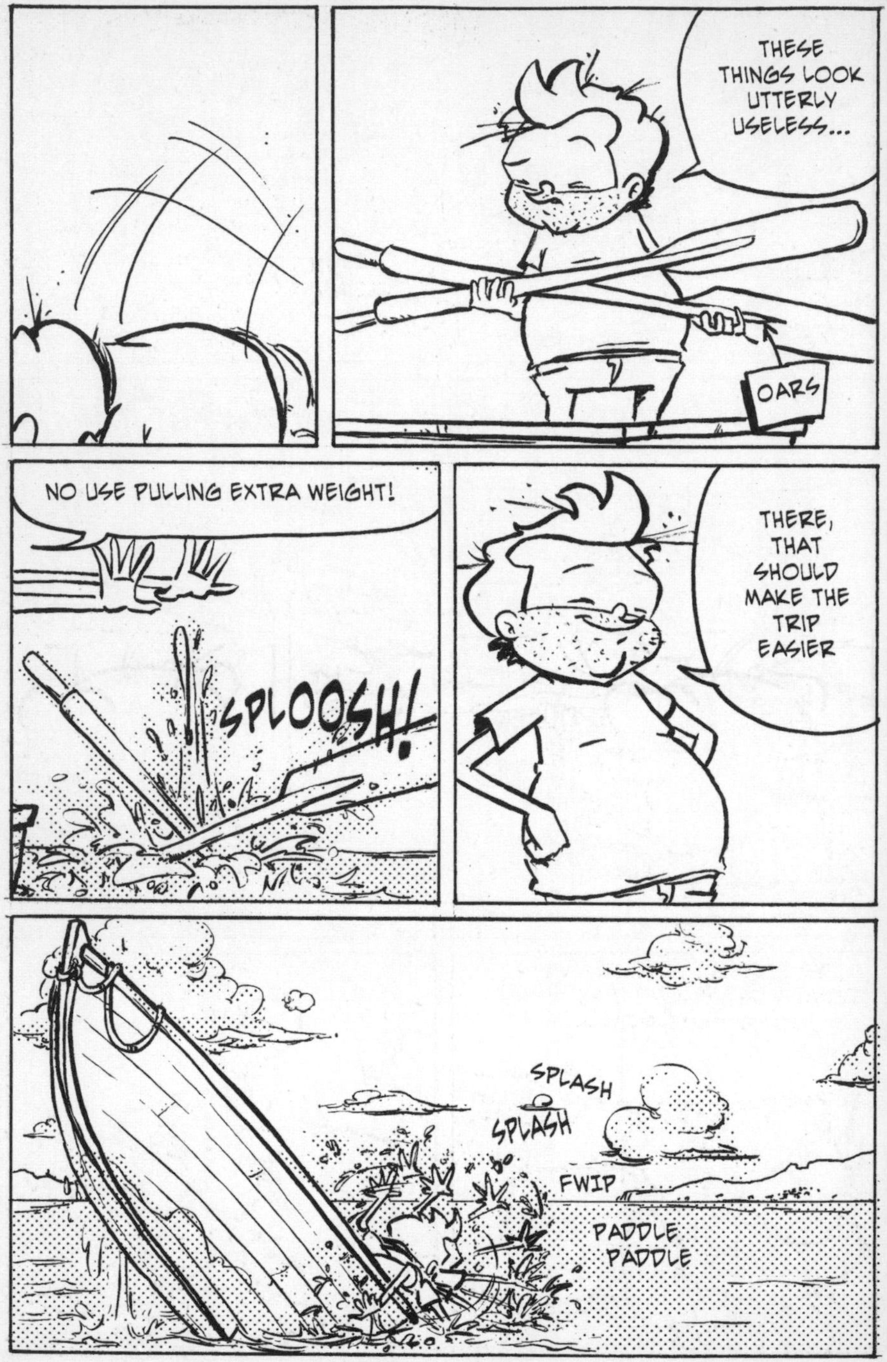
THESE THINGS LOOK UTTERLY USELESS...
OARS
NO USE PULLING EXTRA WEIGHT!
SPLOOSH!
THERE, THAT SHOULD MAKE THE TRIP EASIER
SPLASH
SPLASH
FWIP
PADDLE
PADDLE

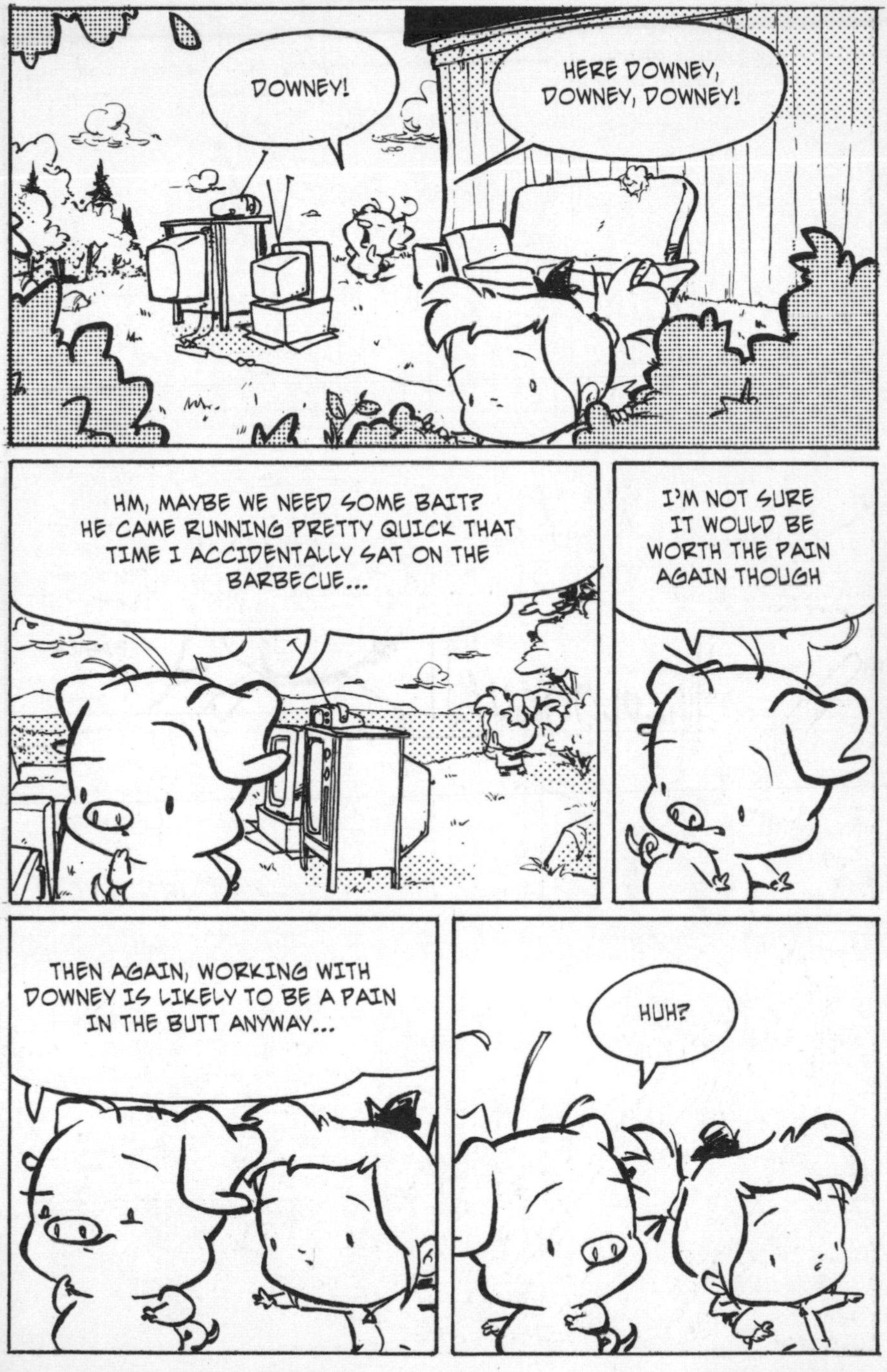
DOWNEY!
HERE DOWNEY, DOWNEY, DOWNEY!
HM, MAYBE WE NEED SOME BAIT? HE CAME RUNNING PRETTY QUICK THAT TIME I ACCIDENTALLY SAT ON THE BARBECUE...
I'M NOT SURE IT WOULD BE WORTH THE PAIN AGAIN THOUGH
THEN AGAIN, WORKING WITH DOWNEY IS LIKELY TO BE A PAIN IN THE BUTT ANYWAY...
HUH?

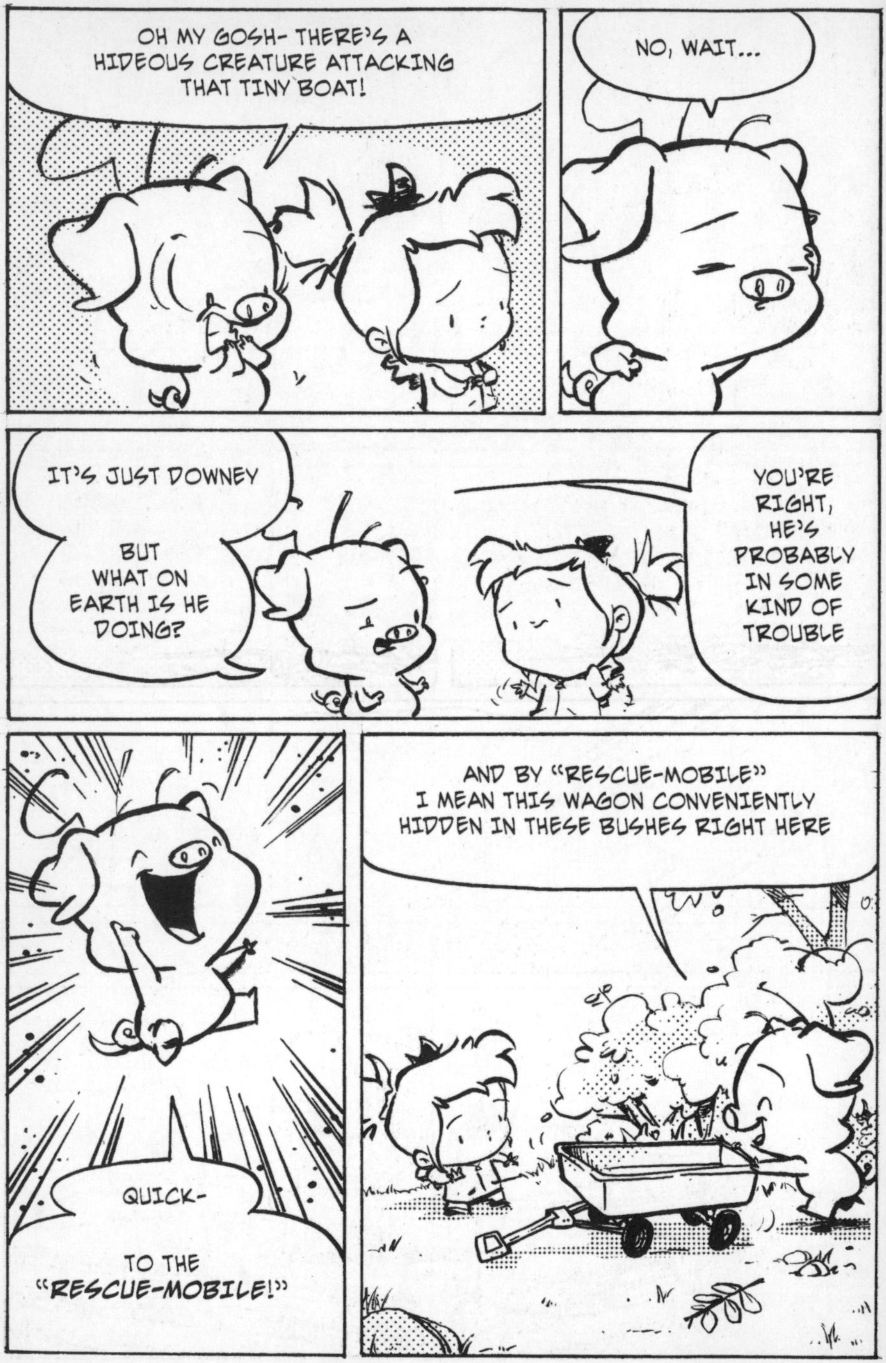
OH MY GOSH- THERE'S A HIDEOUS CREATURE ATTACKING THAT TINY BOAT!
NO, WAIT...
IT'S JUST DOWNEY
BUT WHAT ON EARTH IS HE DOING?
YOU'RE RIGHT, HE'S PROBABLY IN SOME KIND OF TROUBLE
QUICK-
TO THE "RESCUE-MOBILE!"
AND BY "RESCUE-MOBILE" I MEAN THIS WAGON CONVENIENTLY HIDDEN IN THESE BUSHES RIGHT HERE

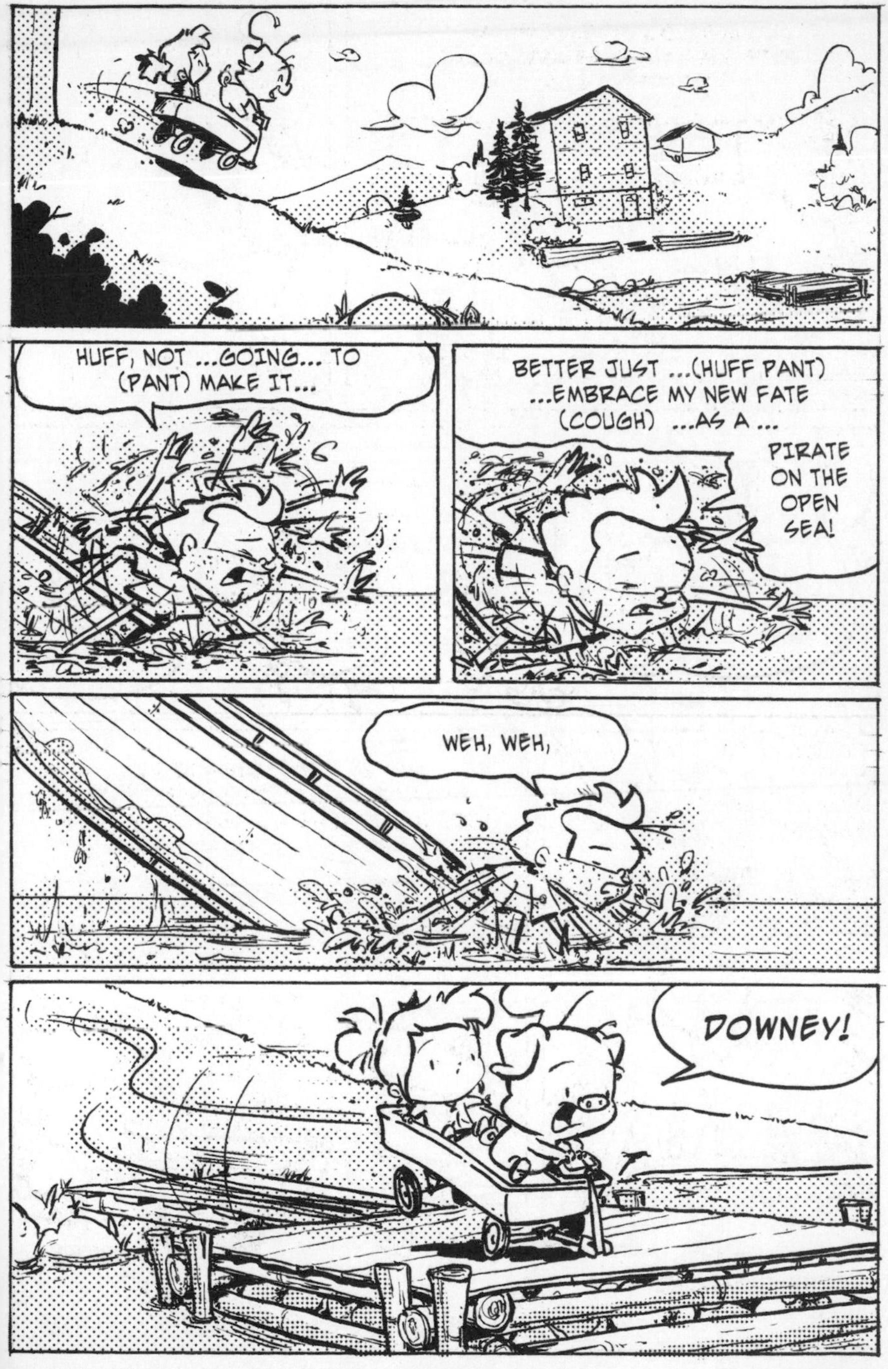
HUFF, NOT ...GOING... TO (PANT) MAKE IT...
BETTER JUST ...(HUFF PANT) ...EMBRACE MY NEW FATE (COUGH) ...AS A ...
PIRATE ON THE OPEN SEA!
WEH, WEH,
DOWNEY!

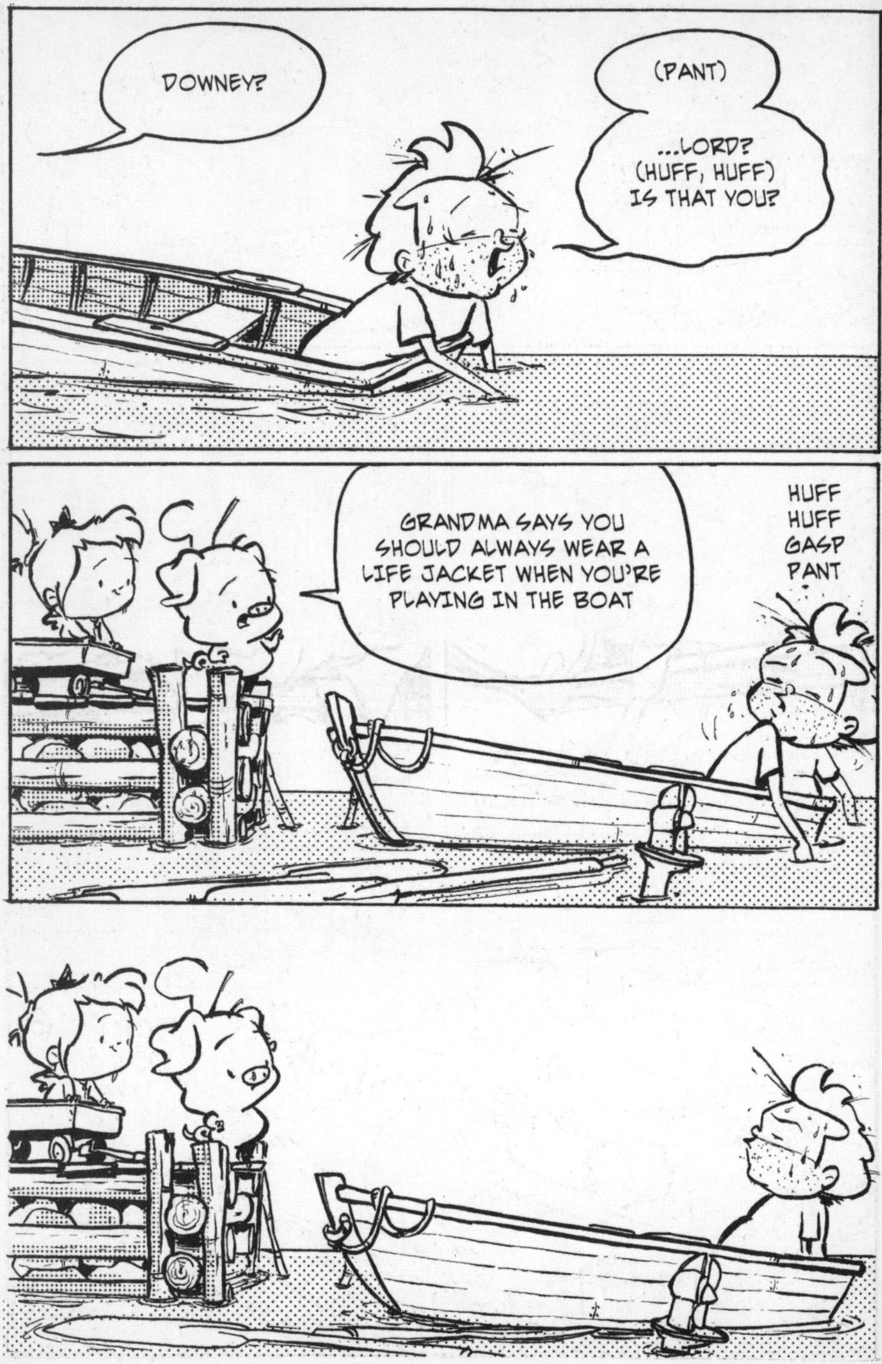
DOWNEY?
(PANT)
...LORD? (HUFF, HUFF) IS THAT YOU?
GRANDMA SAYS YOU SHOULD ALWAYS WEAR A LIFE JACKET WHEN YOU'RE PLAYING IN THE BOAT
HUFF HUFF GASP PANT

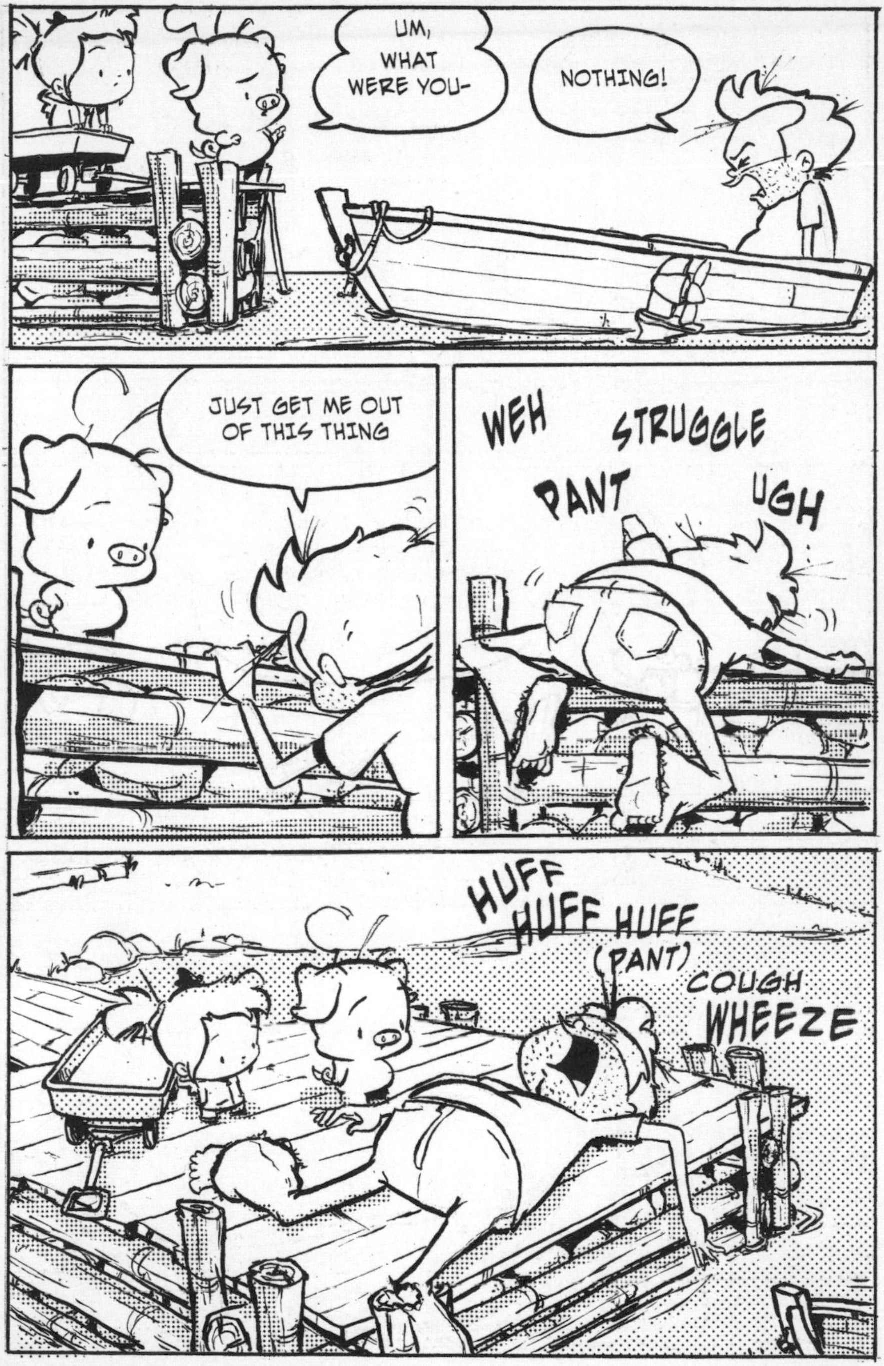
UM, WHAT WERE YOU-
NOTHING!
JUST GET ME OUT OF THIS THING
WEH
STRUGGLE
PANT
UGH
HUFF
HUFF HUFF
(PANT)
COUGH
WHEEZE

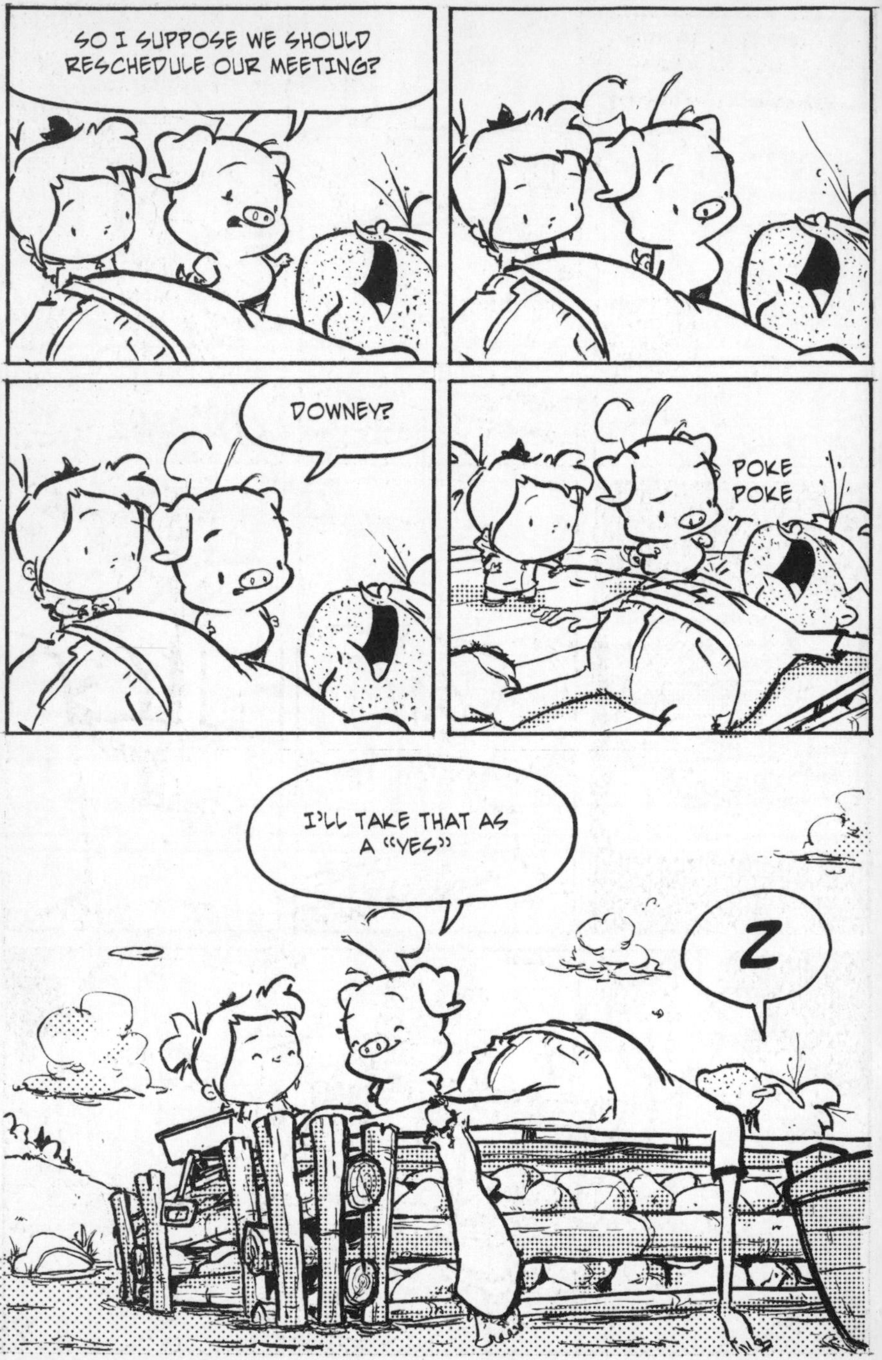
SO I SUPPOSE WE SHOULD RESCHEDULE OUR MEETING?
DOWNEY?
POKE POKE
I'LL TAKE THAT AS A "YES"
Z

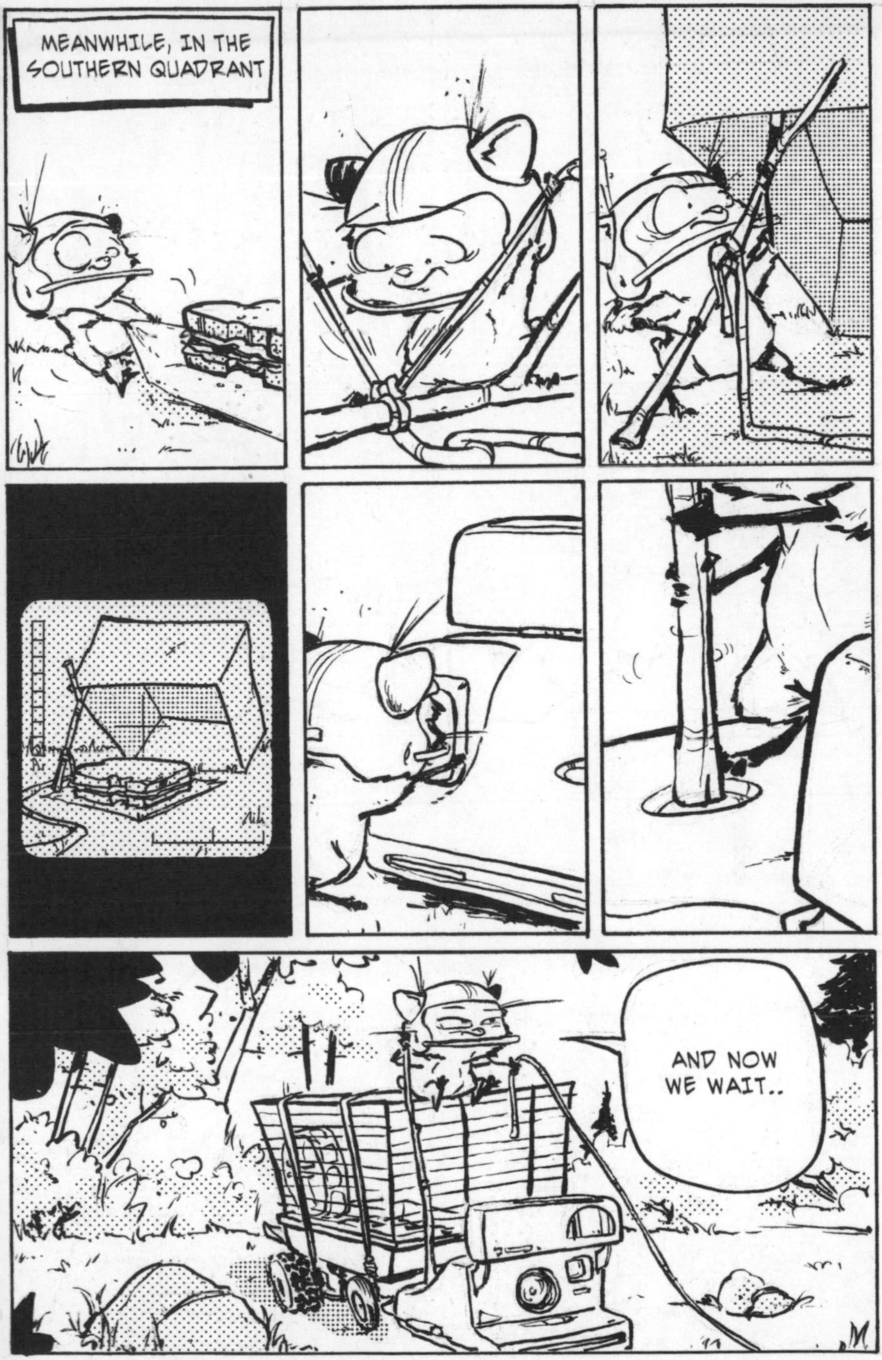
MEANWHILE, IN THE SOUTHERN QUADRANT
AND NOW WE WAIT..

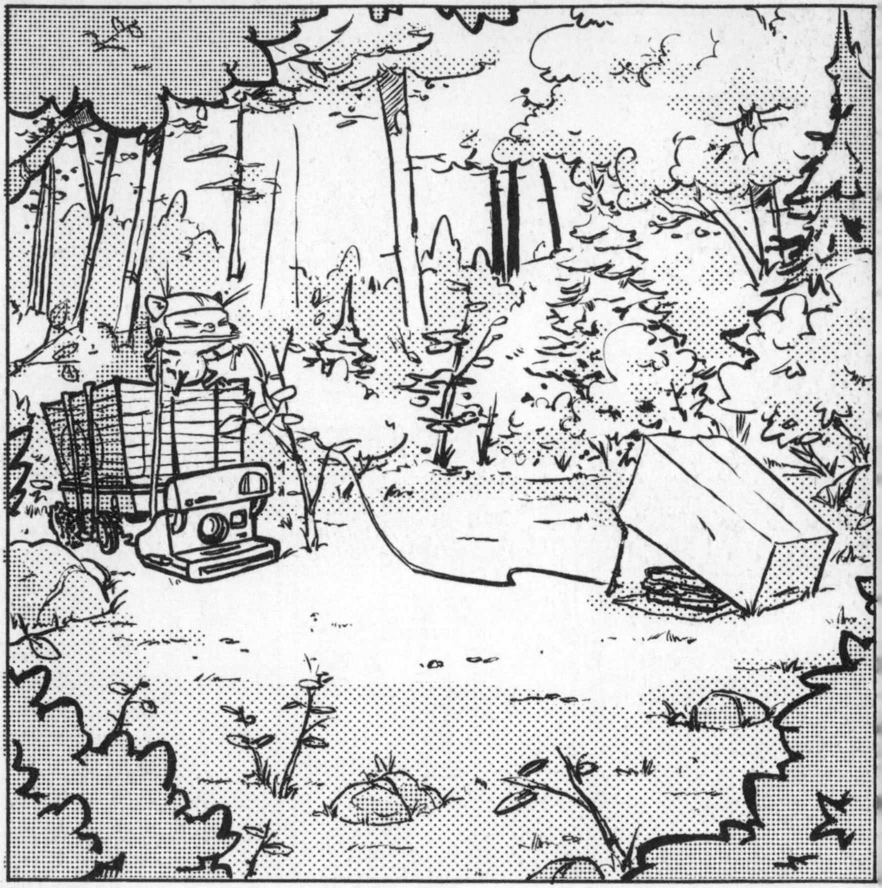

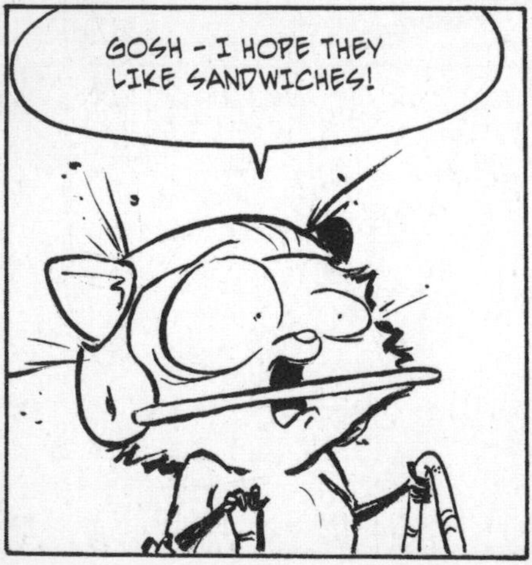
GOSH - I HOPE THEY LIKE SANDWICHES!

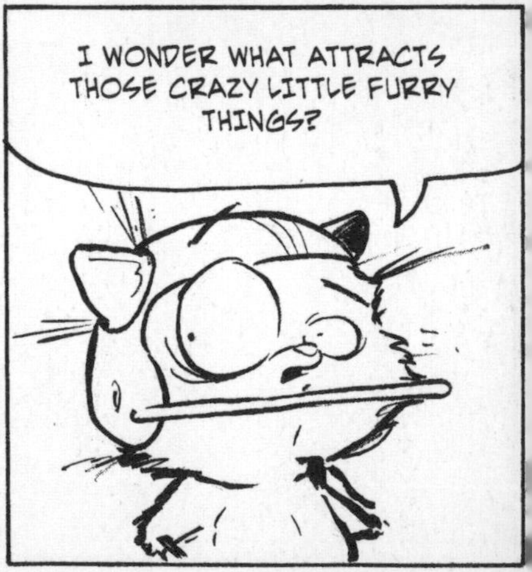
I WONDER WHAT ATTRACTS THOSE CRAZY LITTLE FURRY THINGS?

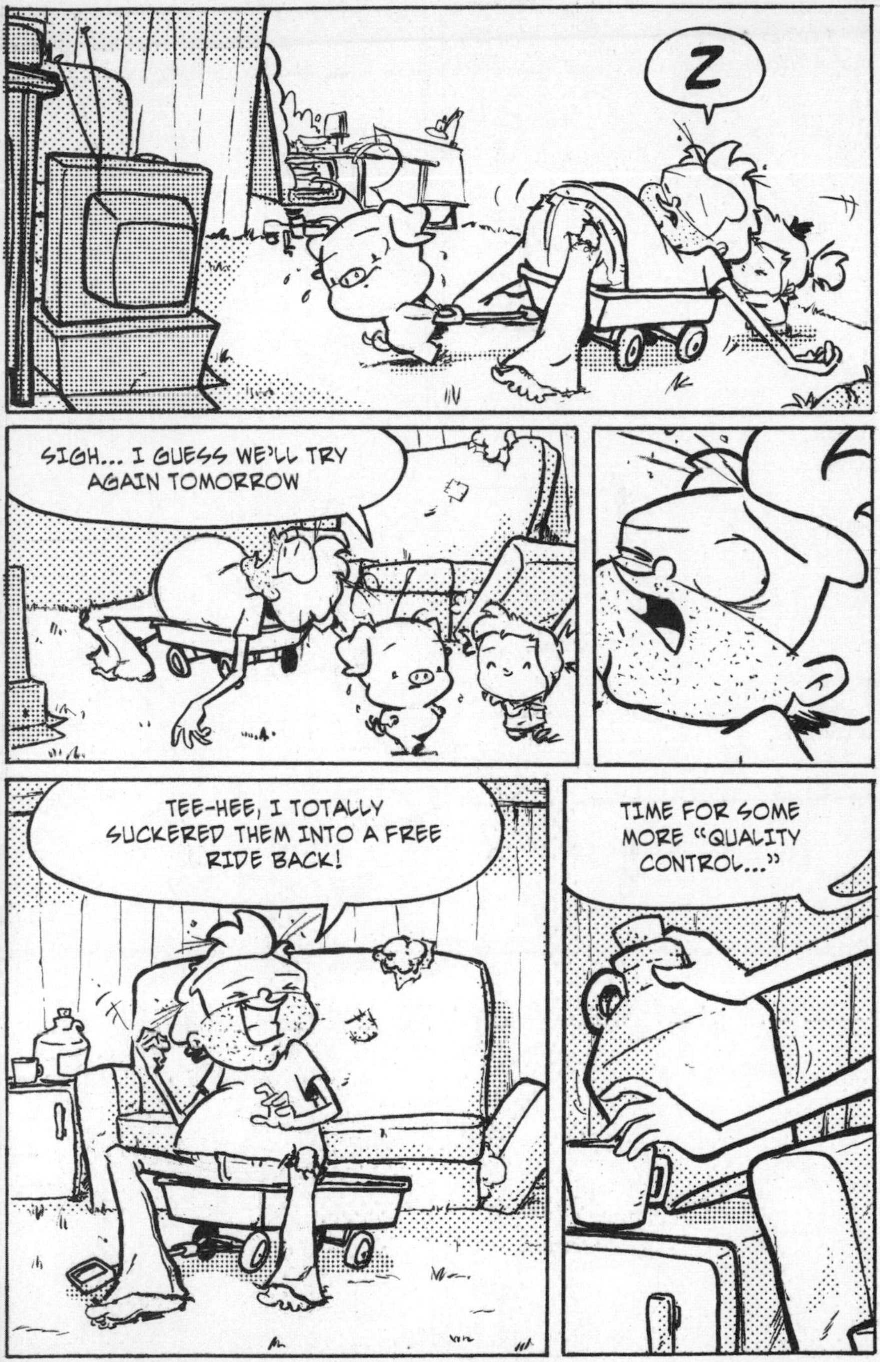
Z
SIGH... I GUESS WE'LL TRY AGAIN TOMORROW
TEE-HEE, I TOTALLY SUCKERED THEM INTO A FREE RIDE BACK!
TIME FOR SOME MORE "QUALITY CONTROL..."

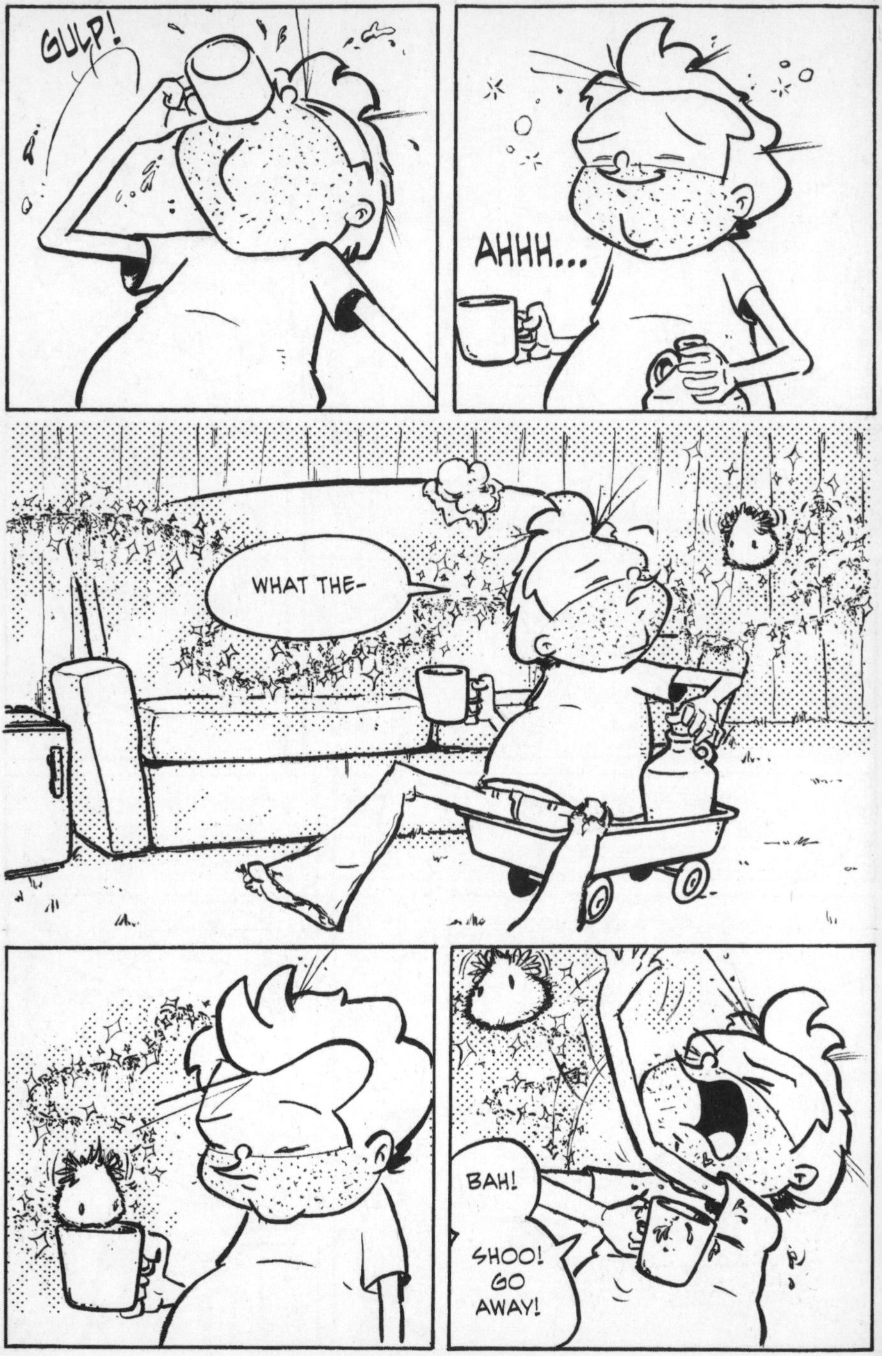
GULP!
AHHH...
WHAT THE-
BAH!
SHOO! GO AWAY!

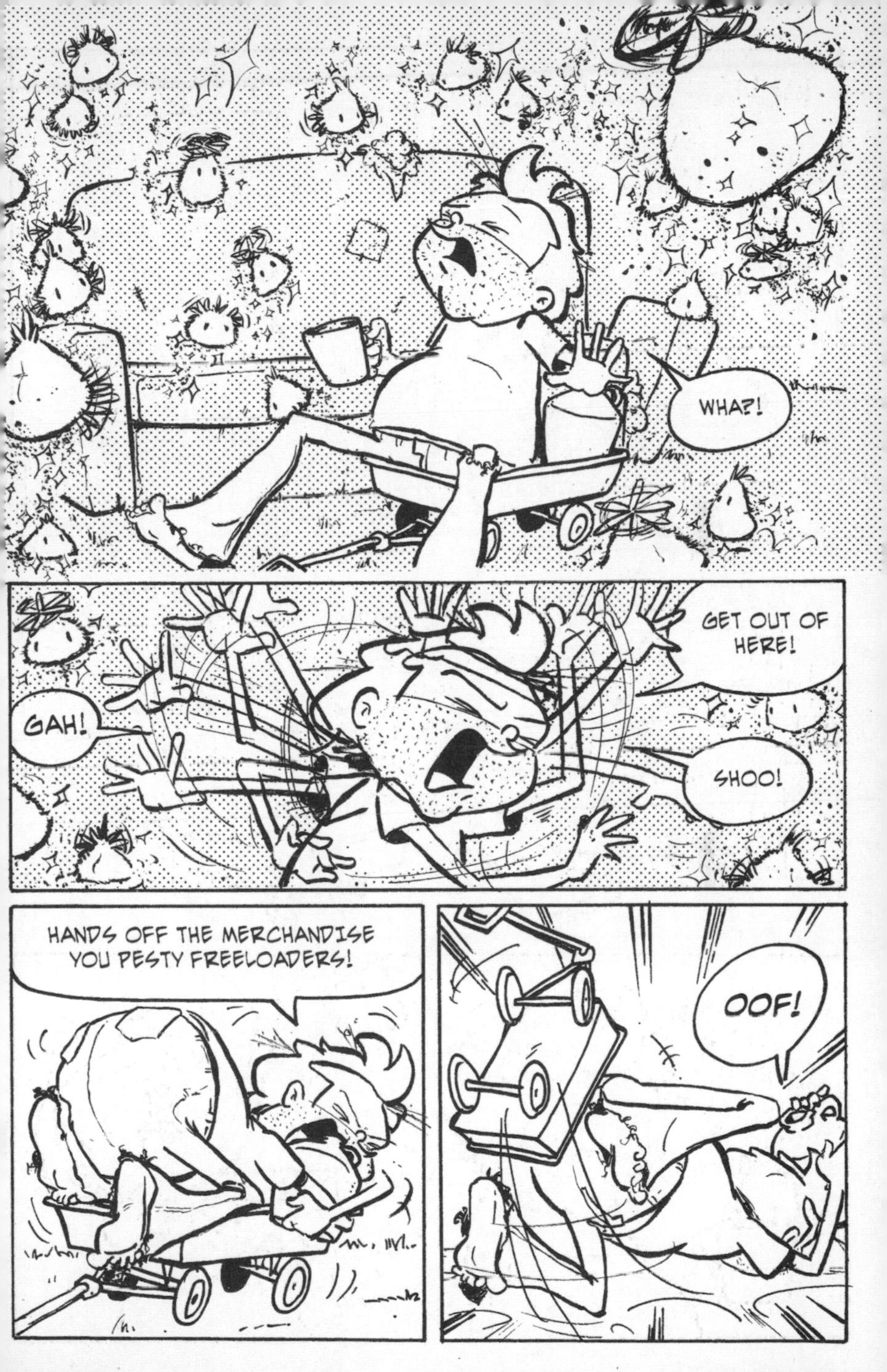
WHA?!
GET OUT OF HERE!
GAH!
SHOO!
HANDS OFF THE MERCHANDISE YOU PESTY FREELOADERS!
OOF!

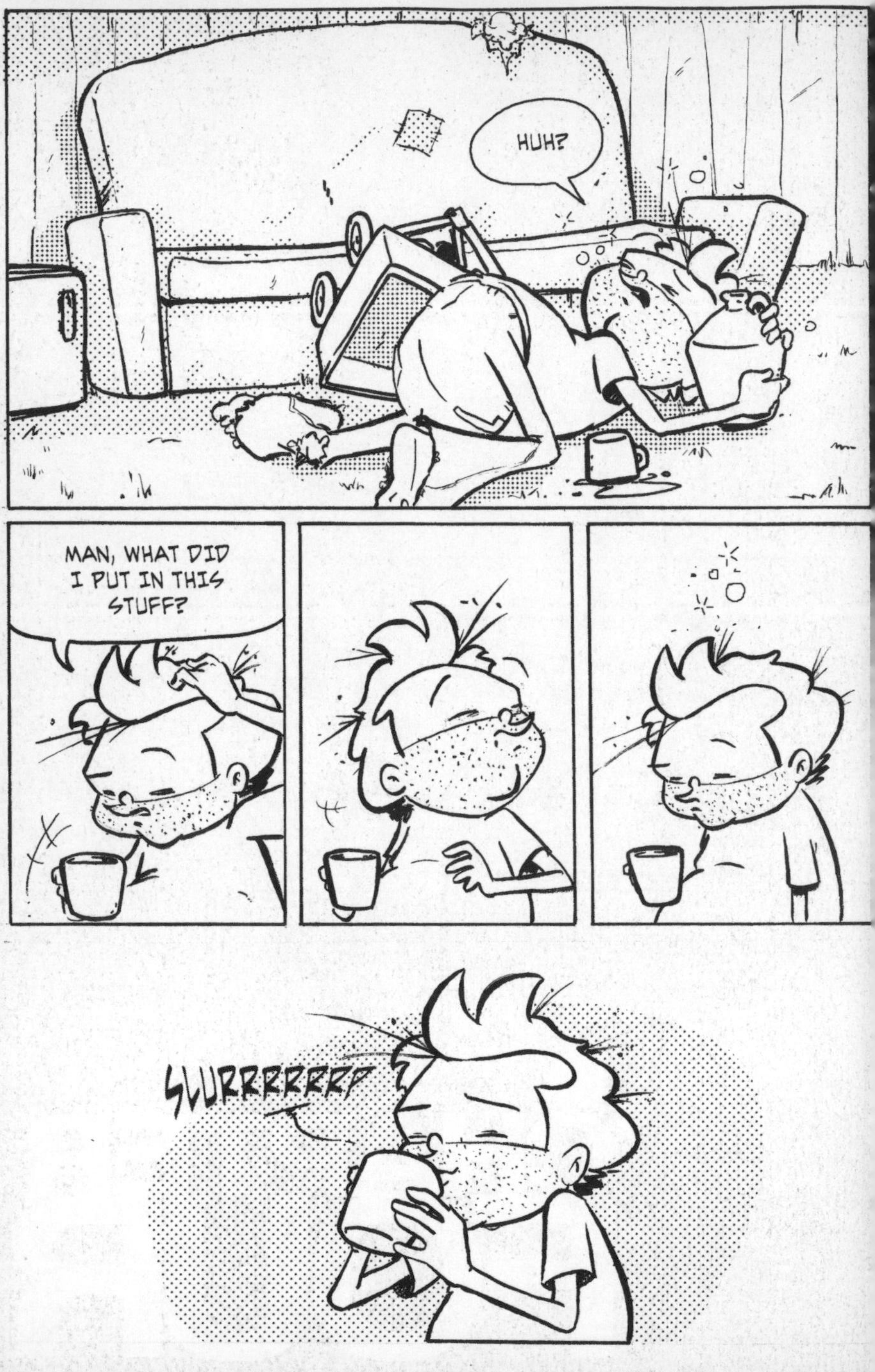
HUH?
MAN, WHAT DID I PUT IN THIS STUFF?
SLURRRRRRP

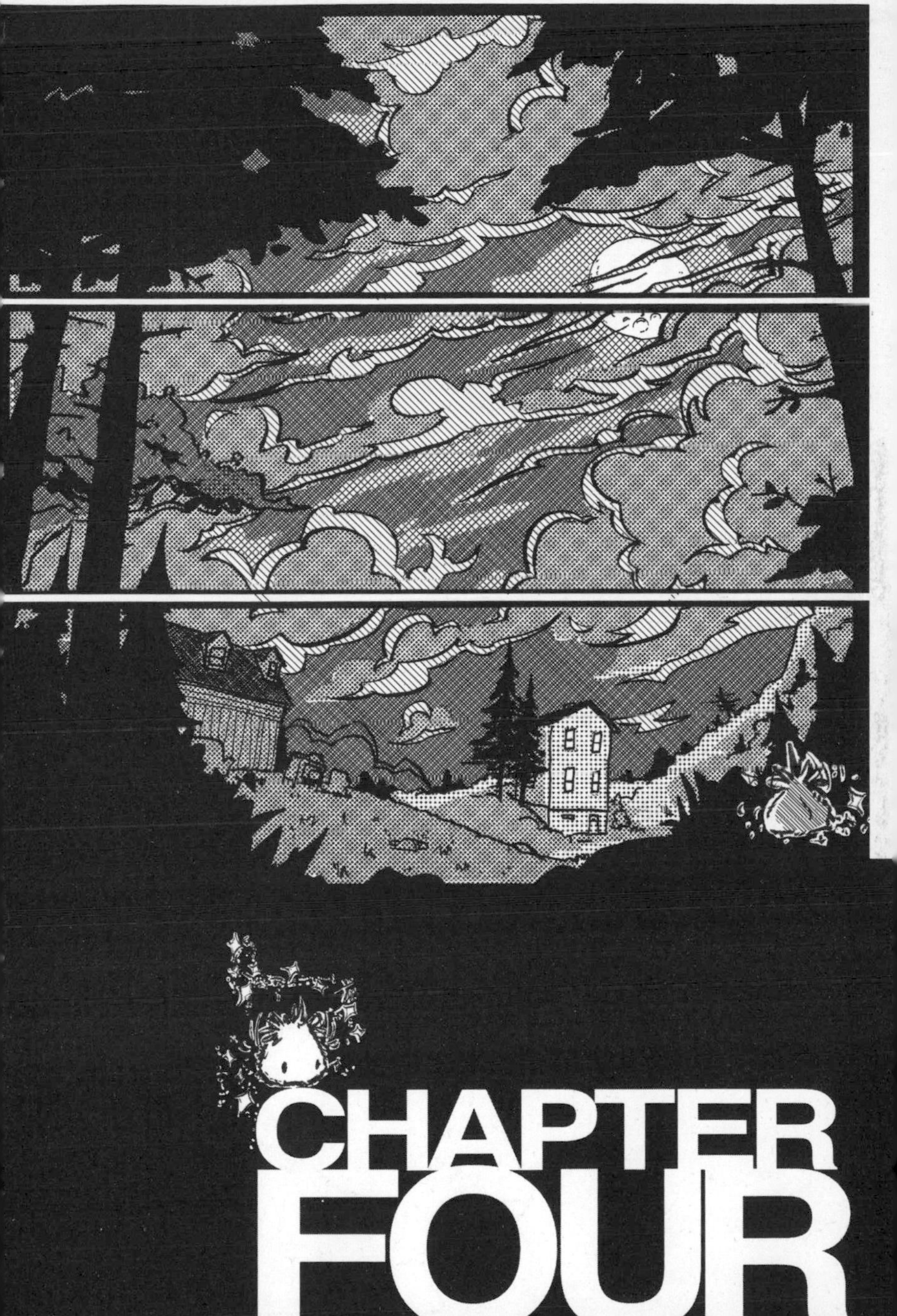

CHAPTER FOUR

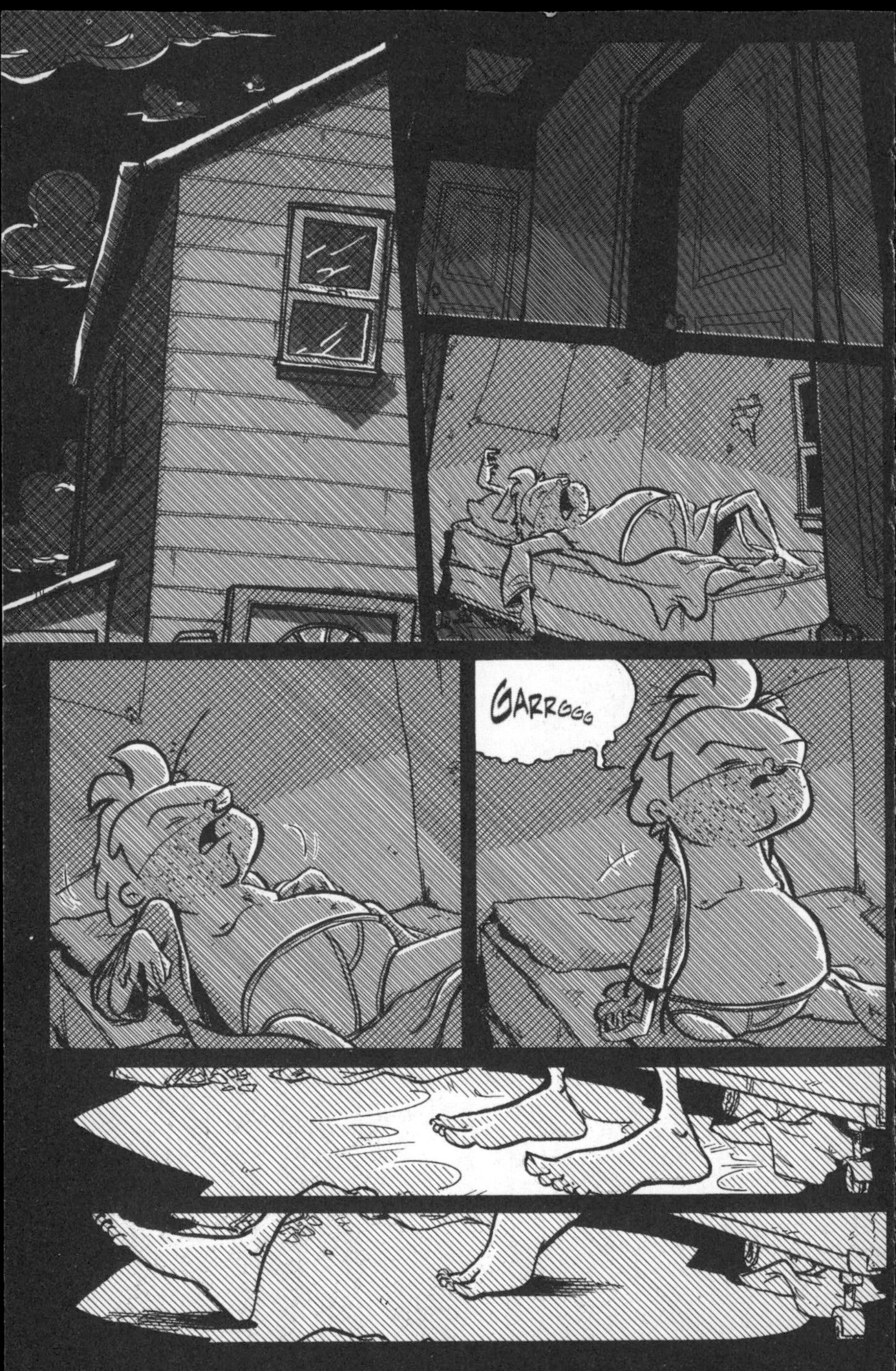
GARRGGG

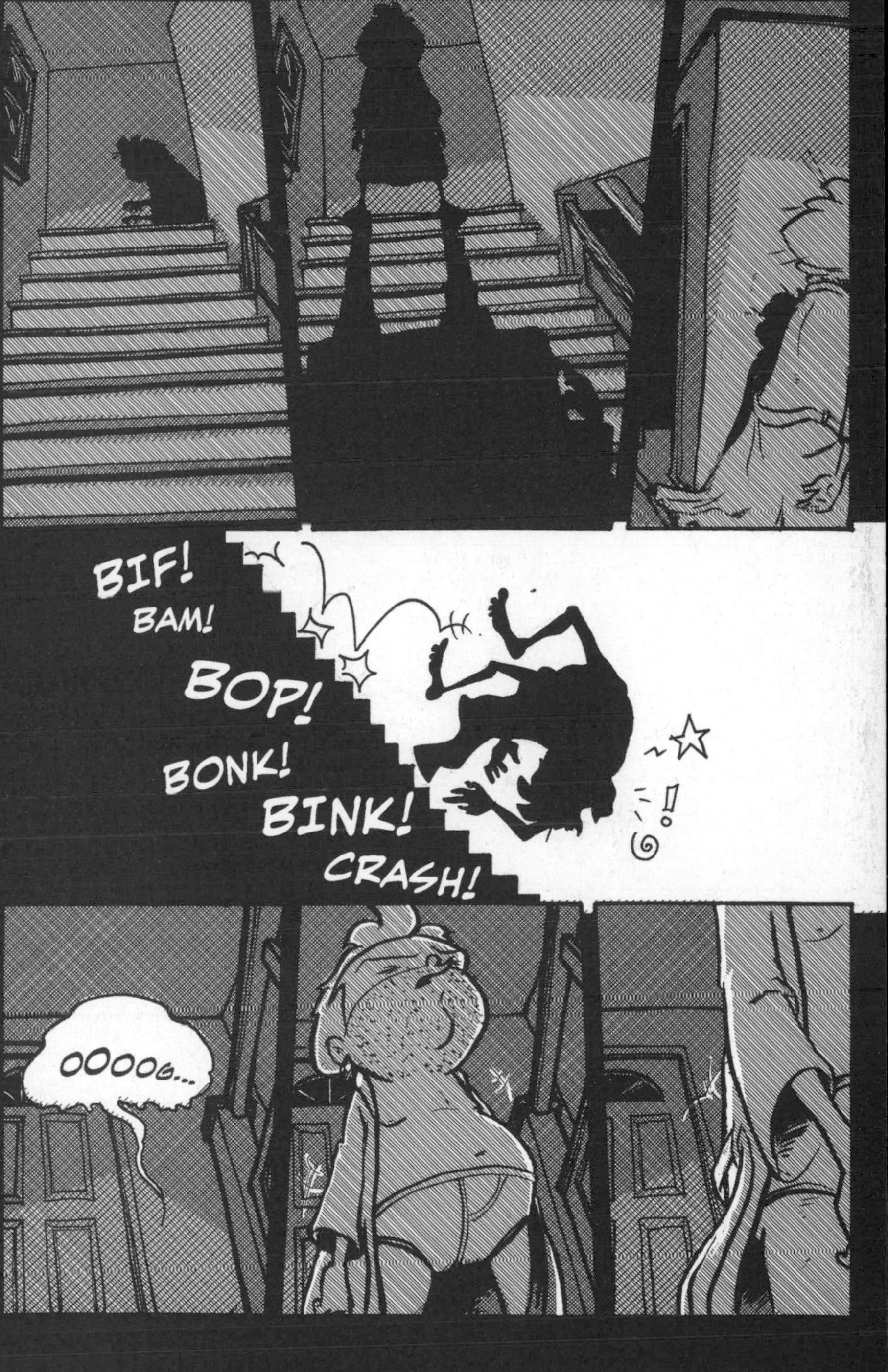
BIF!
BAM!
BOP!
BONK!
BINK!
CRASH!
OOOOG...

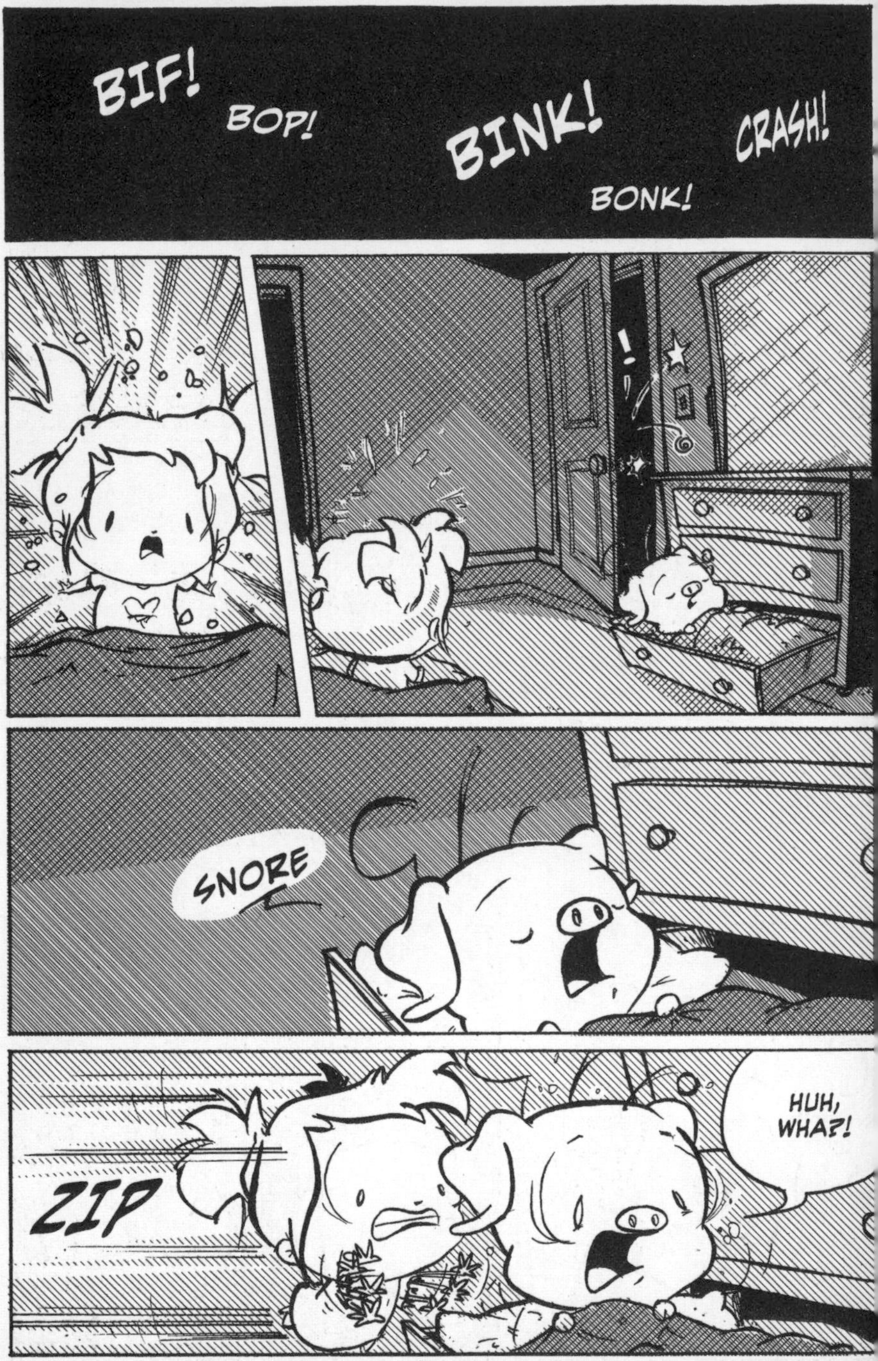
BIF!
BOP!
BINK!
BONK!
CRASH!
!
SNORE
ZIP
HUH, WHA?!

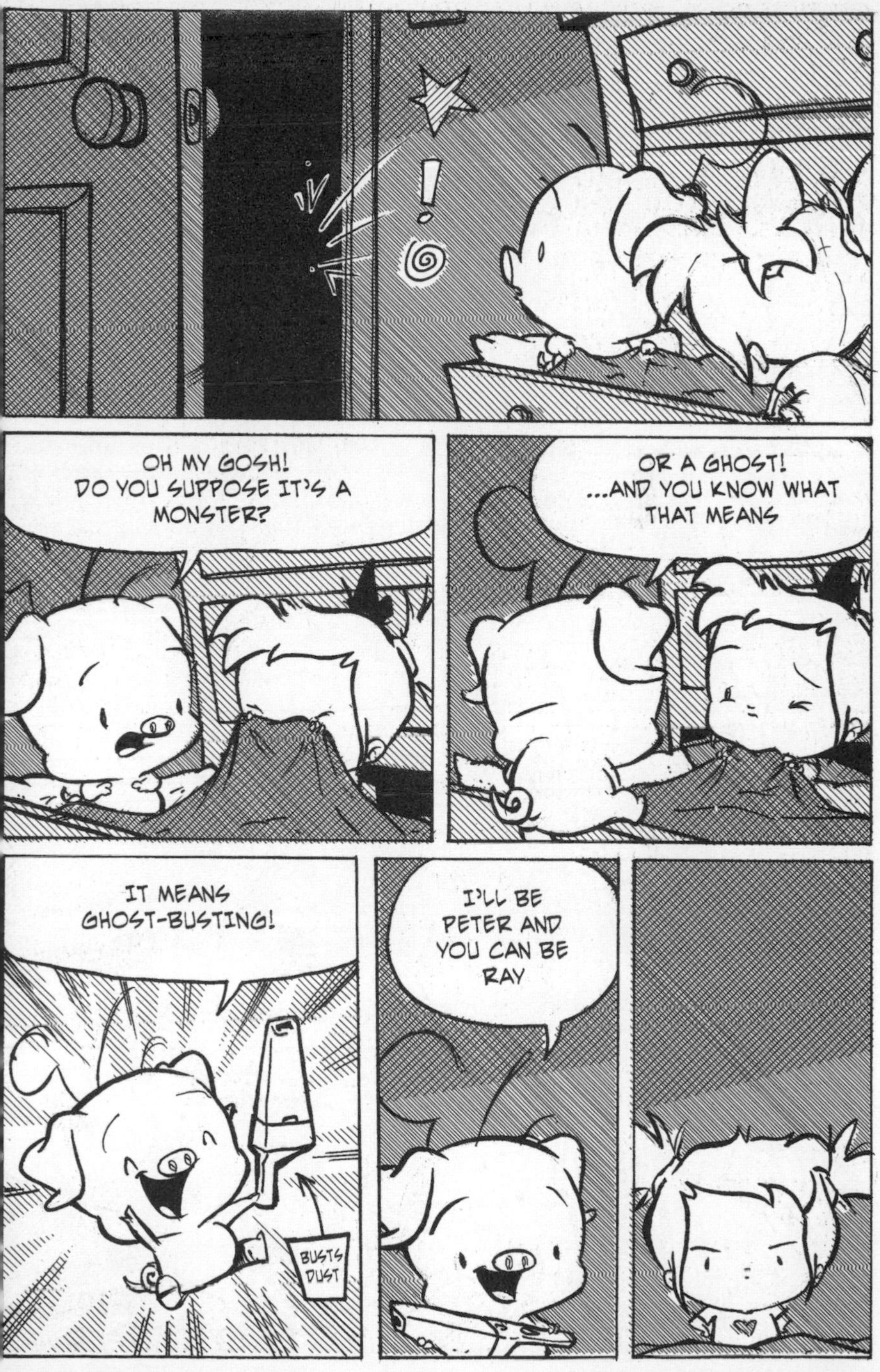
OH MY GOSH! DO YOU SUPPOSE IT'S A MONSTER?
OR A GHOST! ...AND YOU KNOW WHAT THAT MEANS
IT MEANS GHOST-BUSTING!
BUSTS DUST
I'LL BE PETER AND YOU CAN BE RAY

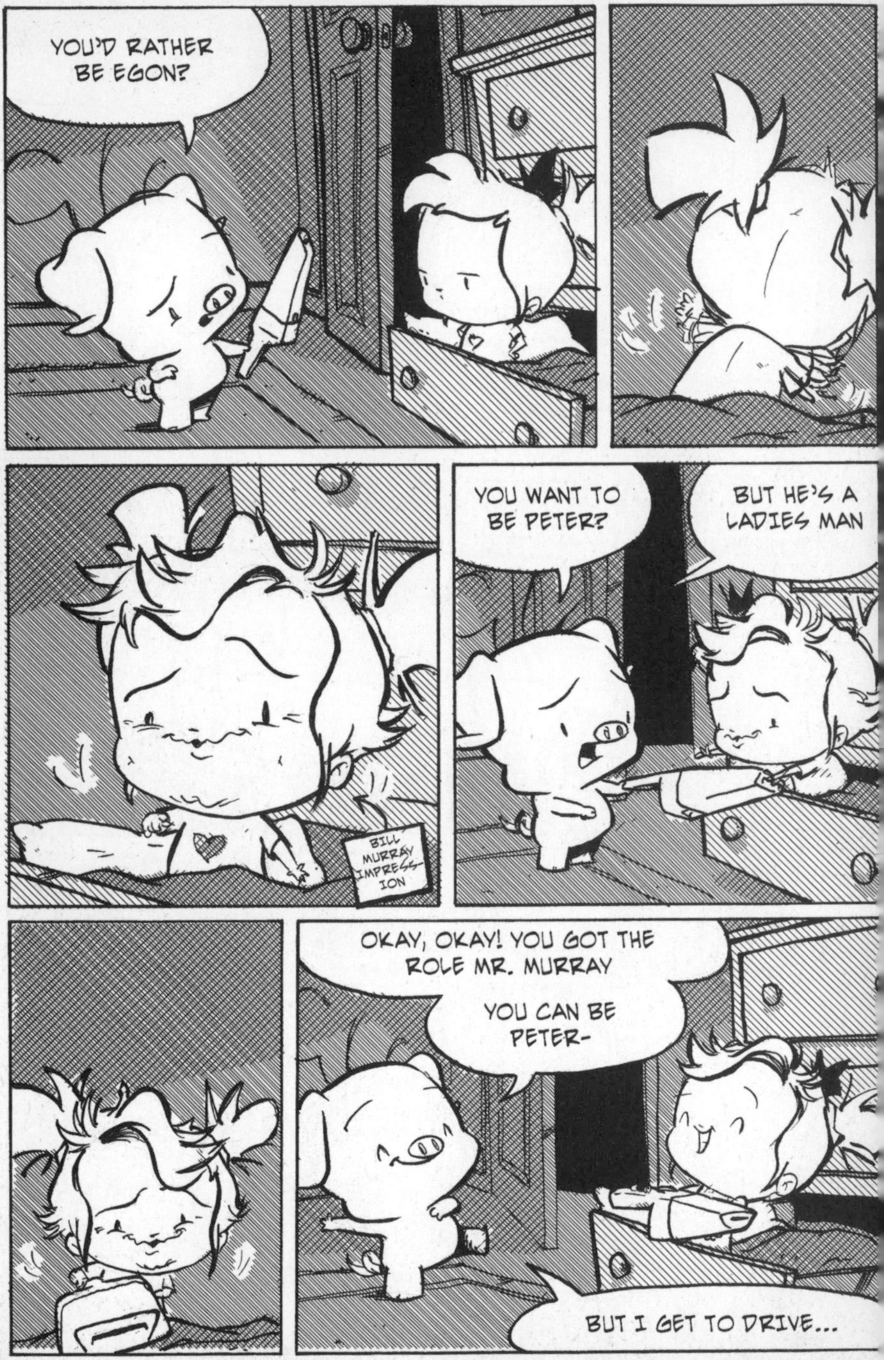
YOU'D RATHER BE EGON?
YOU WANT TO BE PETER?
BUT HE'S A LADIES MAN
BILL MURRAY IMPRESS-ION
OKAY, OKAY! YOU GOT THE ROLE MR. MURRAY
YOU CAN BE PETER-
BUT I GET TO DRIVE...

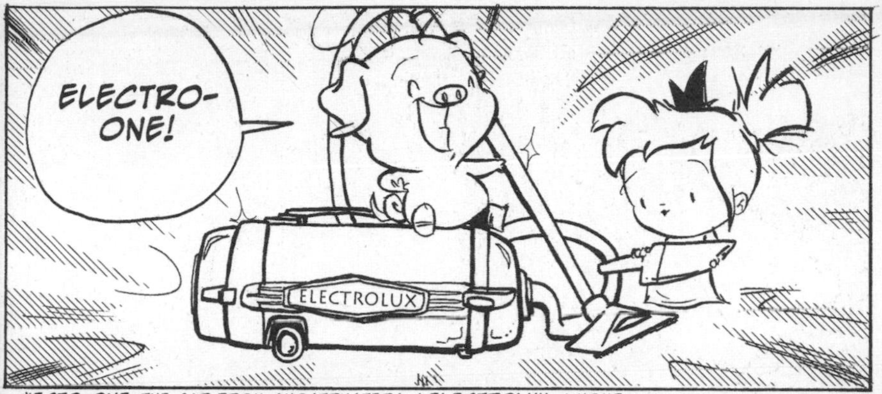
ELECTRO-ONE!
ELECTROLUX

*ECTO-ONE: THE CAR FROM GHOSTBUSTERS / ELECTROLUX: A HOME APPLIANCE MANUFACTURER & AN AWESOME BAND CIRCA '95-'96

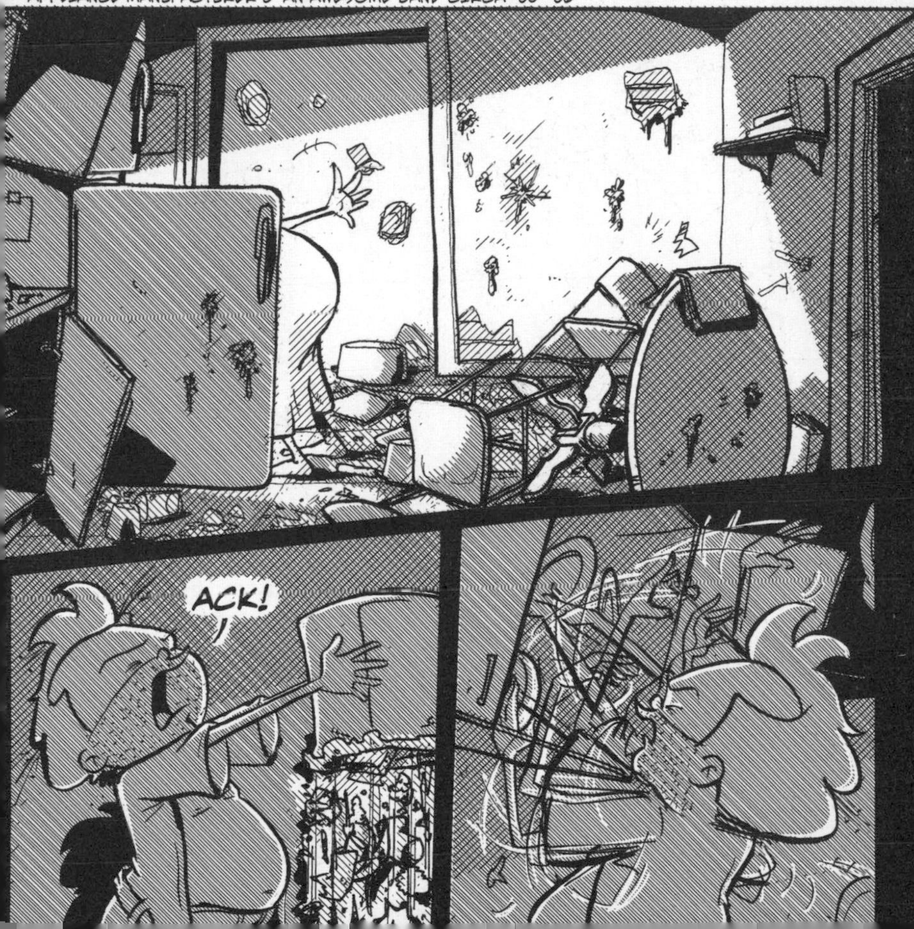
ACK!

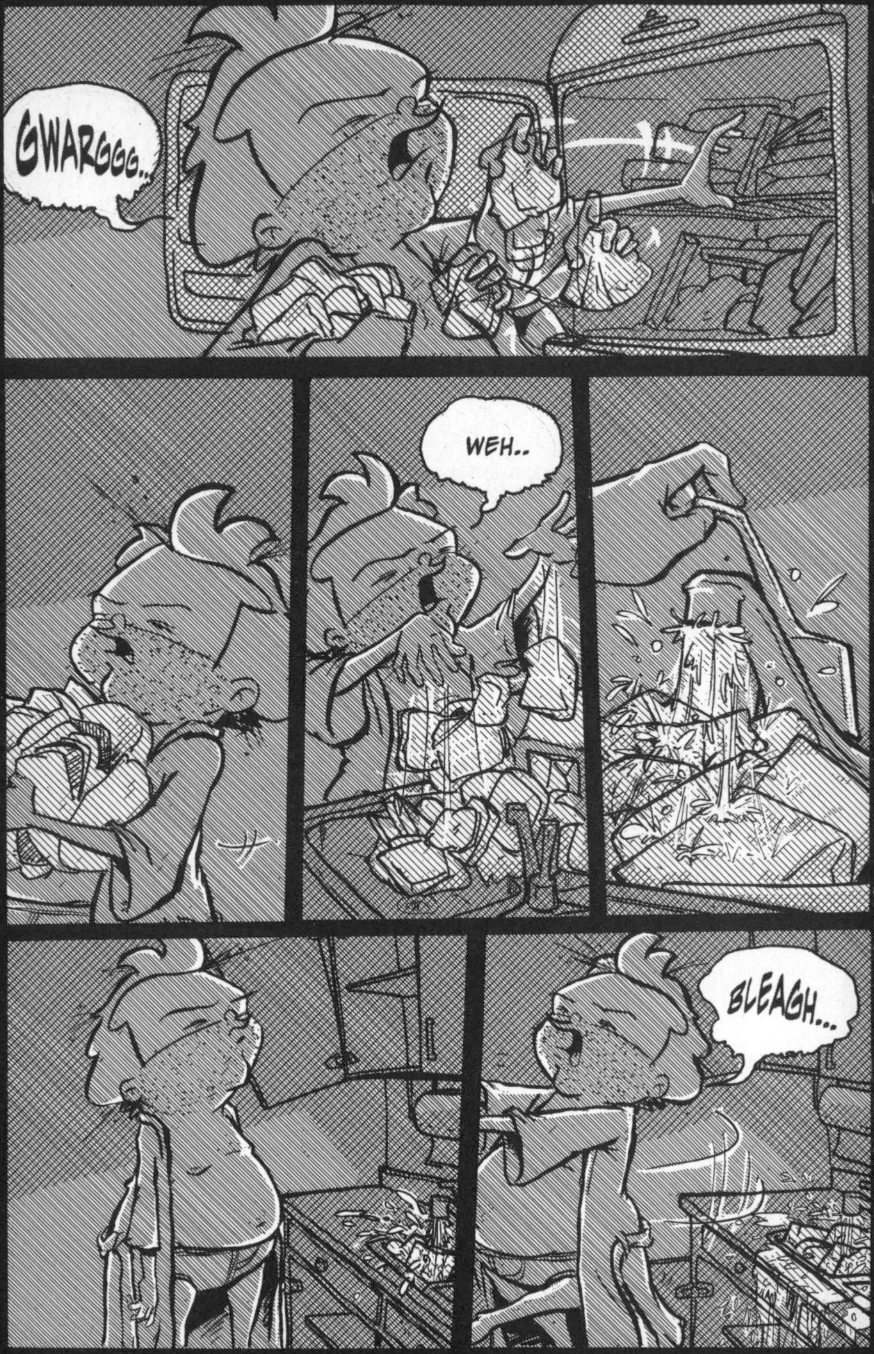
GWARGGG..
WEH..
BLEAGH...

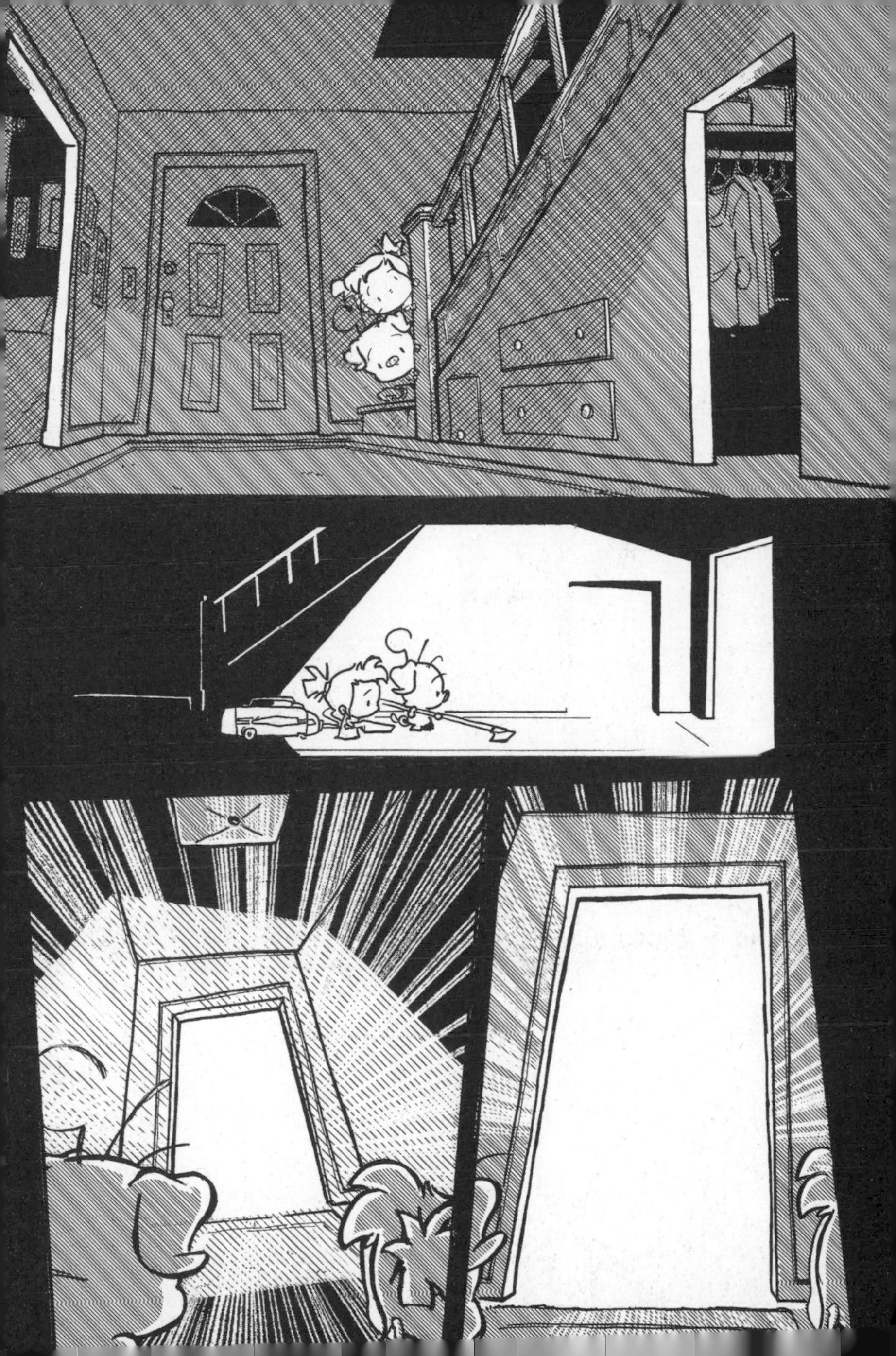

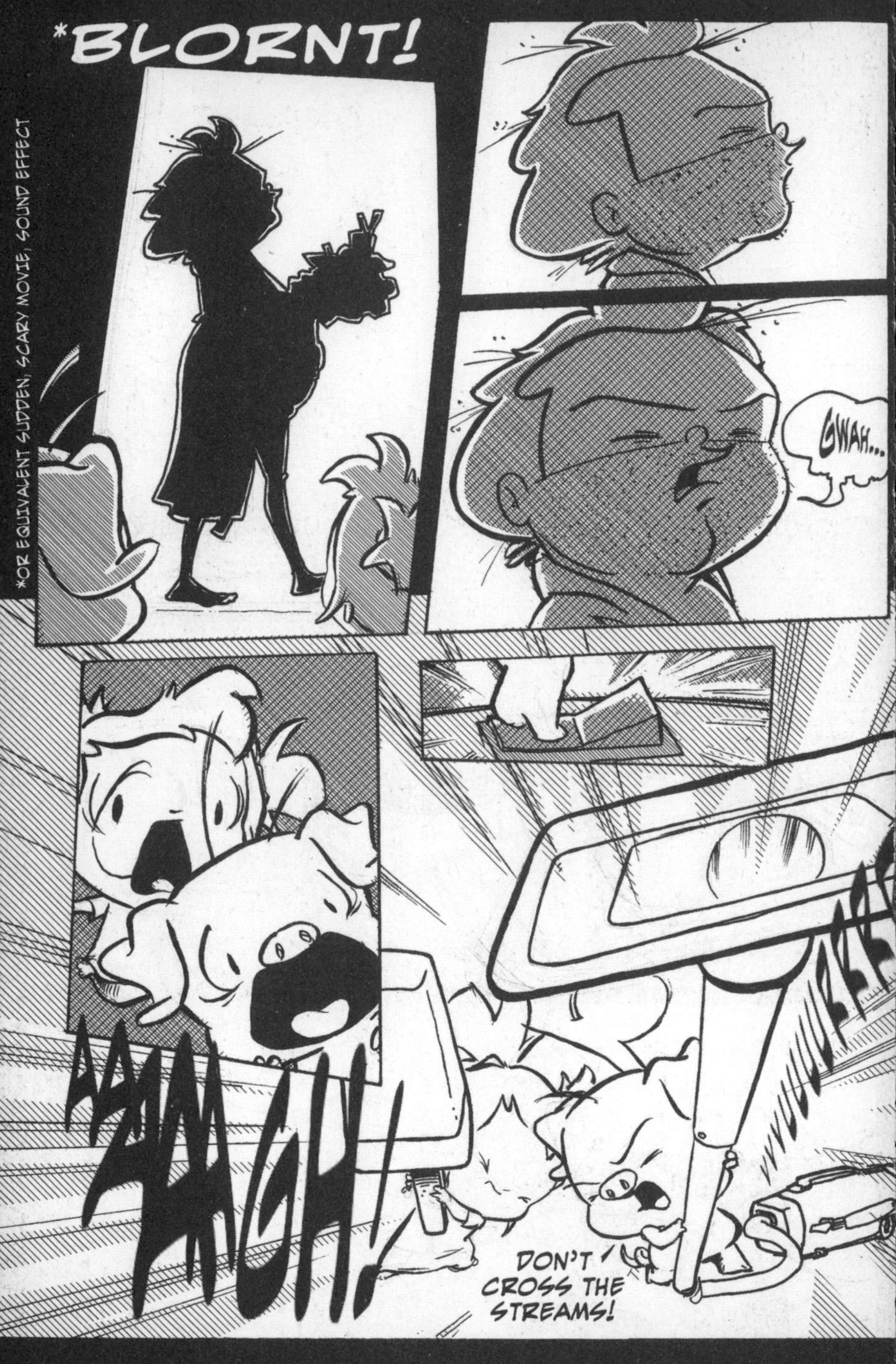
*BLORNT!
*OR EQUIVALENT SUDDEN, SCARY MOVIE, SOUND EFFECT
GWAH...
BAAAHH!
DON'T CROSS THE STREAMS!

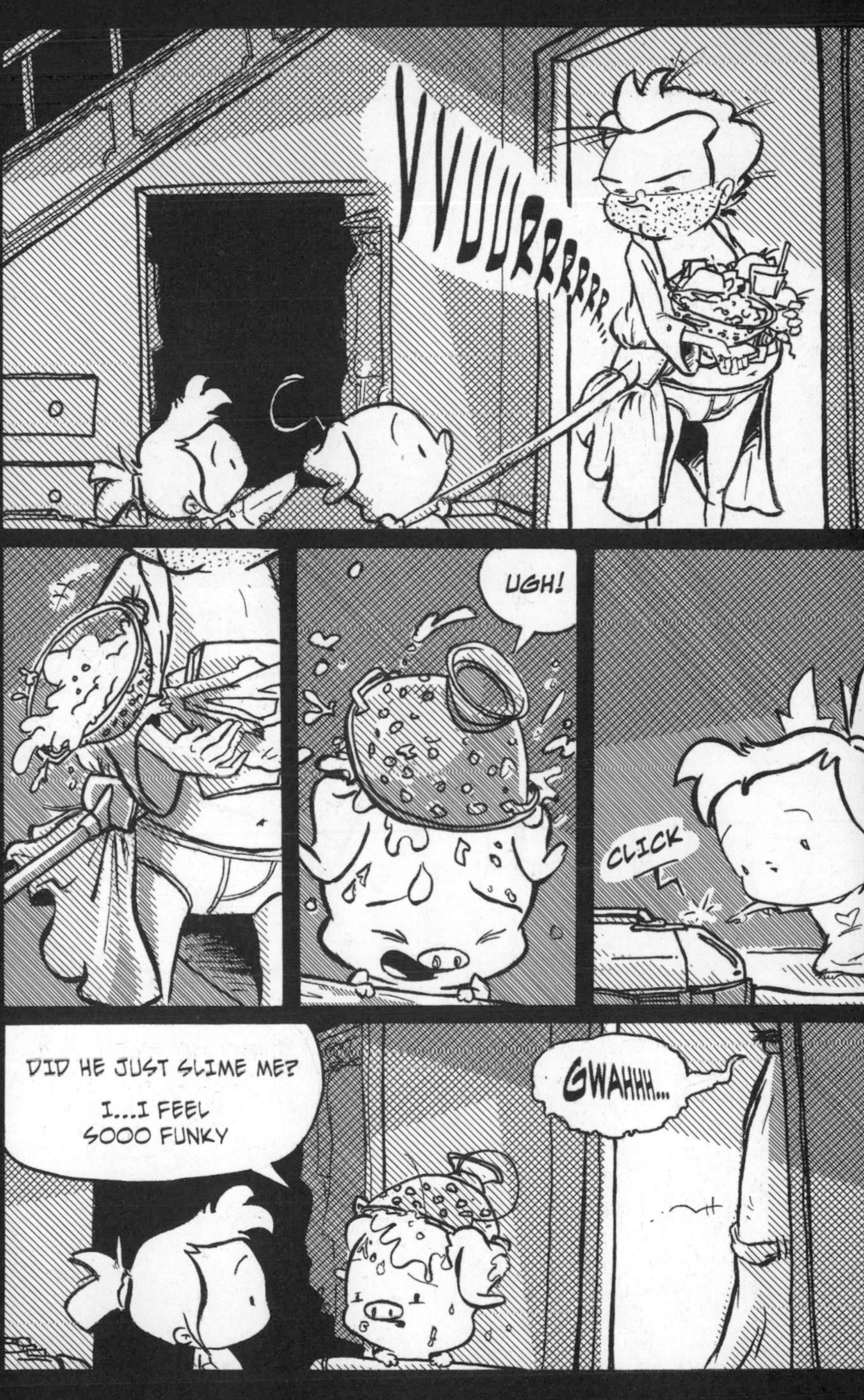
VVUURRRRRRR...
UGH!
CLICK
DID HE JUST SLIME ME?
I...I FEEL SOOO FUNKY
GWAHHH...

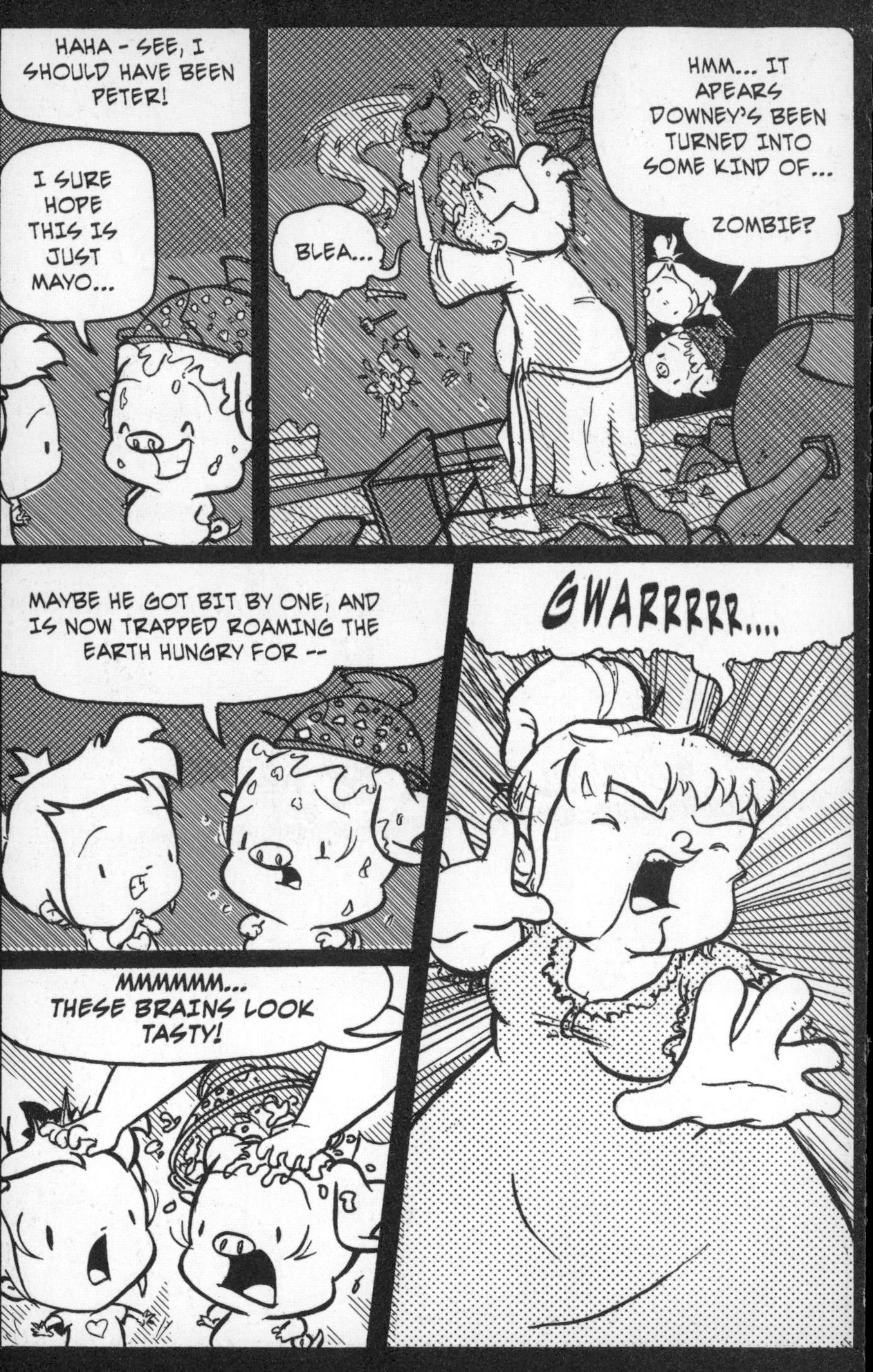
HAHA - SEE, I SHOULD HAVE BEEN PETER!
I SURE HOPE THIS IS JUST MAYO...
BLEA...
HMM... IT APEARS DOWNEY'S BEEN TURNED INTO SOME KIND OF...
ZOMBIE?
MAYBE HE GOT BIT BY ONE, AND IS NOW TRAPPED ROAMING THE EARTH HUNGRY FOR --
GWARRRRR....
MMMMMM... THESE BRAINS LOOK TASTY!

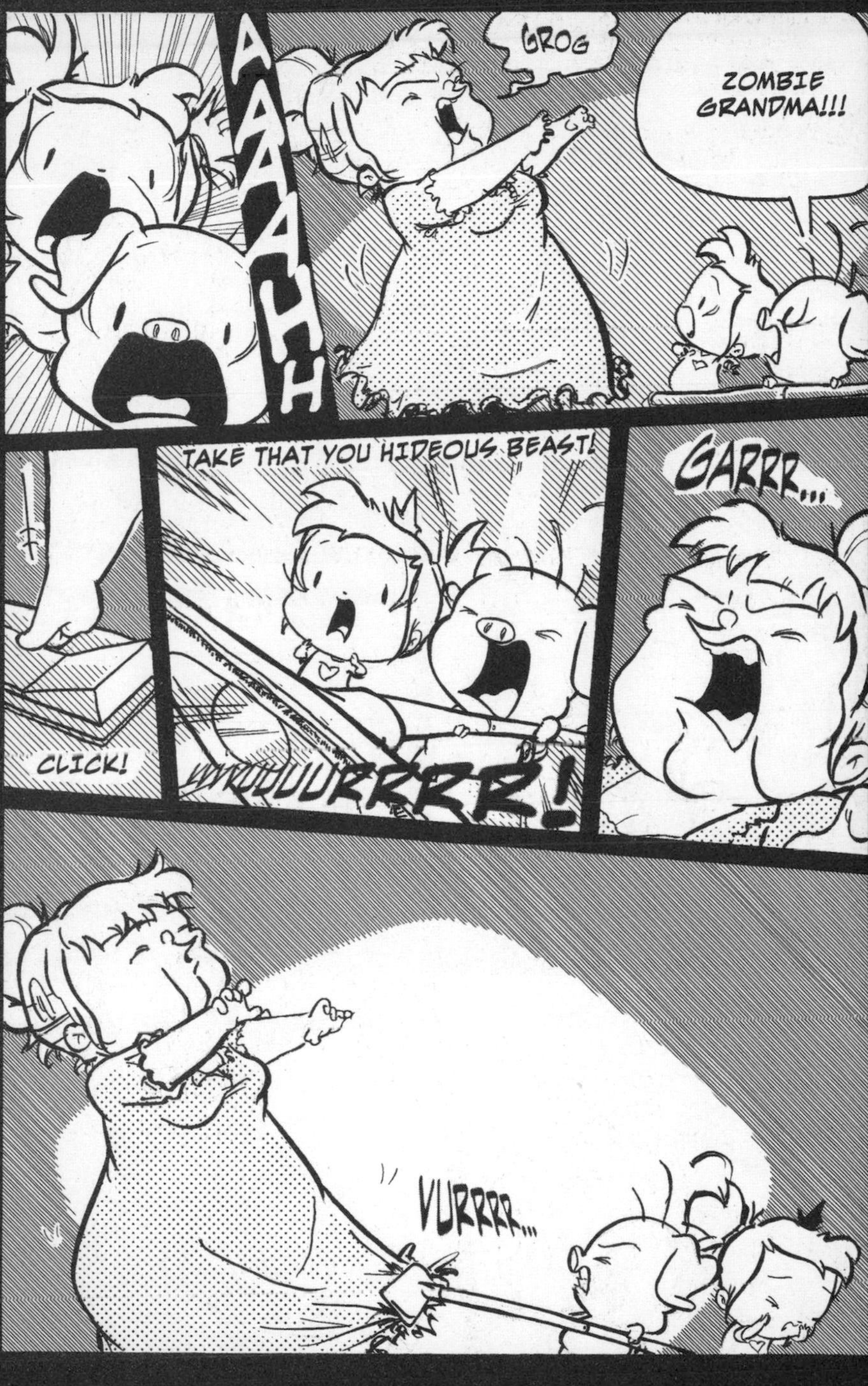
AAAAAHH
GROG
ZOMBIE GRANDMA!!!
!
CLICK!
TAKE THAT YOU HIDEOUS BEAST!
WWUUUURRRRR!
GARRR...
VURRRR...

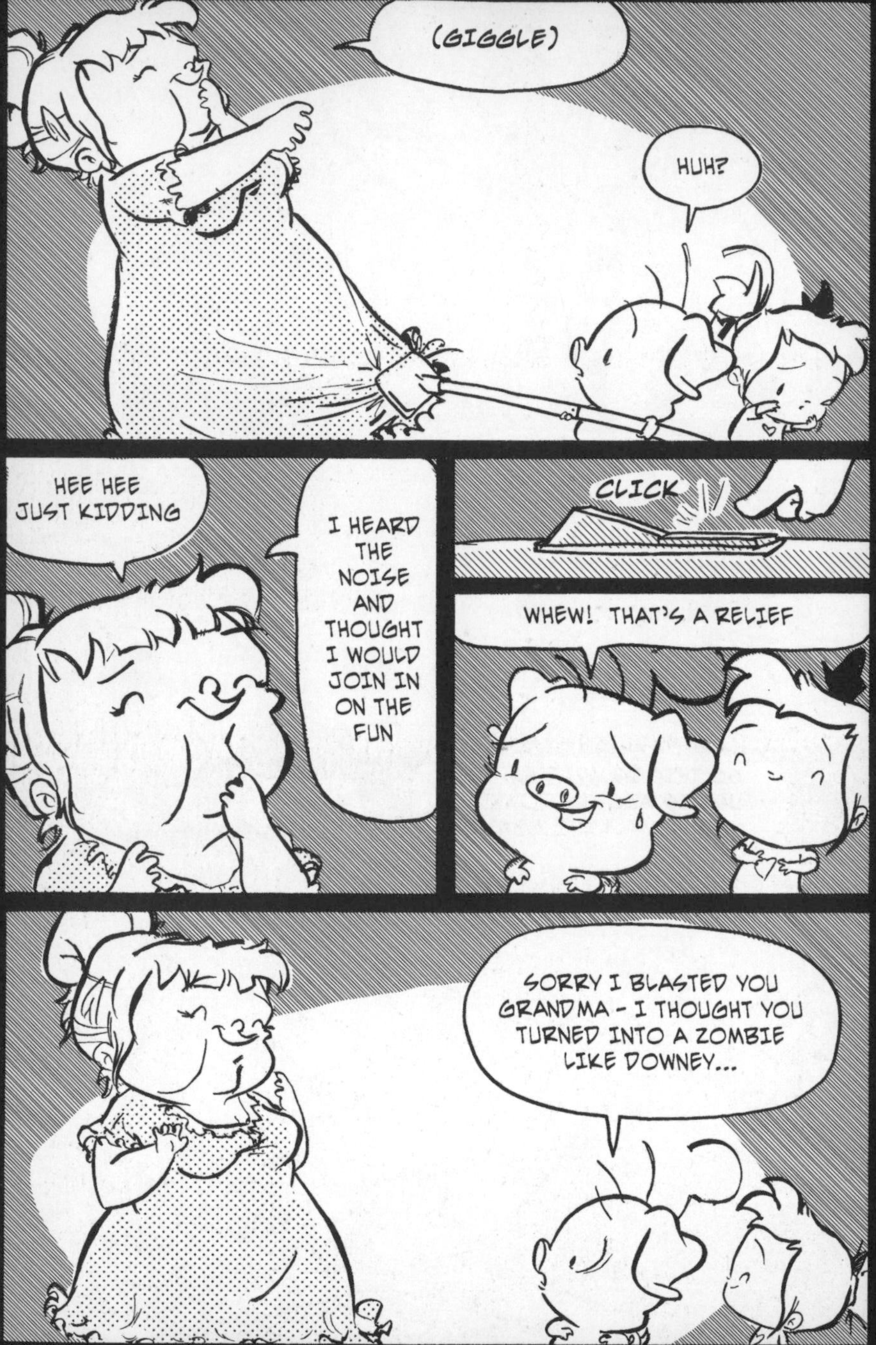
(GIGGLE)
HUH?
HEE HEE JUST KIDDING
I HEARD THE NOISE AND THOUGHT I WOULD JOIN IN ON THE FUN
CLICK
WHEW! THAT'S A RELIEF
SORRY I BLASTED YOU GRANDMA - I THOUGHT YOU TURNED INTO A ZOMBIE LIKE DOWNEY...

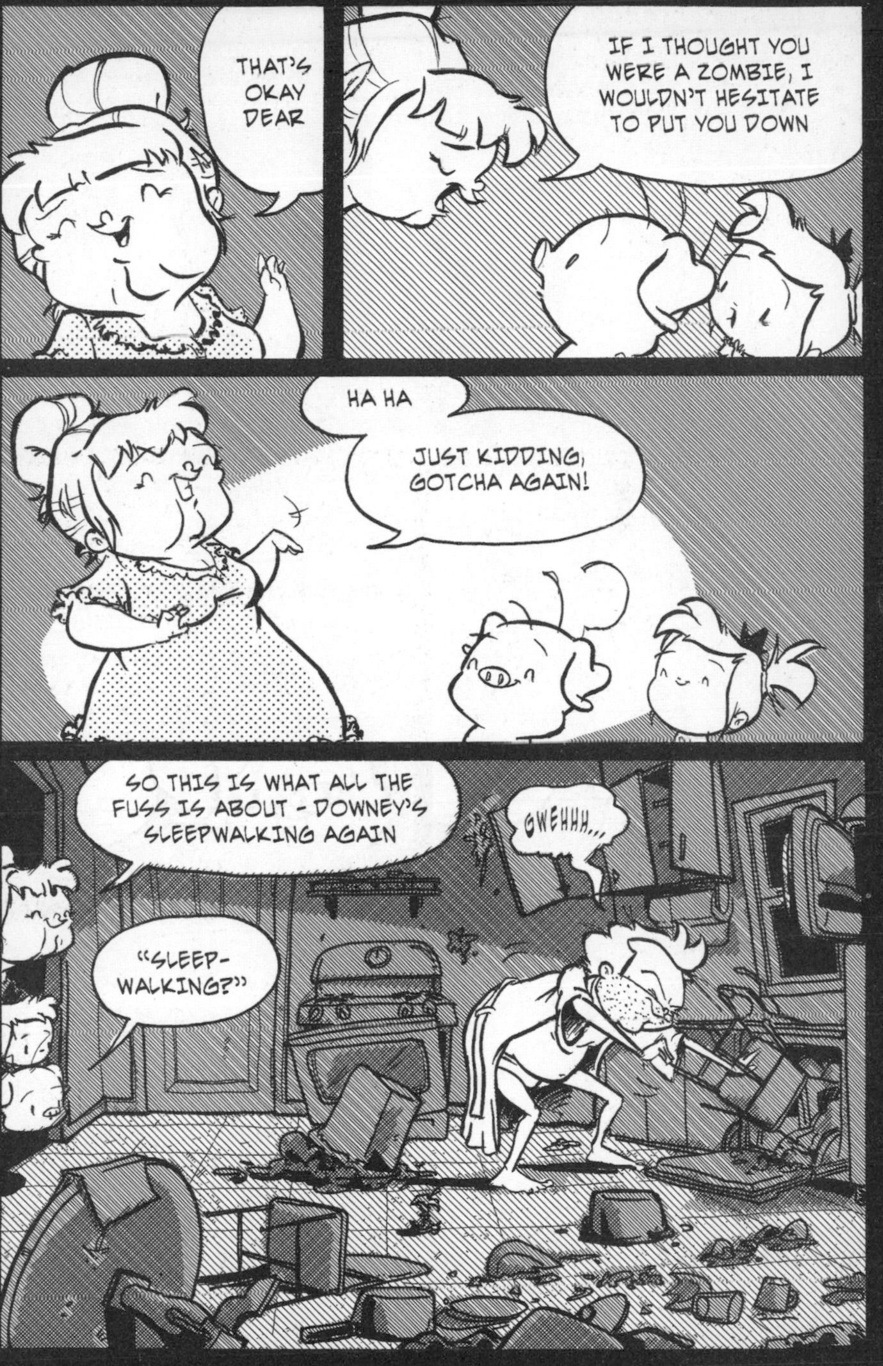
THAT'S OKAY DEAR
IF I THOUGHT YOU WERE A ZOMBIE, I WOULDN'T HESITATE TO PUT YOU DOWN
HA HA
JUST KIDDING, GOTCHA AGAIN!
SO THIS IS WHAT ALL THE FUSS IS ABOUT - DOWNEY'S SLEEPWALKING AGAIN
GWEHHH...
"SLEEP-WALKING?"

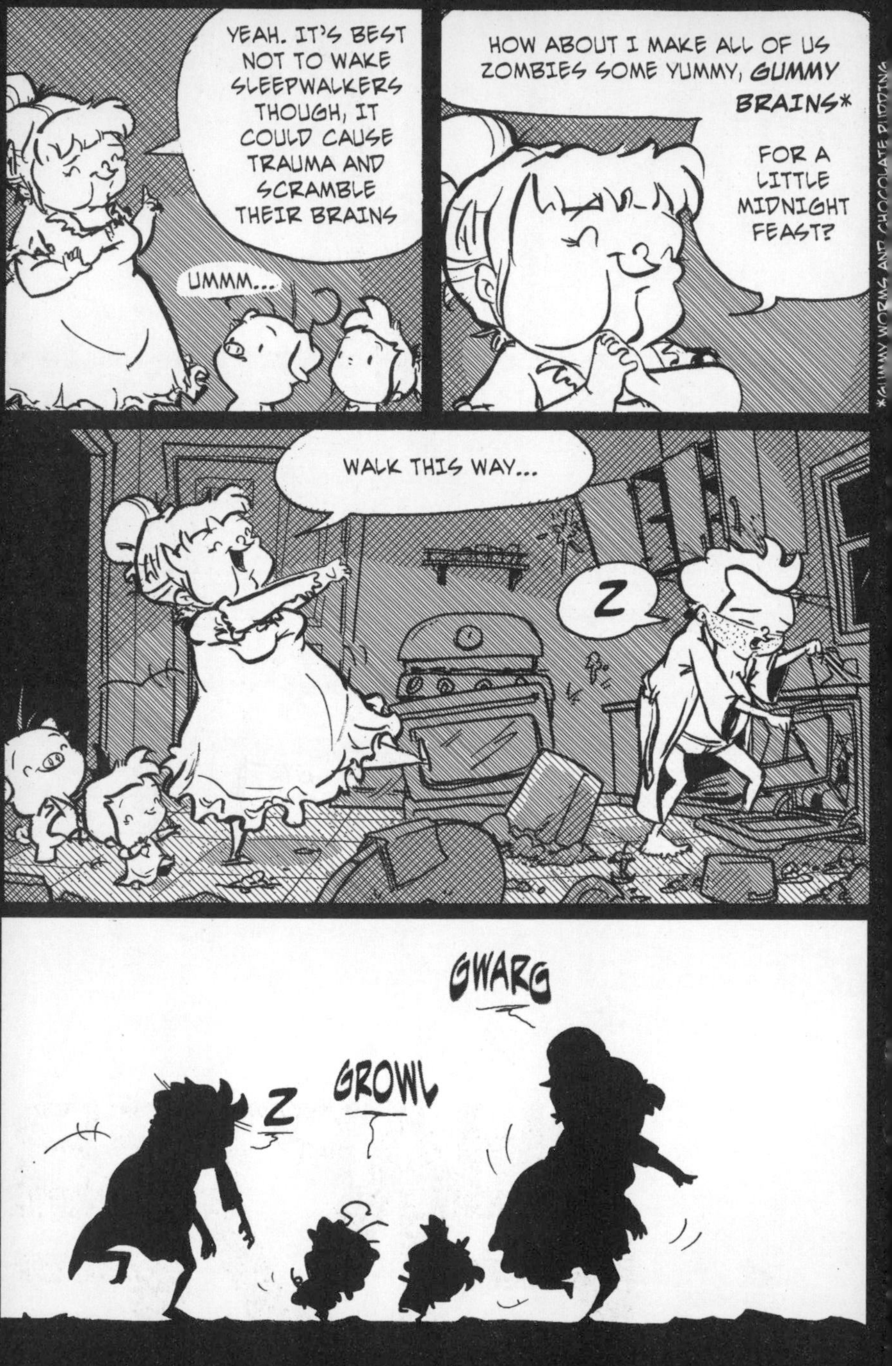
YEAH. IT'S BEST NOT TO WAKE SLEEPWALKERS THOUGH, IT COULD CAUSE TRAUMA AND SCRAMBLE THEIR BRAINS
UMMM...
HOW ABOUT I MAKE ALL OF US ZOMBIES SOME YUMMY, GUMMY BRAINS*
FOR A LITTLE MIDNIGHT FEAST?
*GUMMY WORMS AND CHOCOLATE PUDDING
WALK THIS WAY...
Z
GWARG
Z
GROWL

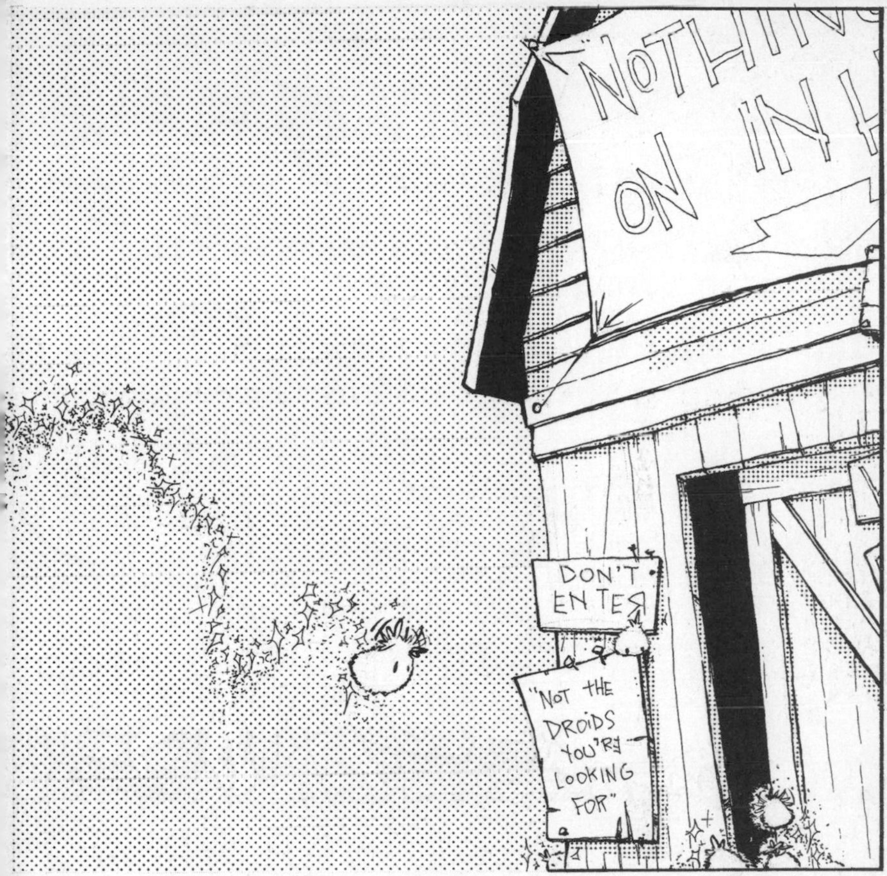
NOTHIN
ON IN H
DON'T ENTER
"NOT THE DROIDS YOU'RE LOOKING FOR"

CHAPTER FIVE

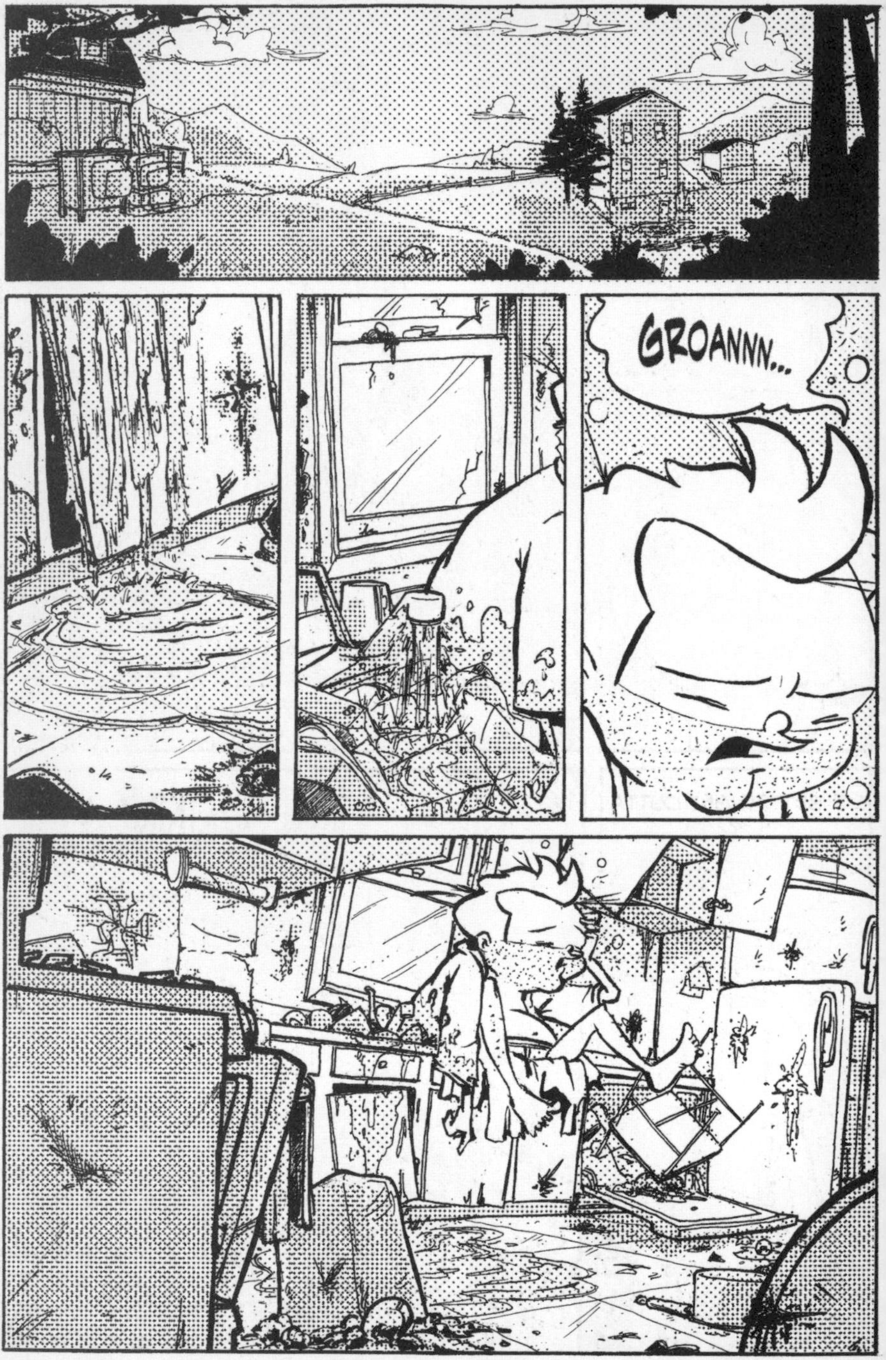
GROANNN...

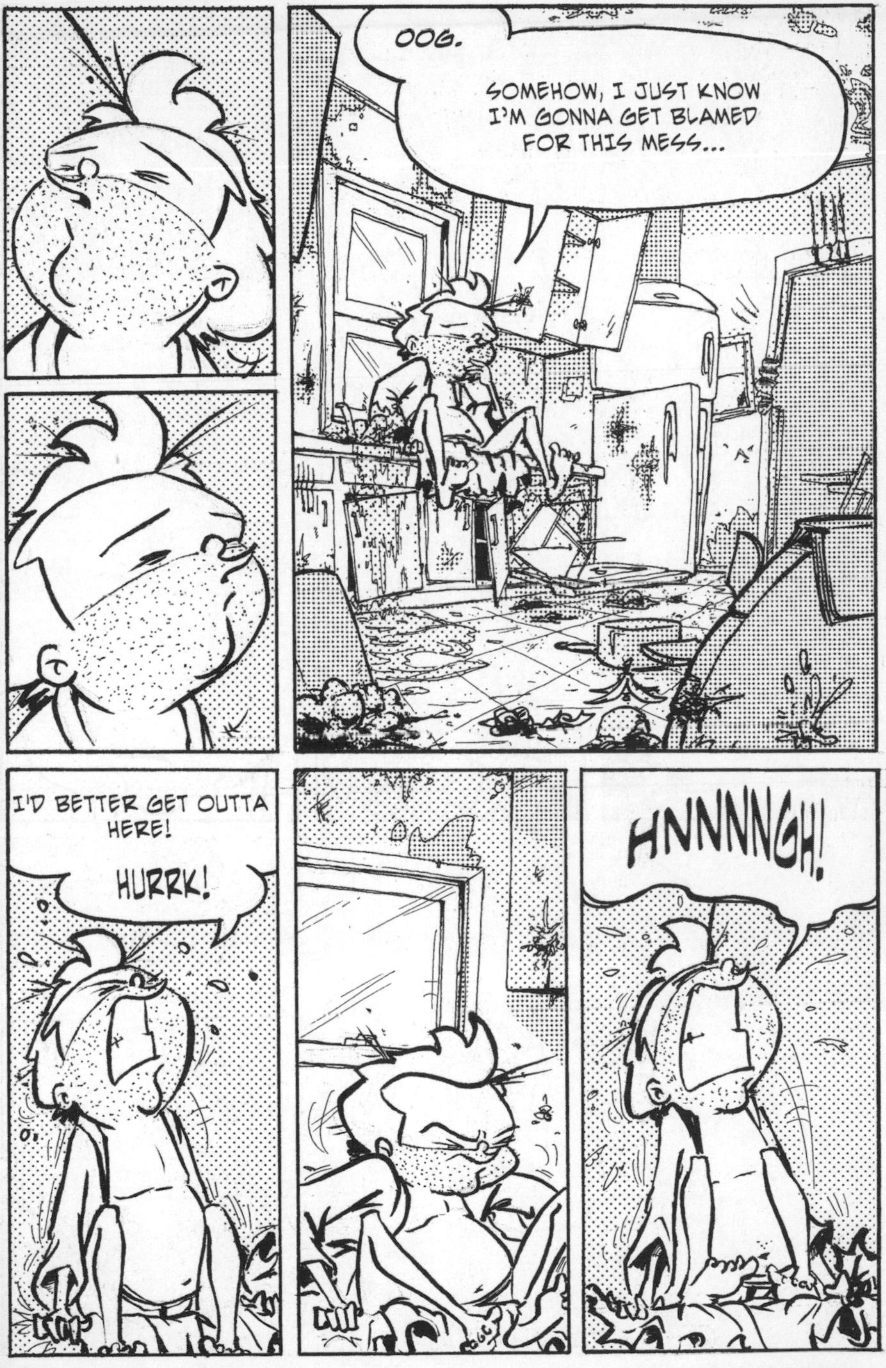
OOG.
SOMEHOW, I JUST KNOW I'M GONNA GET BLAMED FOR THIS MESS...
I'D BETTER GET OUTTA HERE!
HURRK!
HNNNNGH!

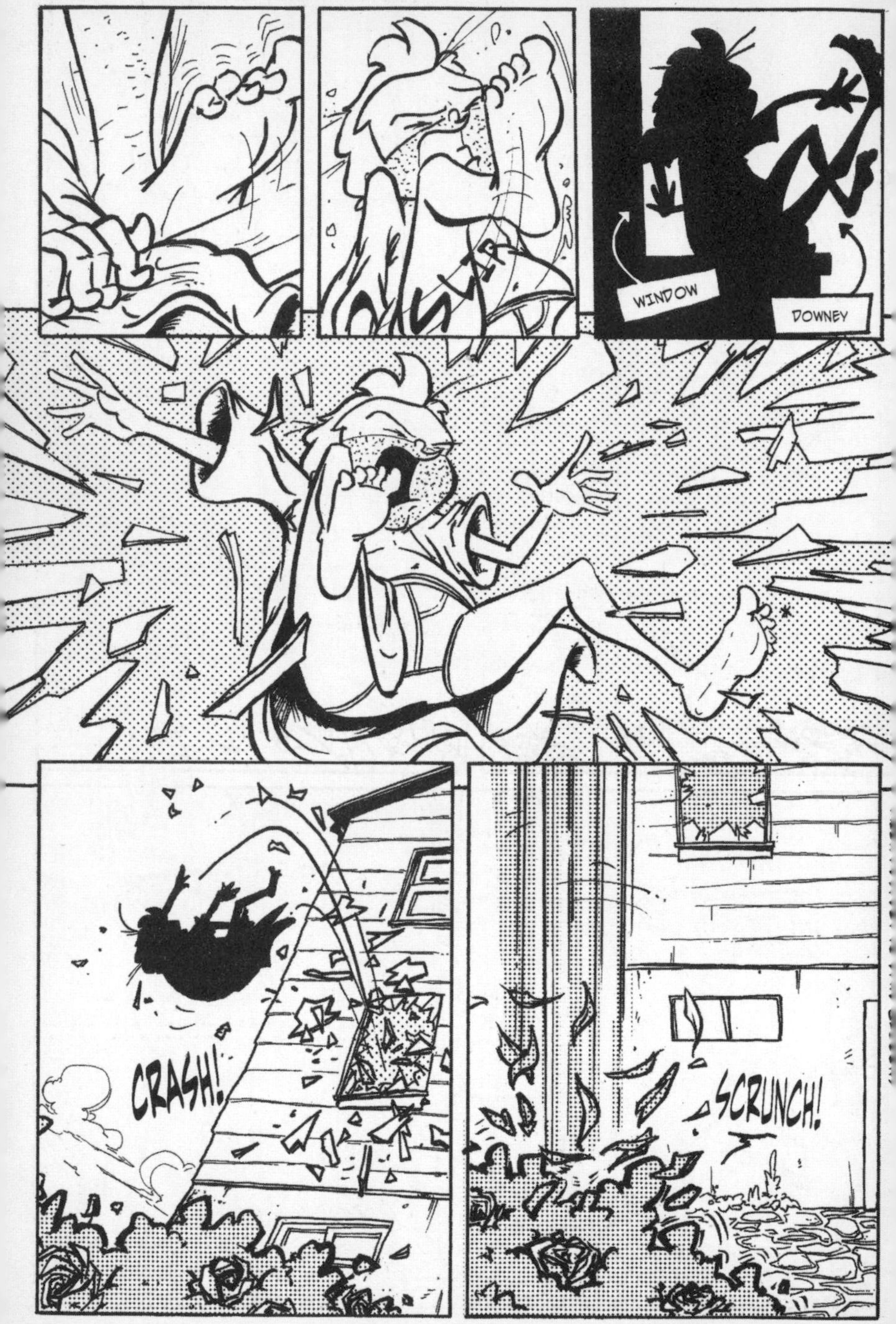
WINDOW
DOWNEY
CRASH!
SCRUNCH!

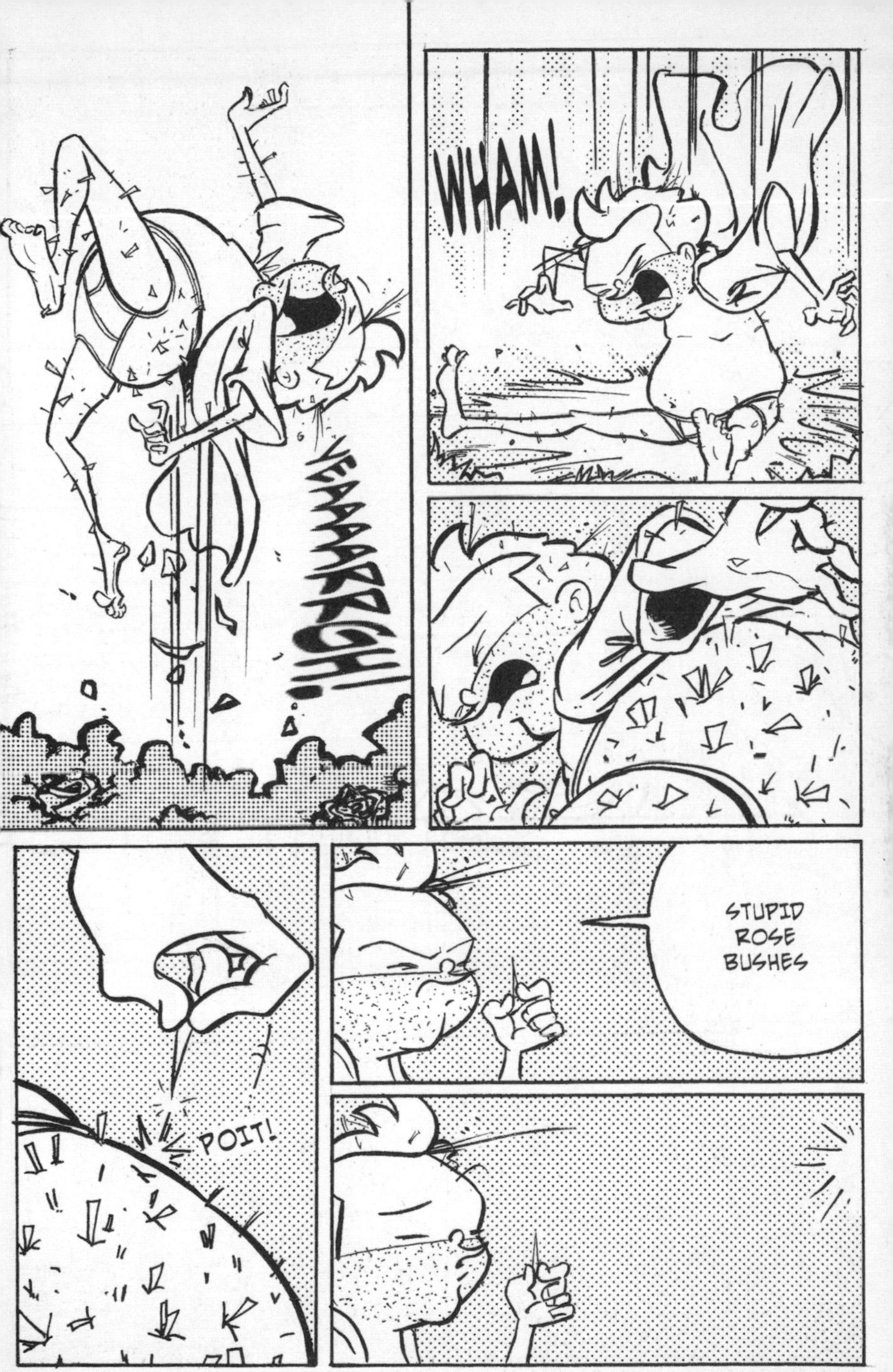

YEAAAARRRGH!
WHAM!
STUPID ROSE BUSHES
POIT!

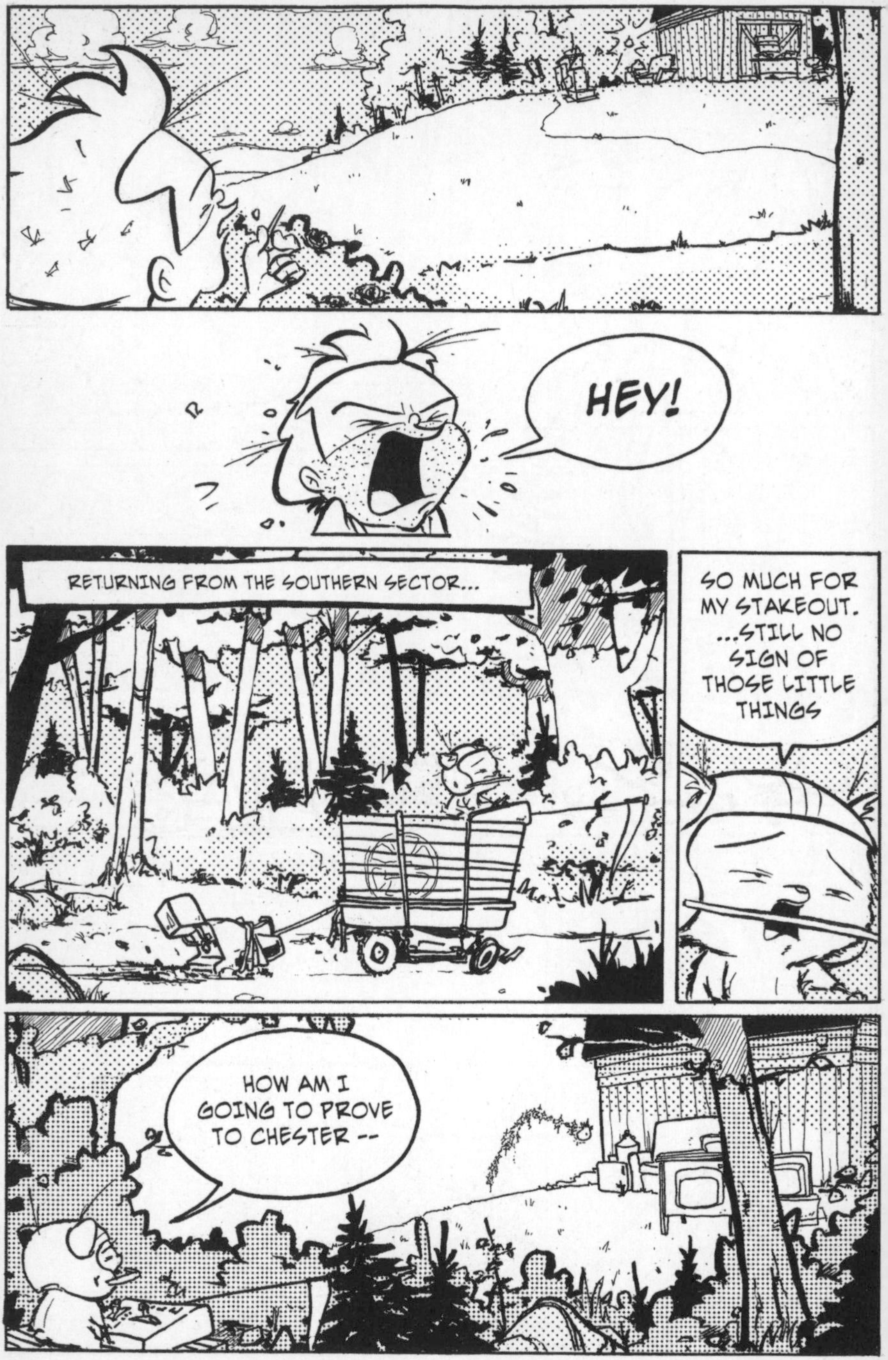
HEY!
RETURNING FROM THE SOUTHERN SECTOR...
SO MUCH FOR MY STAKEOUT. ...STILL NO SIGN OF THOSE LITTLE THINGS
HOW AM I GOING TO PROVE TO CHESTER --

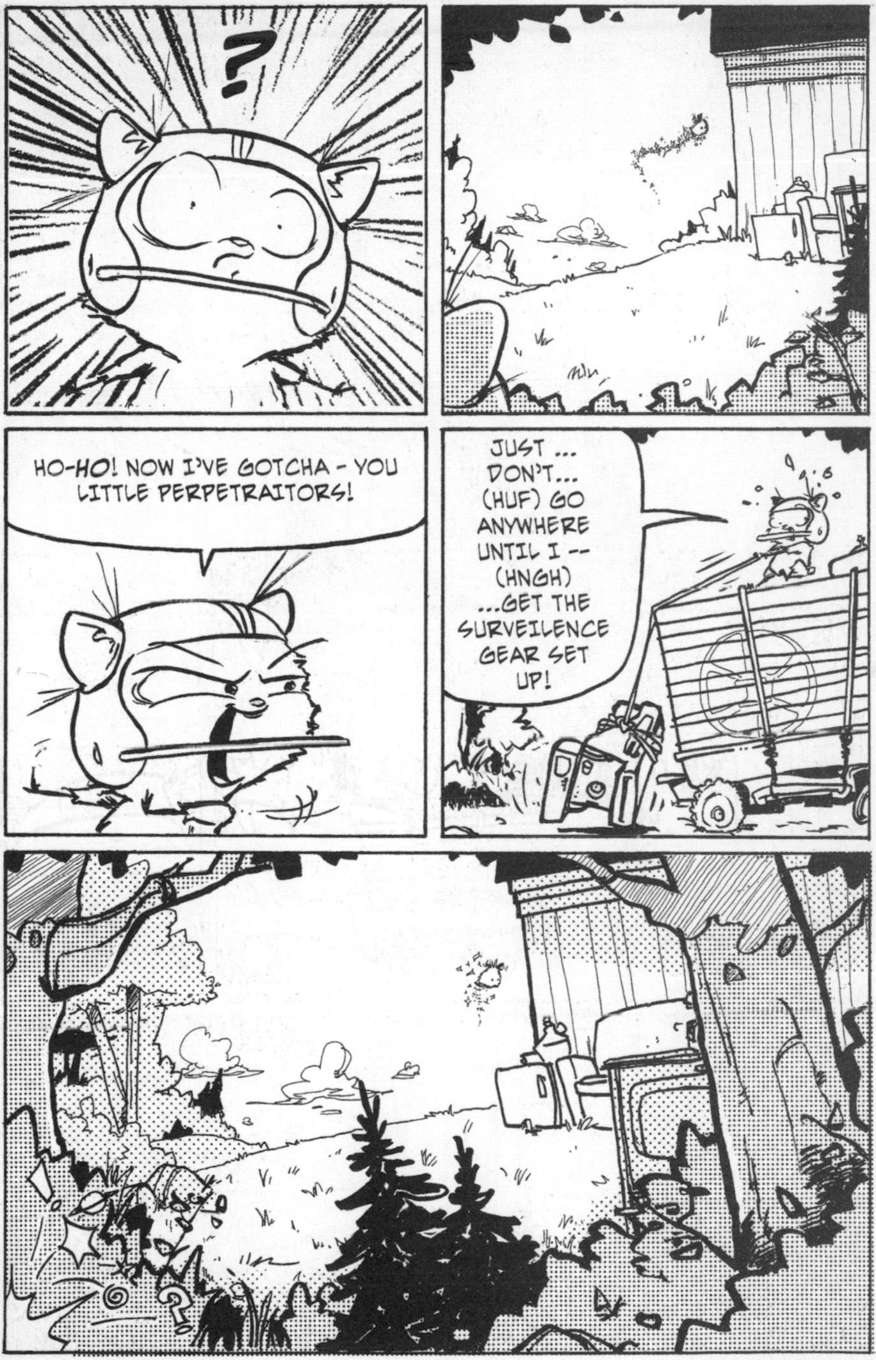
?
HO-HO! NOW I'VE GOTCHA - YOU LITTLE PERPETRAITORS!
JUST ... DON'T... (HUF) GO ANYWHERE UNTIL I -- (HNGH) ...GET THE SURVEILENCE GEAR SET UP!

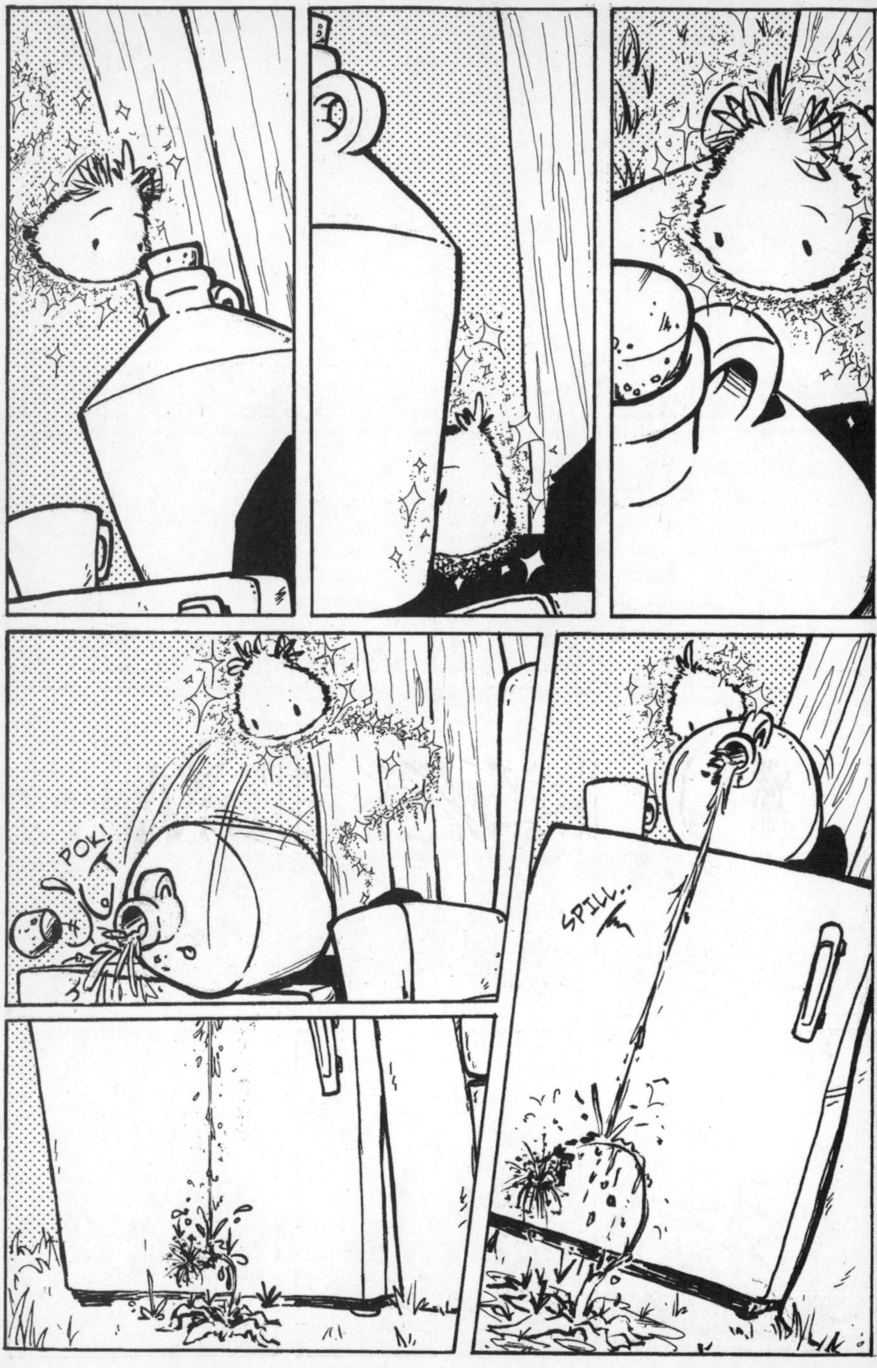
POK!
SPILL..

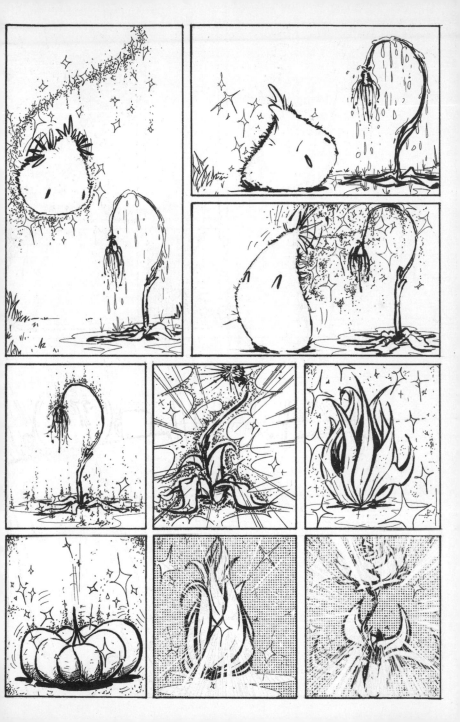

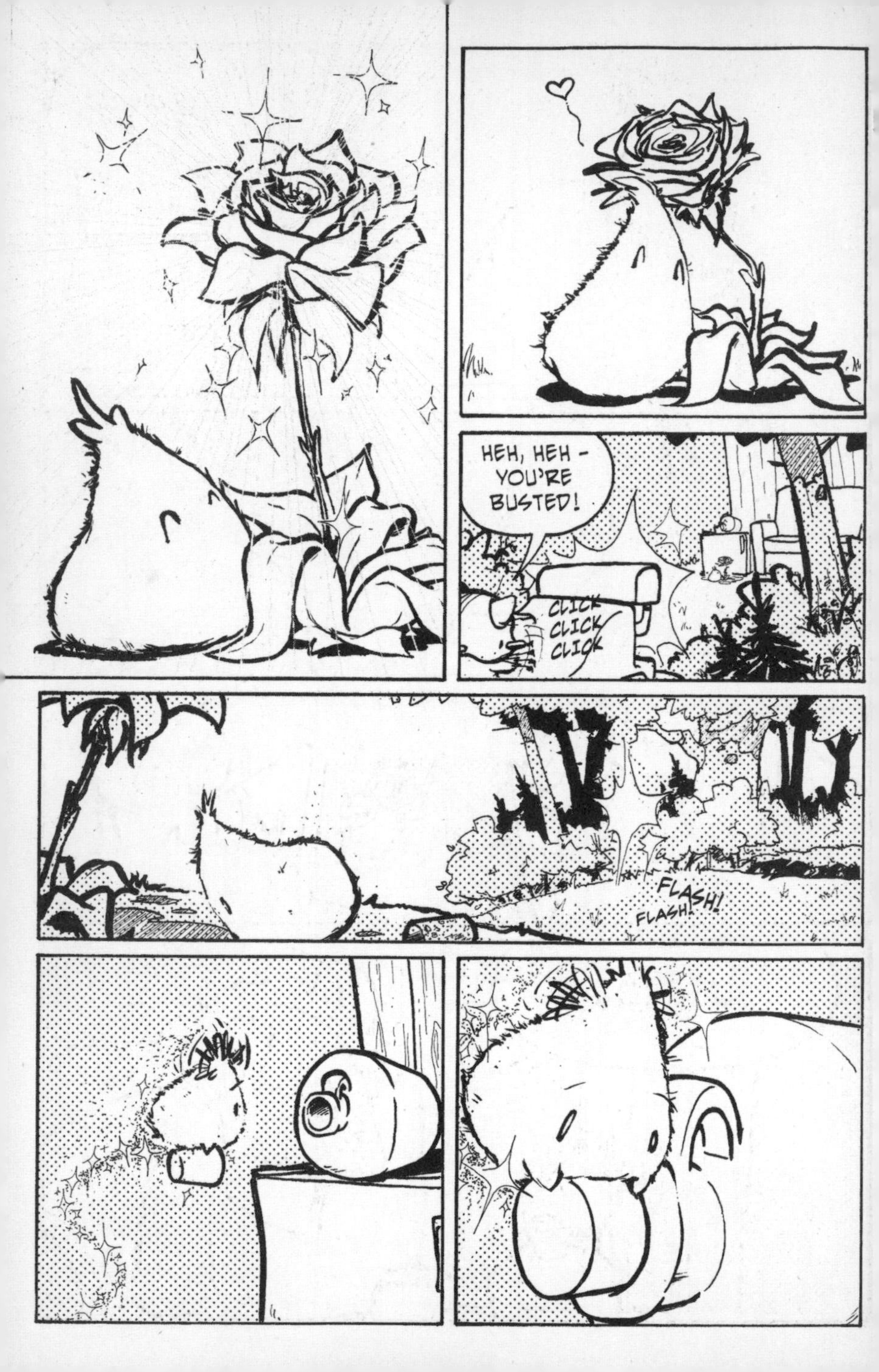
HEH, HEH - YOU'RE BUSTED!
CLICK CLICK CLICK
FLASH! FLASH!

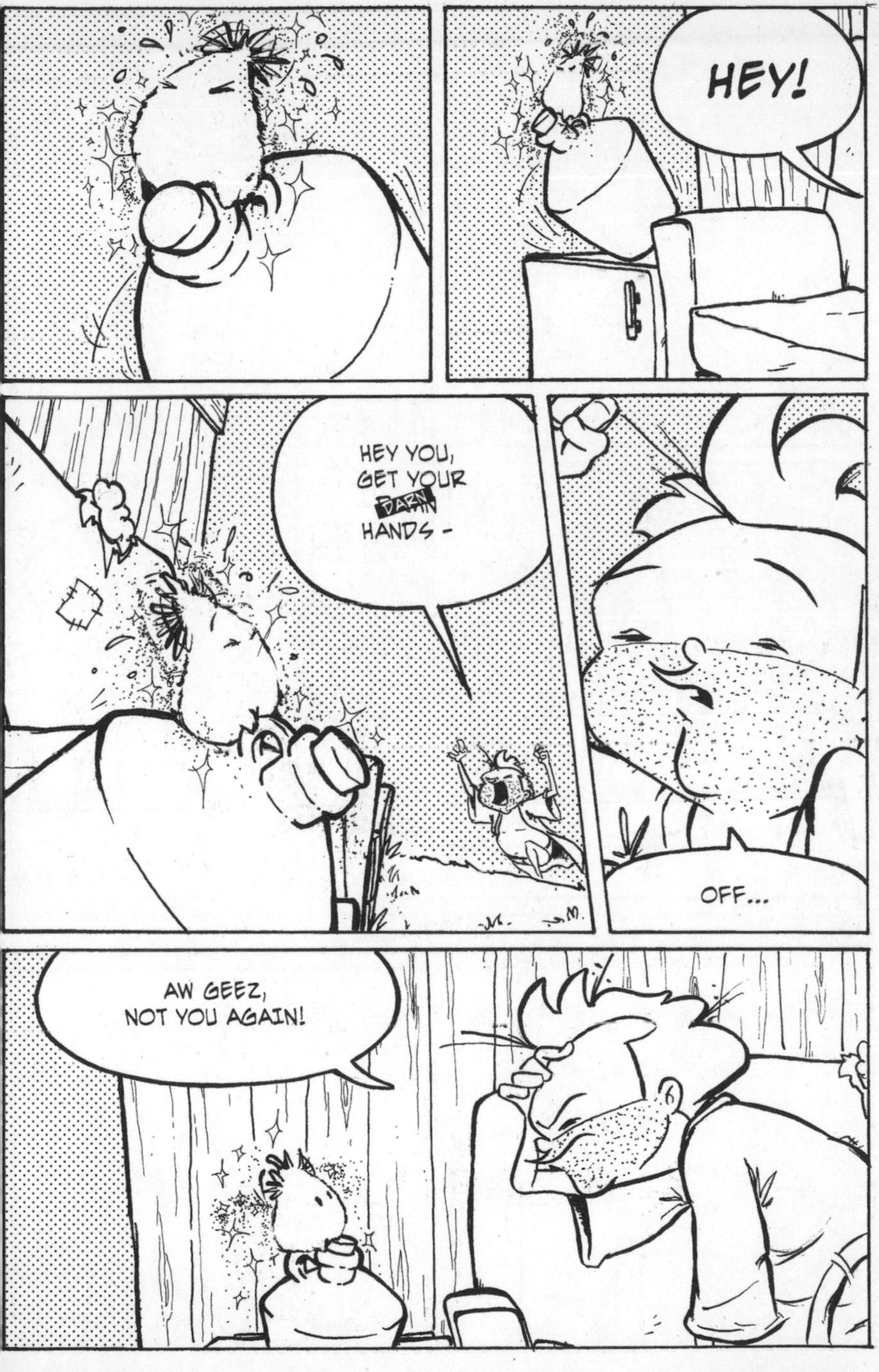
HEY!
HEY YOU, GET YOUR [redacted] HANDS -
OFF...
AW GEEZ, NOT YOU AGAIN!

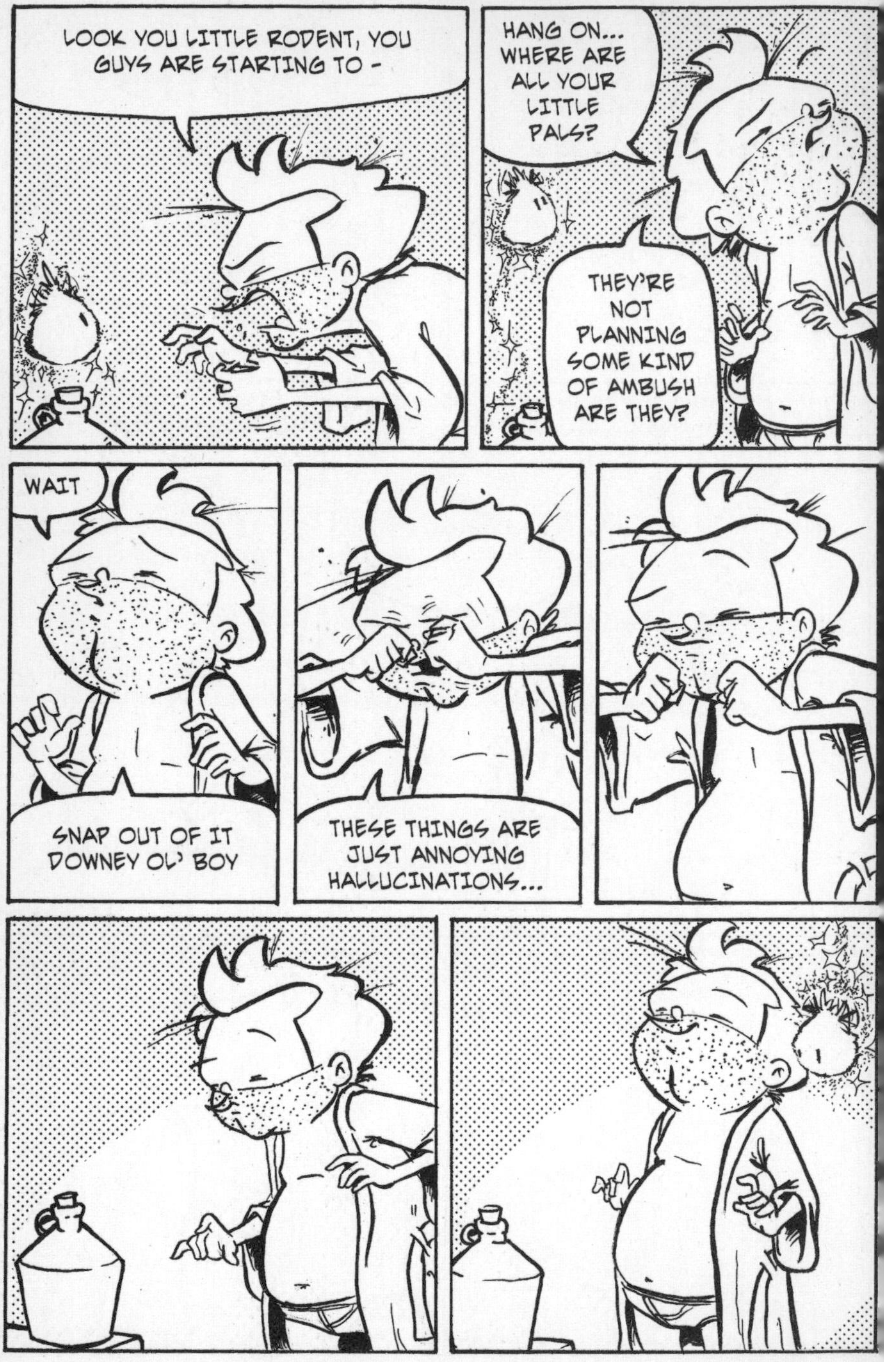
LOOK YOU LITTLE RODENT, YOU GUYS ARE STARTING TO -
HANG ON... WHERE ARE ALL YOUR LITTLE PALS?
THEY'RE NOT PLANNING SOME KIND OF AMBUSH ARE THEY?
WAIT
SNAP OUT OF IT DOWNEY OL' BOY
THESE THINGS ARE JUST ANNOYING HALLUCINATIONS...

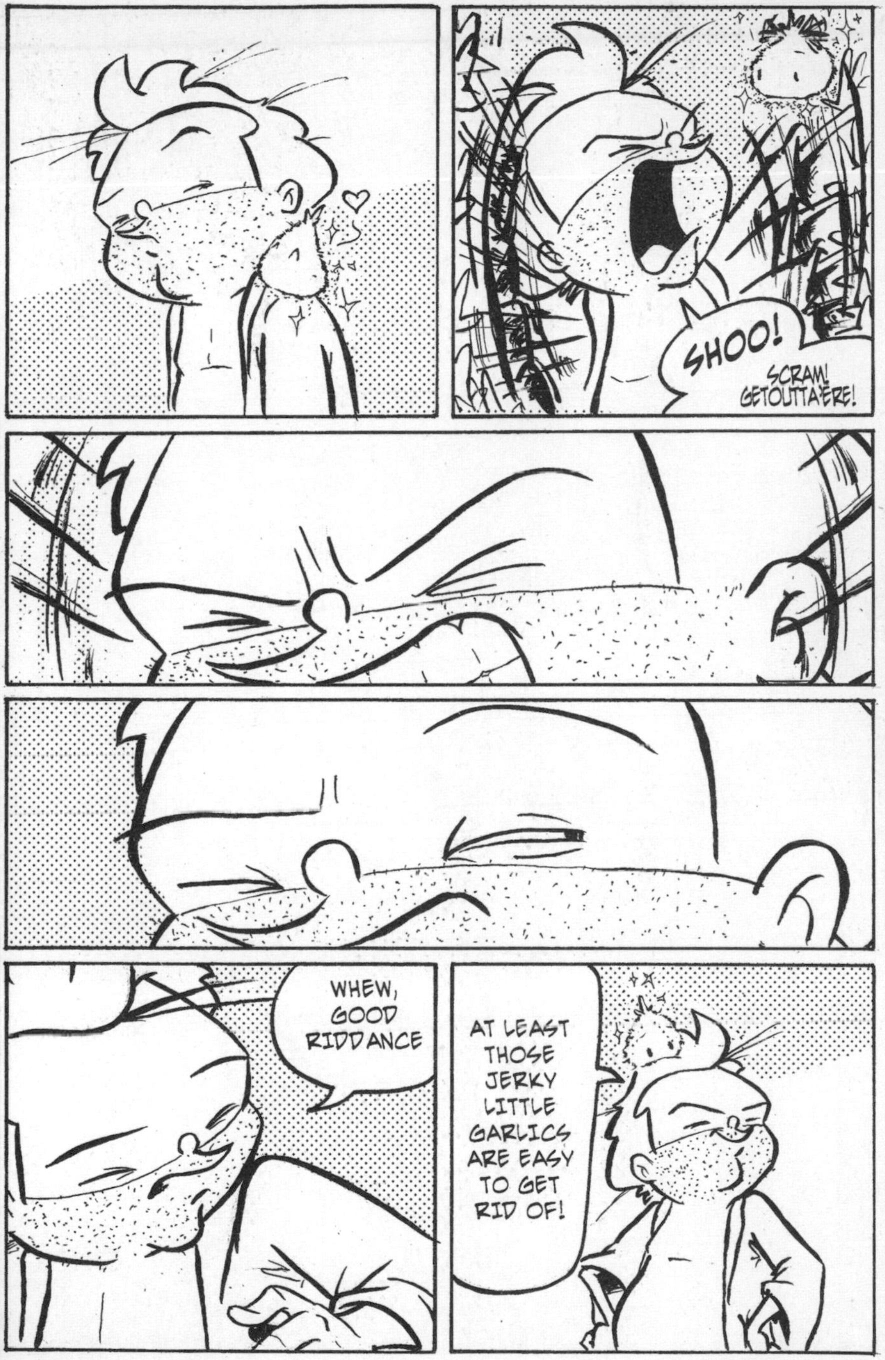
SHOO!
SCRAM! GETOUTTA'ERE!
WHEW, GOOD RIDDANCE
AT LEAST THOSE JERKY LITTLE GARLICS ARE EASY TO GET RID OF!

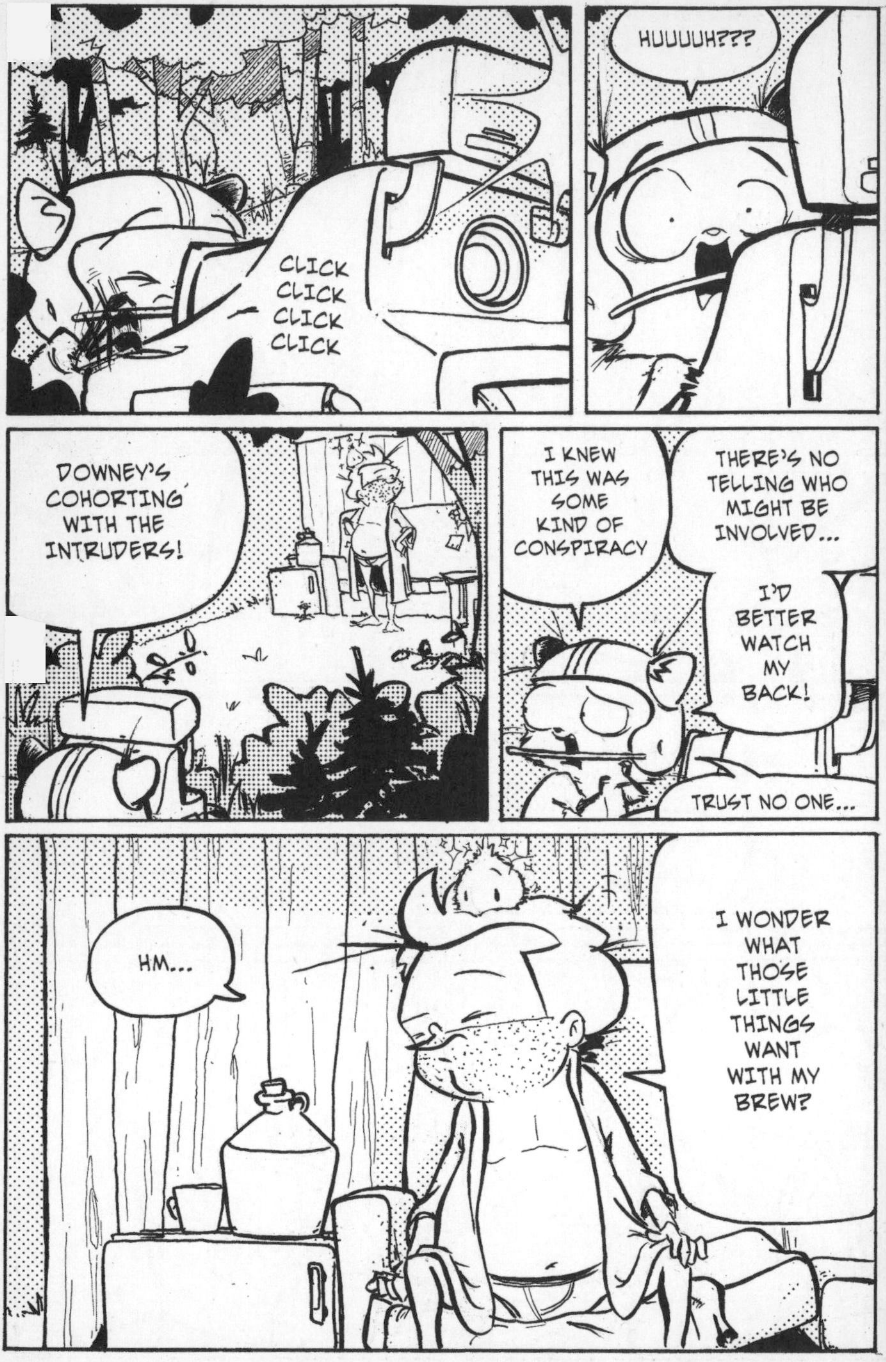
CLICK
CLICK
CLICK
CLICK
HUUUUH???
DOWNEY'S COHORTING WITH THE INTRUDERS!
I KNEW THIS WAS SOME KIND OF CONSPIRACY
THERE'S NO TELLING WHO MIGHT BE INVOLVED...
I'D BETTER WATCH MY BACK!
TRUST NO ONE...
HM...
I WONDER WHAT THOSE LITTLE THINGS WANT WITH MY BREW?

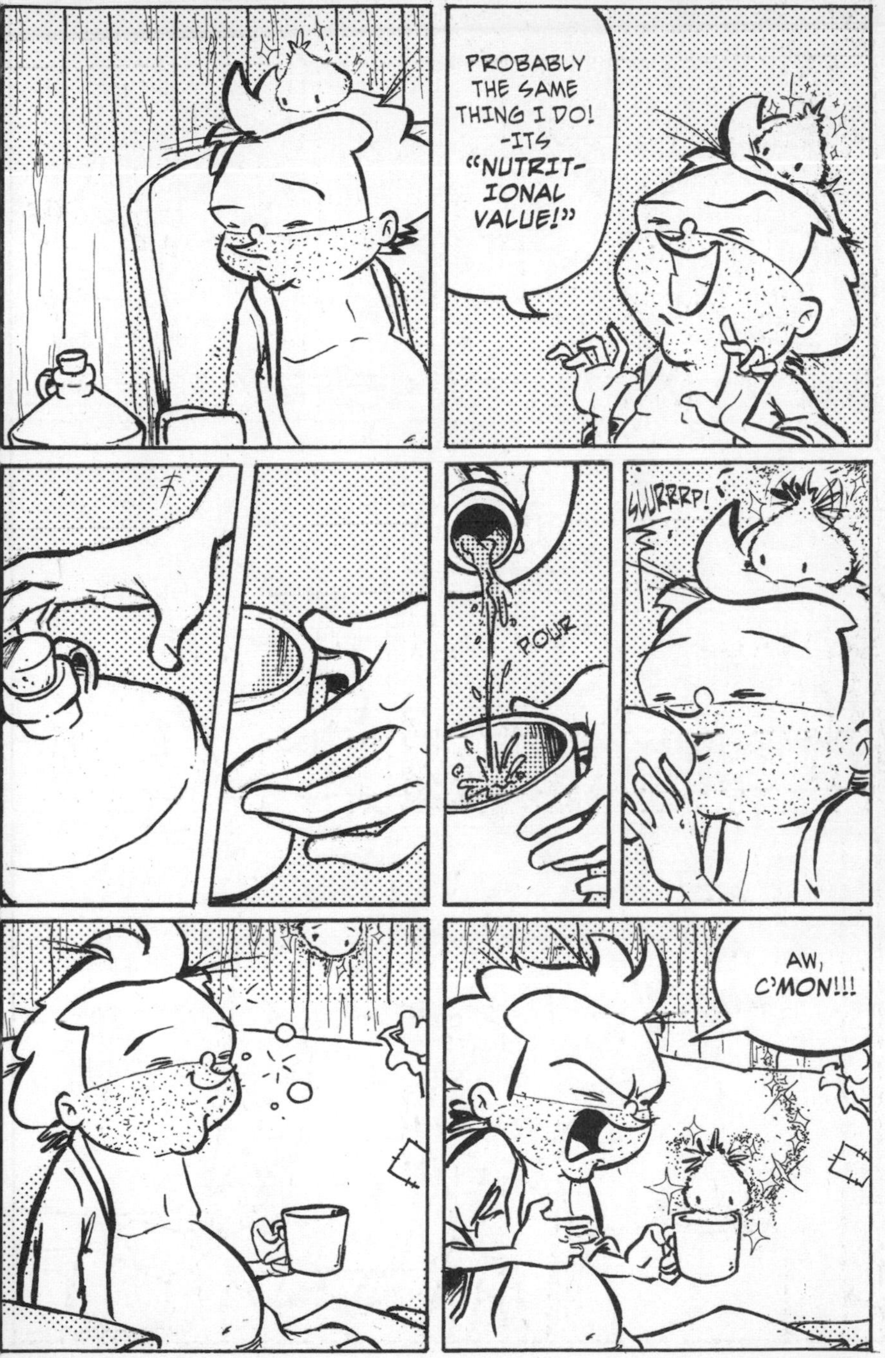
PROBABLY THE SAME THING I DO! -ITS "NUTRIT-IONAL VALUE!"
POUR
SLURRRP!
AW, C'MON!!!

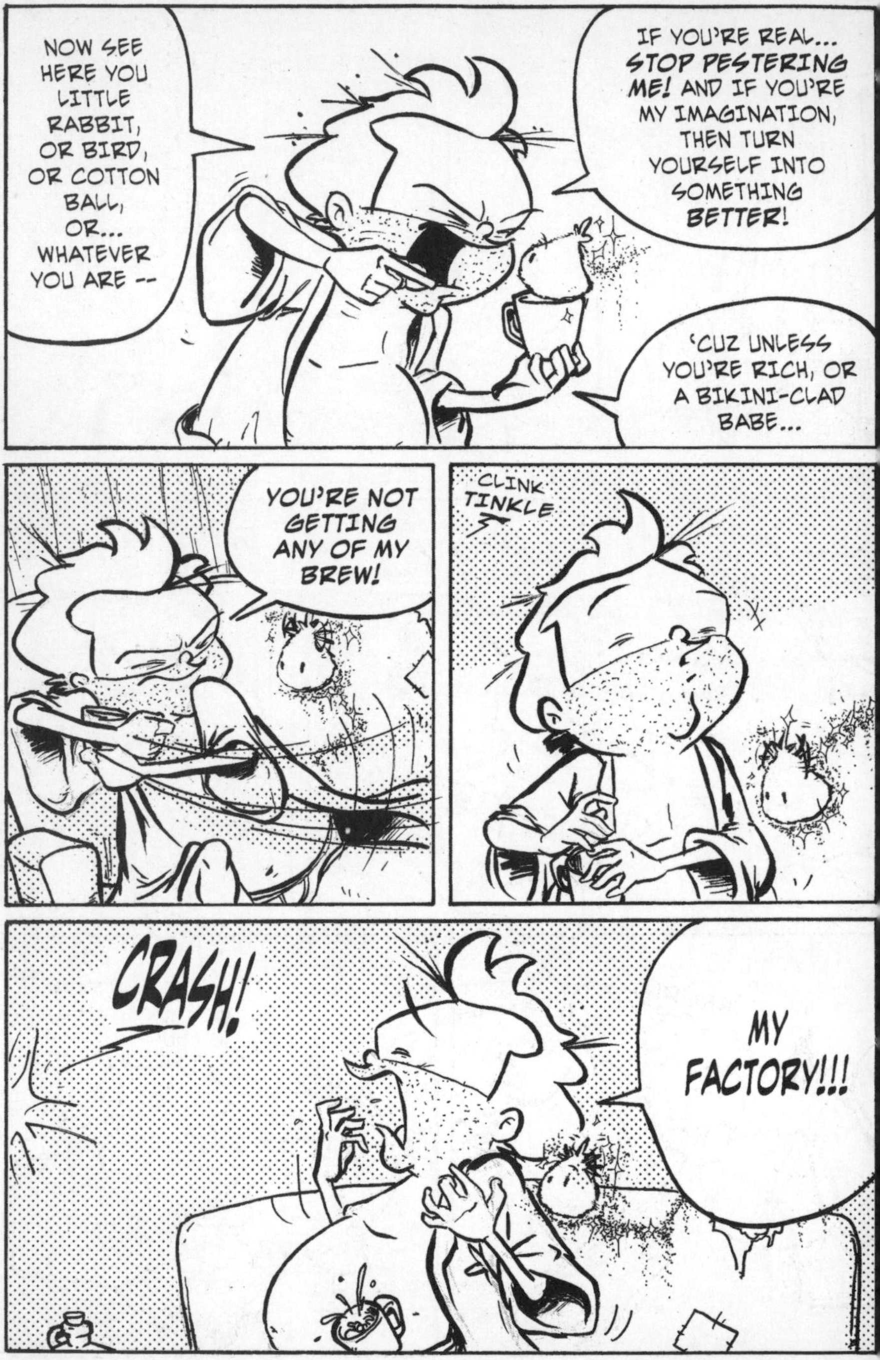
NOW SEE HERE YOU LITTLE RABBIT, OR BIRD, OR COTTON BALL, OR... WHATEVER YOU ARE --
IF YOU'RE REAL... STOP PESTERING ME! AND IF YOU'RE MY IMAGINATION, THEN TURN YOURSELF INTO SOMETHING BETTER!
'CUZ UNLESS YOU'RE RICH, OR A BIKINI-CLAD BABE...
YOU'RE NOT GETTING ANY OF MY BREW!
CLINK
TINKLE
CRASH!
MY FACTORY!!!

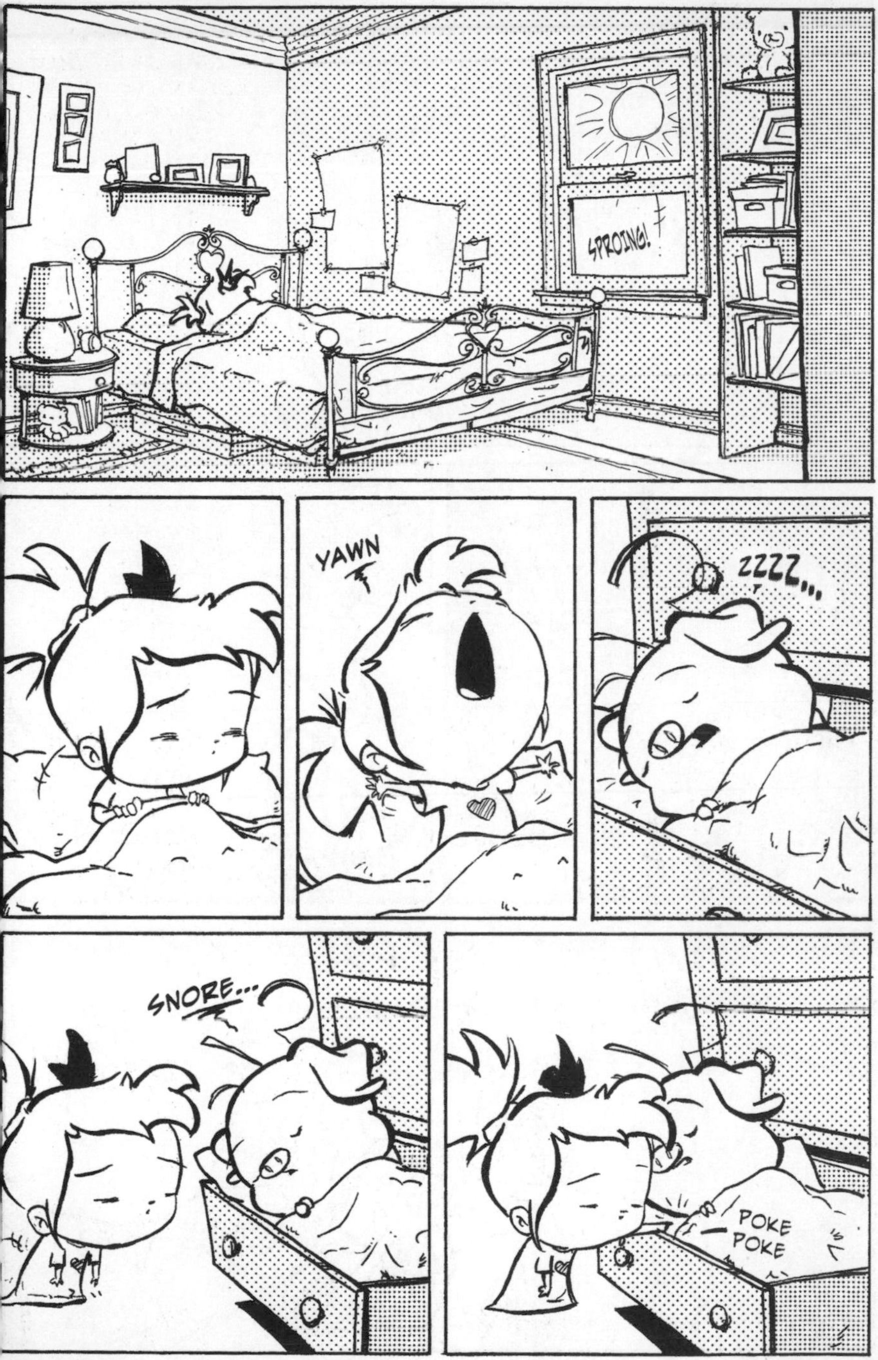
SPROING!
YAWN
ZZZZ...
SNORE...
POKE
POKE

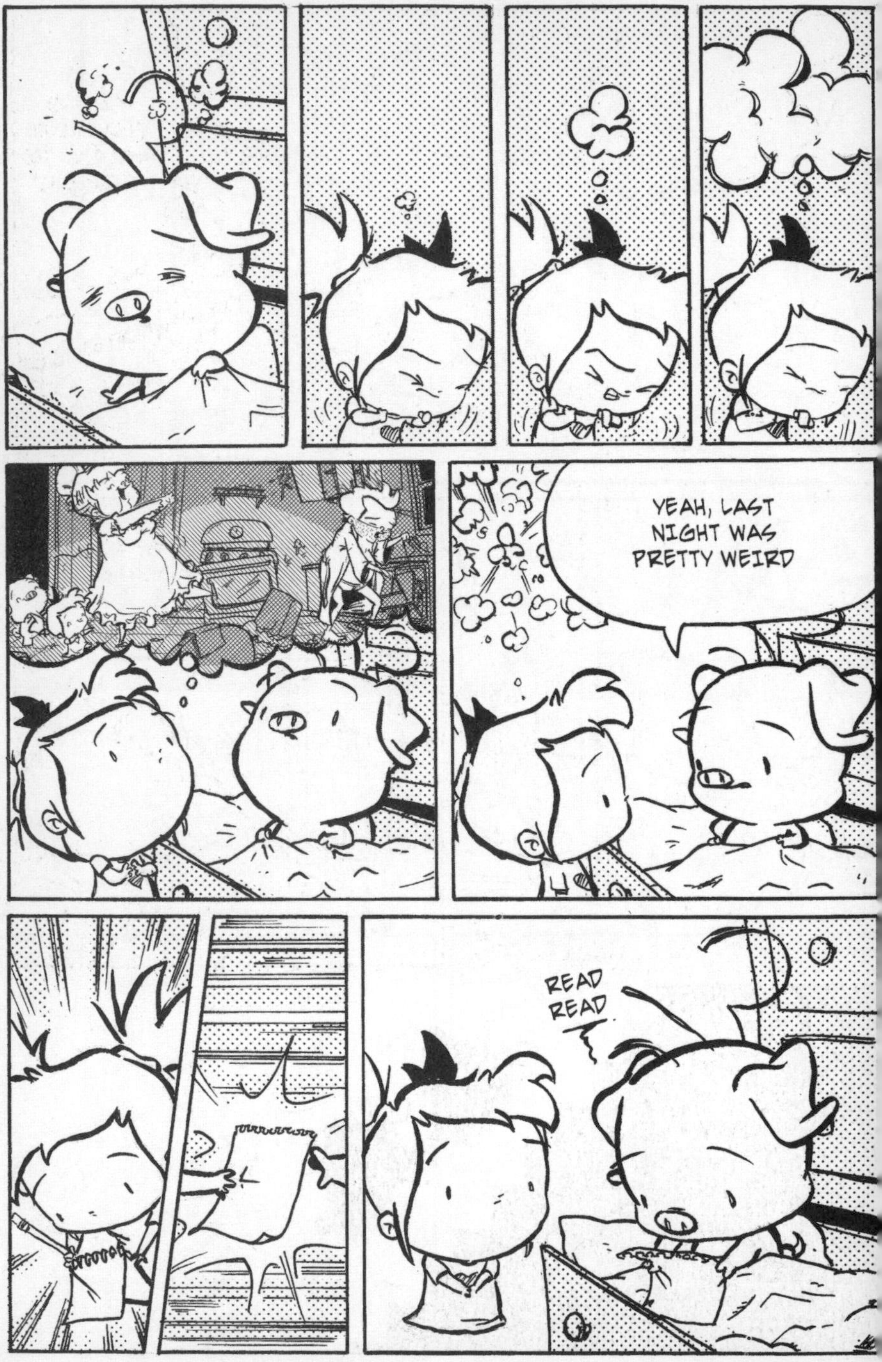
YEAH, LAST NIGHT WAS PRETTY WEIRD
READ READ

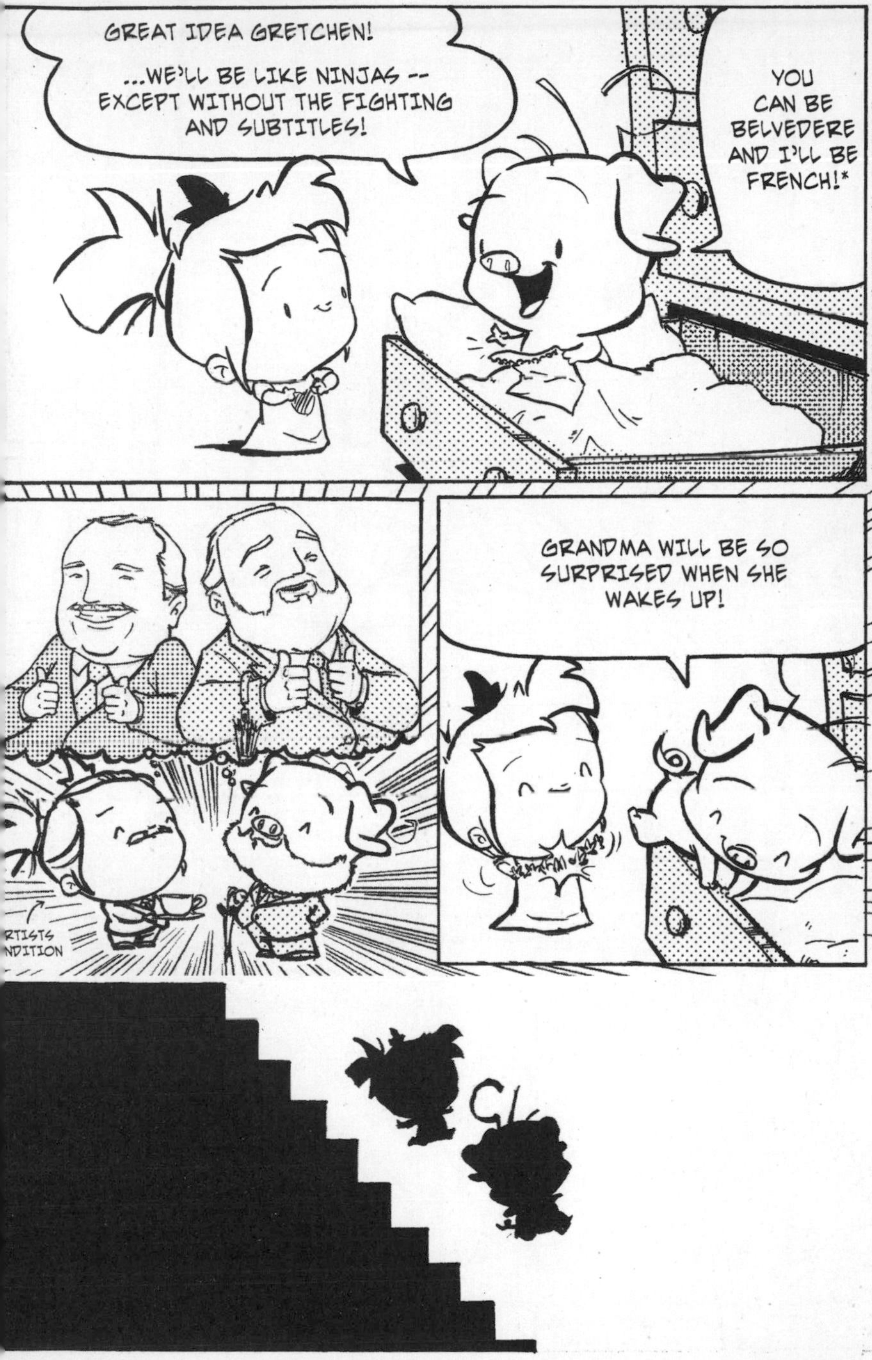
GREAT IDEA GRETCHEN!
...WE'LL BE LIKE NINJAS -- EXCEPT WITHOUT THE FIGHTING AND SUBTITLES!
YOU CAN BE BELVEDERE AND I'LL BE FRENCH!*
RTISTS NDITION
GRANDMA WILL BE SO SURPRISED WHEN SHE WAKES UP!

* TWO OF TELEVISIONS "GENTLEMAN'S GENTLEMEN" POPULARIZED IN THE LATER 20TH CENTURY

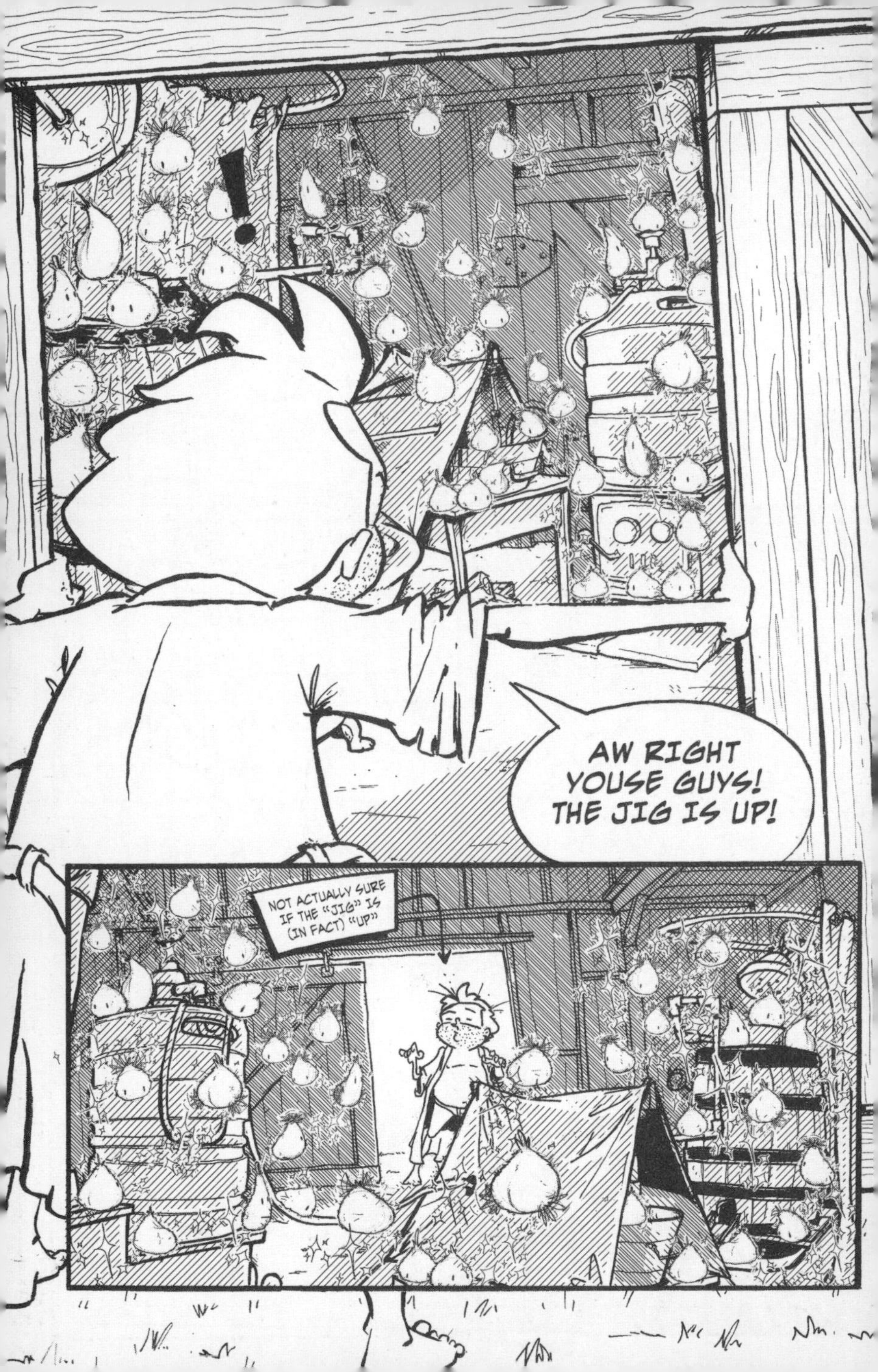
AW RIGHT YOUSE GUYS! THE JIG IS UP!
NOT ACTUALLY SURE IF THE "JIG" IS (IN FACT) "UP"

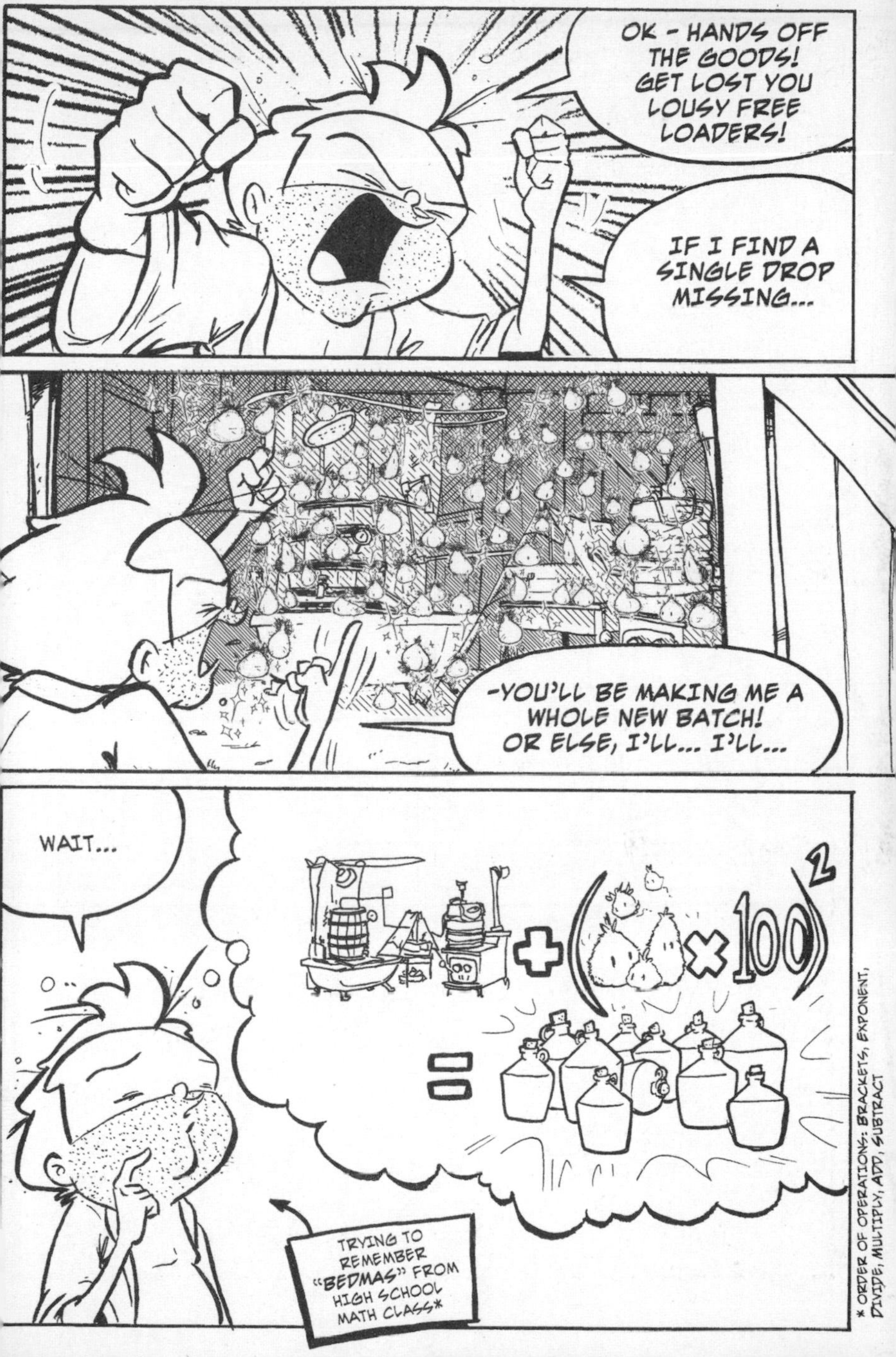
OK - HANDS OFF THE GOODS! GET LOST YOU LOUSY FREE LOADERS!
IF I FIND A SINGLE DROP MISSING...
-YOU'LL BE MAKING ME A WHOLE NEW BATCH! OR ELSE, I'LL... I'LL...
WAIT...
TRYING TO REMEMBER "BEDMAS" FROM HIGH SCHOOL MATH CLASS*

* ORDER OF OPERATIONS: BRACKETS, EXPONENT, DIVIDE, MULTIPLY, ADD, SUBTRACT

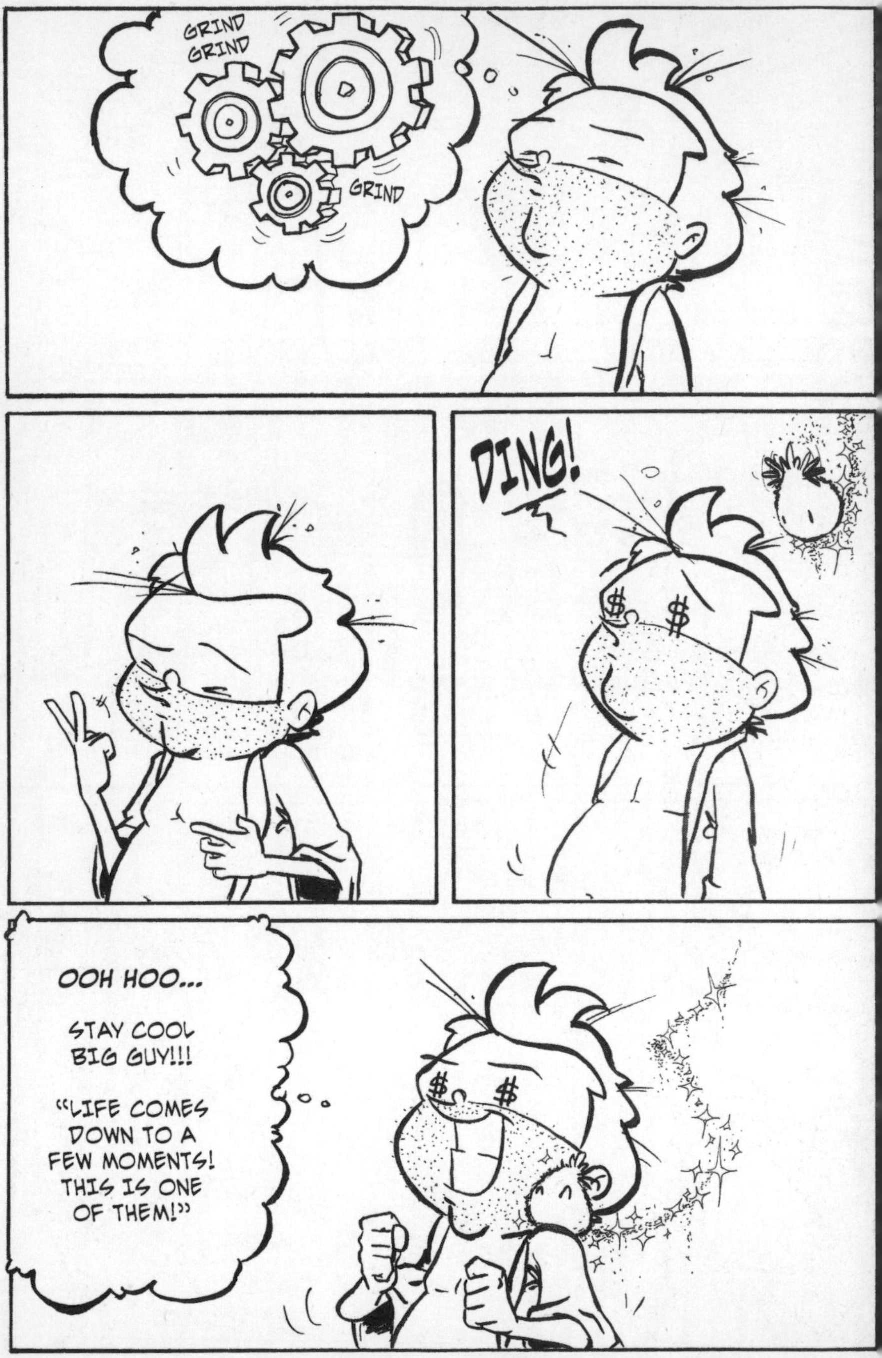
GRIND
GRIND
GRIND
DING!
OOH HOO...
STAY COOL BIG GUY!!!
"LIFE COMES DOWN TO A FEW MOMENTS! THIS IS ONE OF THEM!"

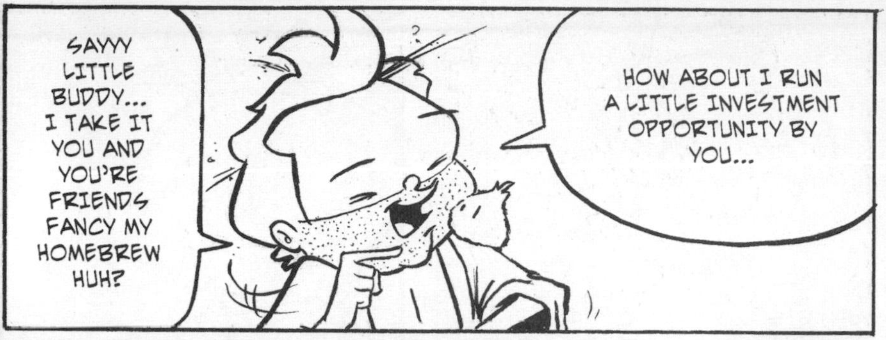
SAYYY LITTLE BUDDY... I TAKE IT YOU AND YOU'RE FRIENDS FANCY MY HOMEBREW HUH?
HOW ABOUT I RUN A LITTLE INVESTMENT OPPORTUNITY BY YOU...

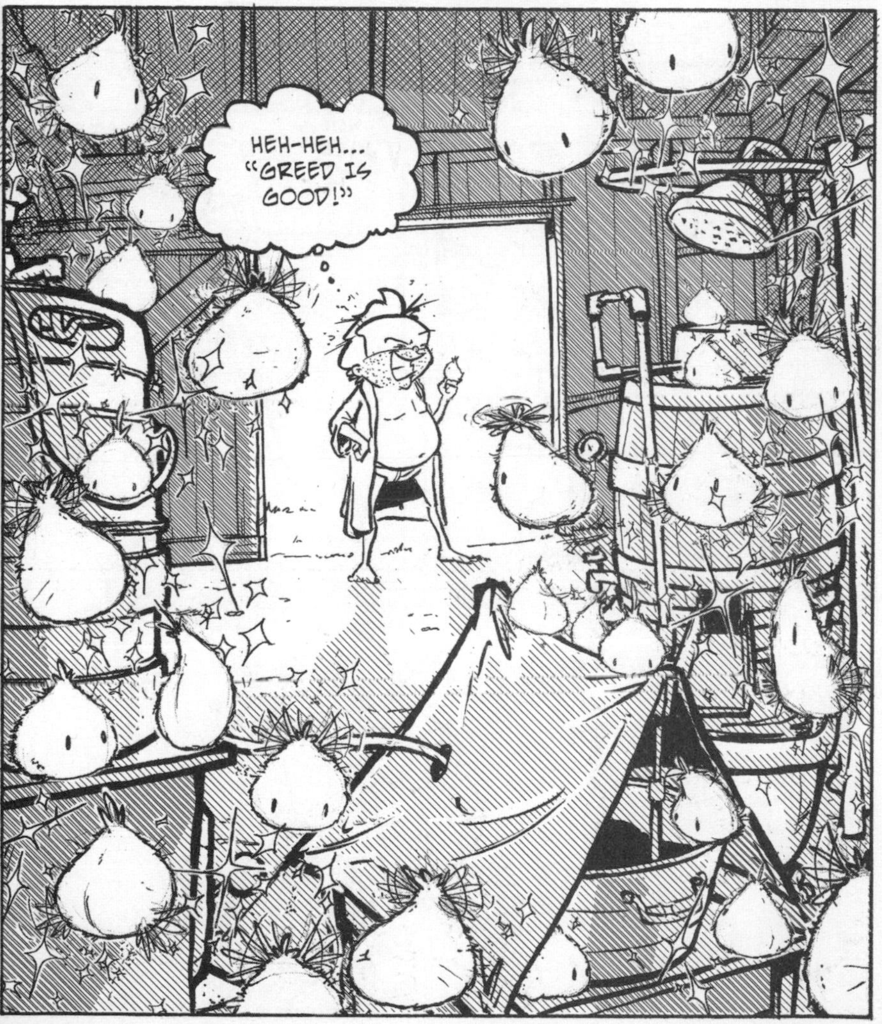
HEH-HEH... "GREED IS GOOD!"

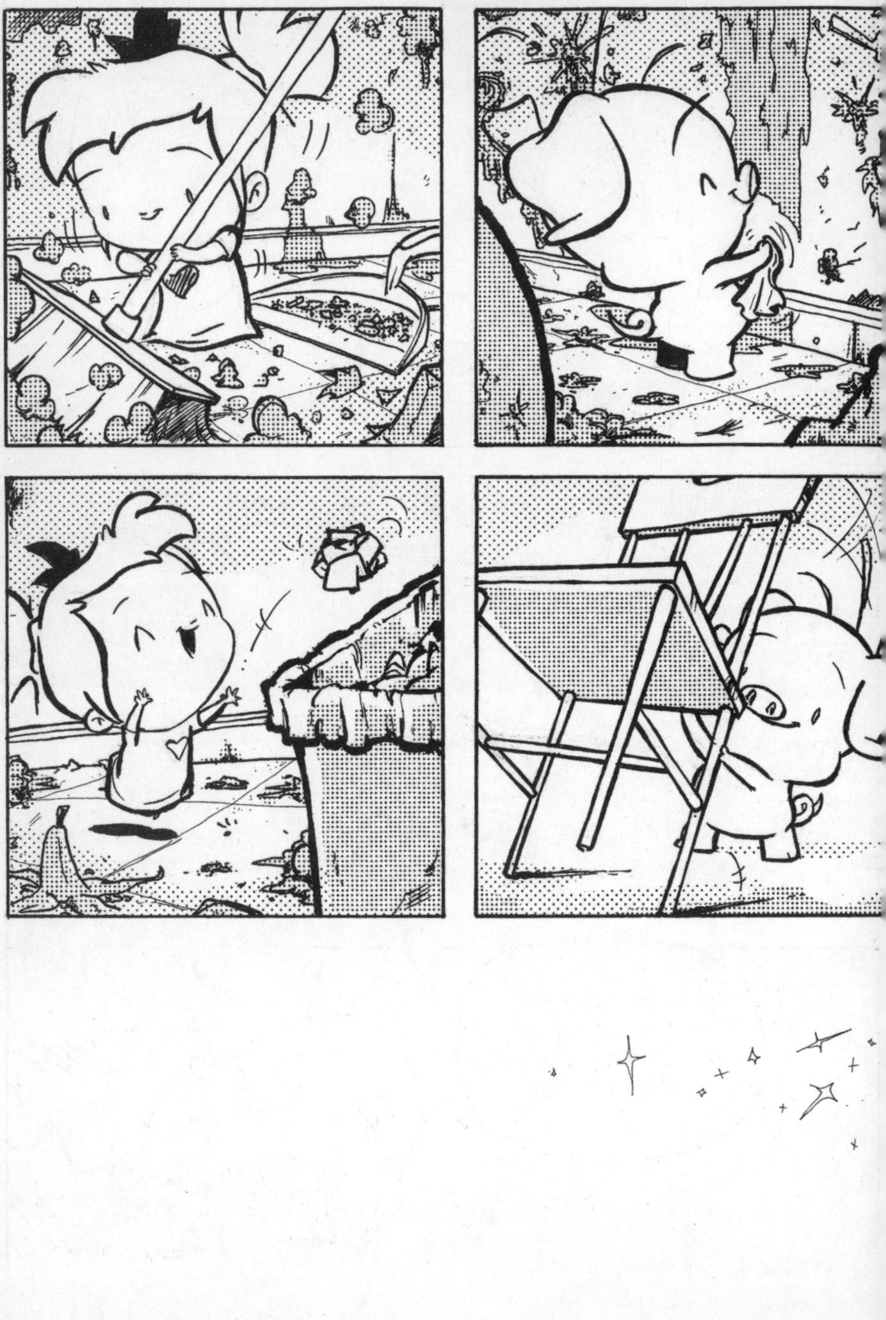

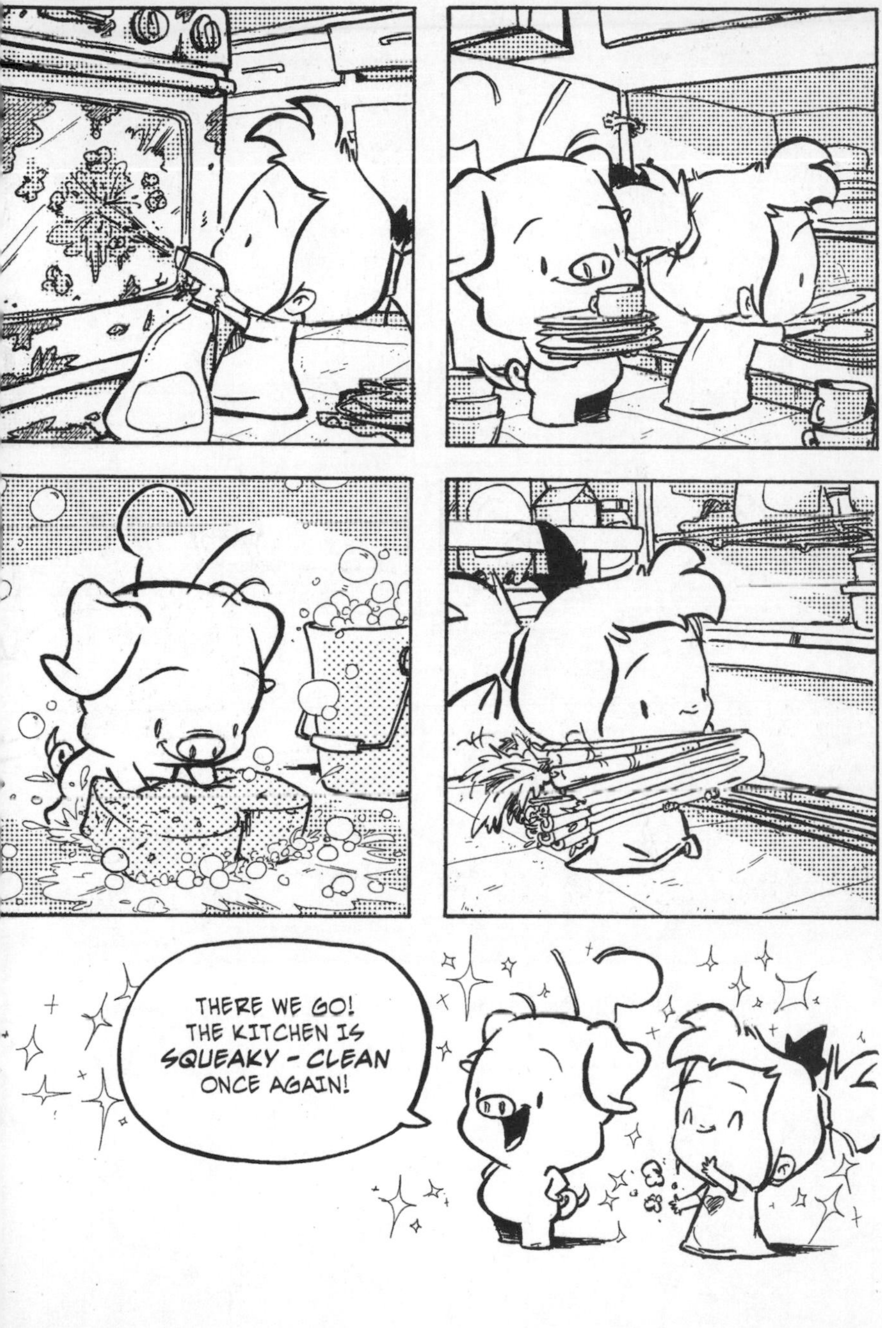
THERE WE GO! THE KITCHEN IS SQUEAKY - CLEAN ONCE AGAIN!

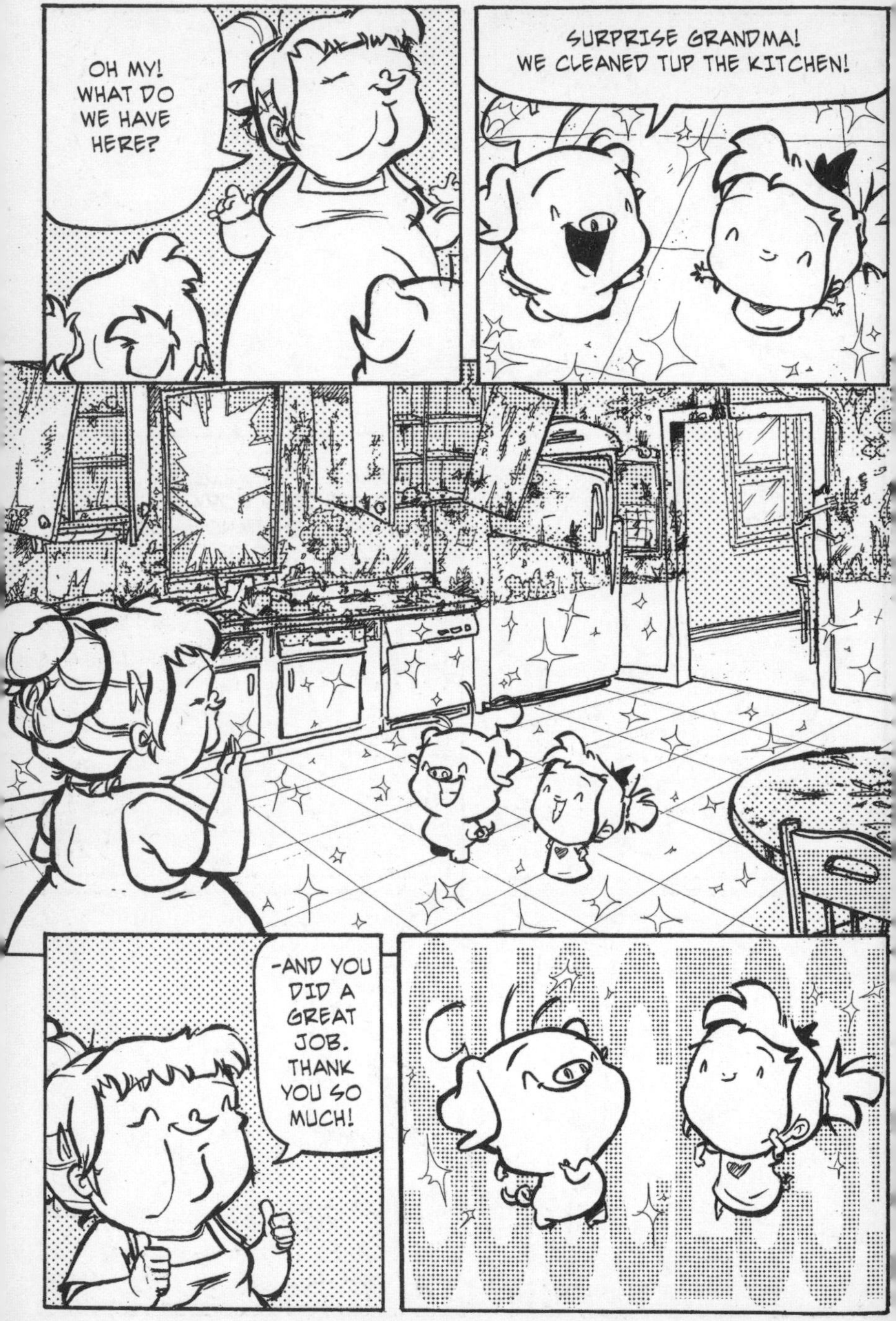
OH MY! WHAT DO WE HAVE HERE?
SURPRISE GRANDMA! WE CLEANED TUP THE KITCHEN!
-AND YOU DID A GREAT JOB. THANK YOU SO MUCH!

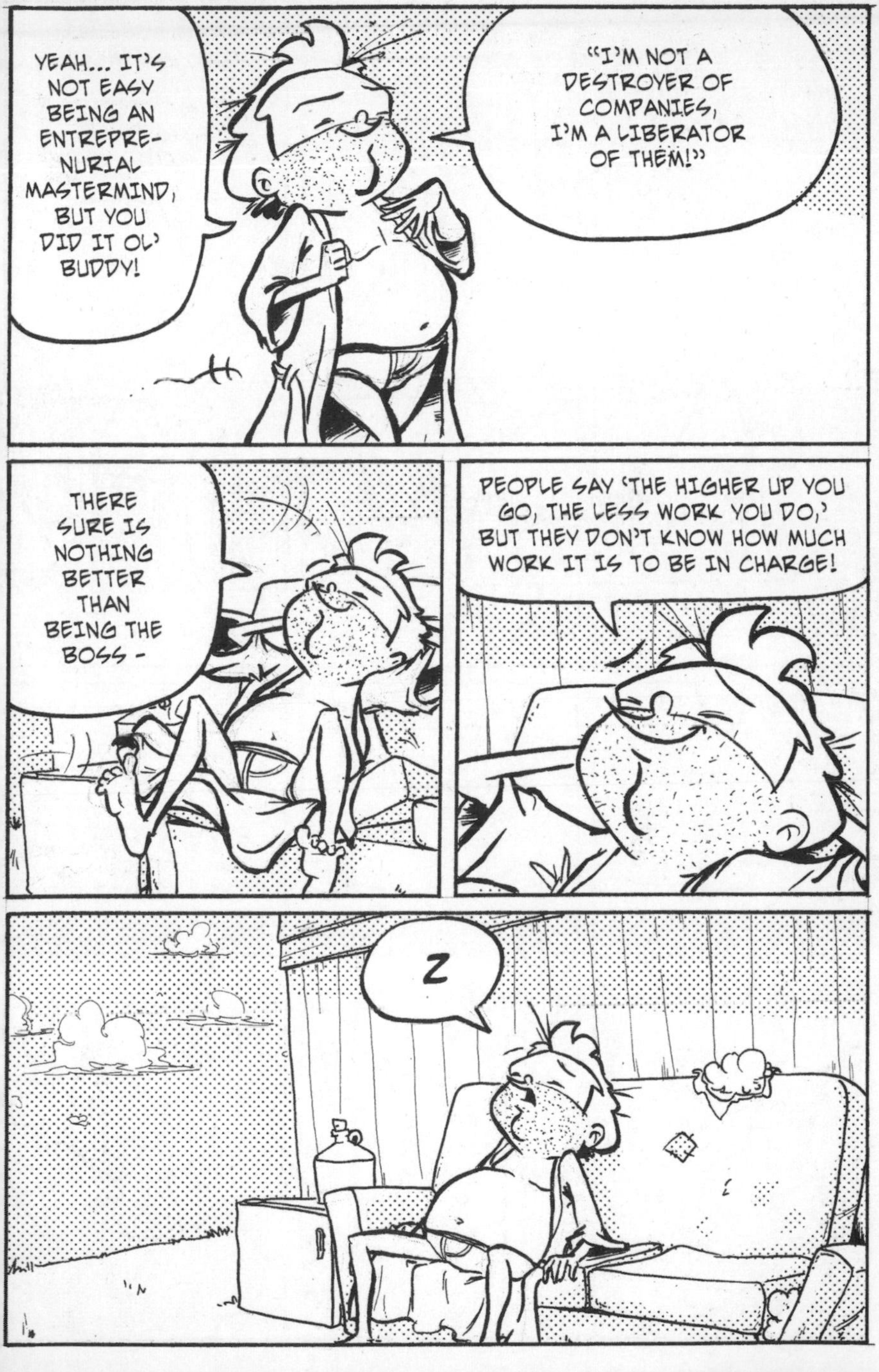
YEAH... IT'S NOT EASY BEING AN ENTREPRE-NURIAL MASTERMIND, BUT YOU DID IT OL' BUDDY!
"I'M NOT A DESTROYER OF COMPANIES, I'M A LIBERATOR OF THEM!"
THERE SURE IS NOTHING BETTER THAN BEING THE BOSS -
PEOPLE SAY 'THE HIGHER UP YOU GO, THE LESS WORK YOU DO,' BUT THEY DON'T KNOW HOW MUCH WORK IT IS TO BE IN CHARGE!
Z

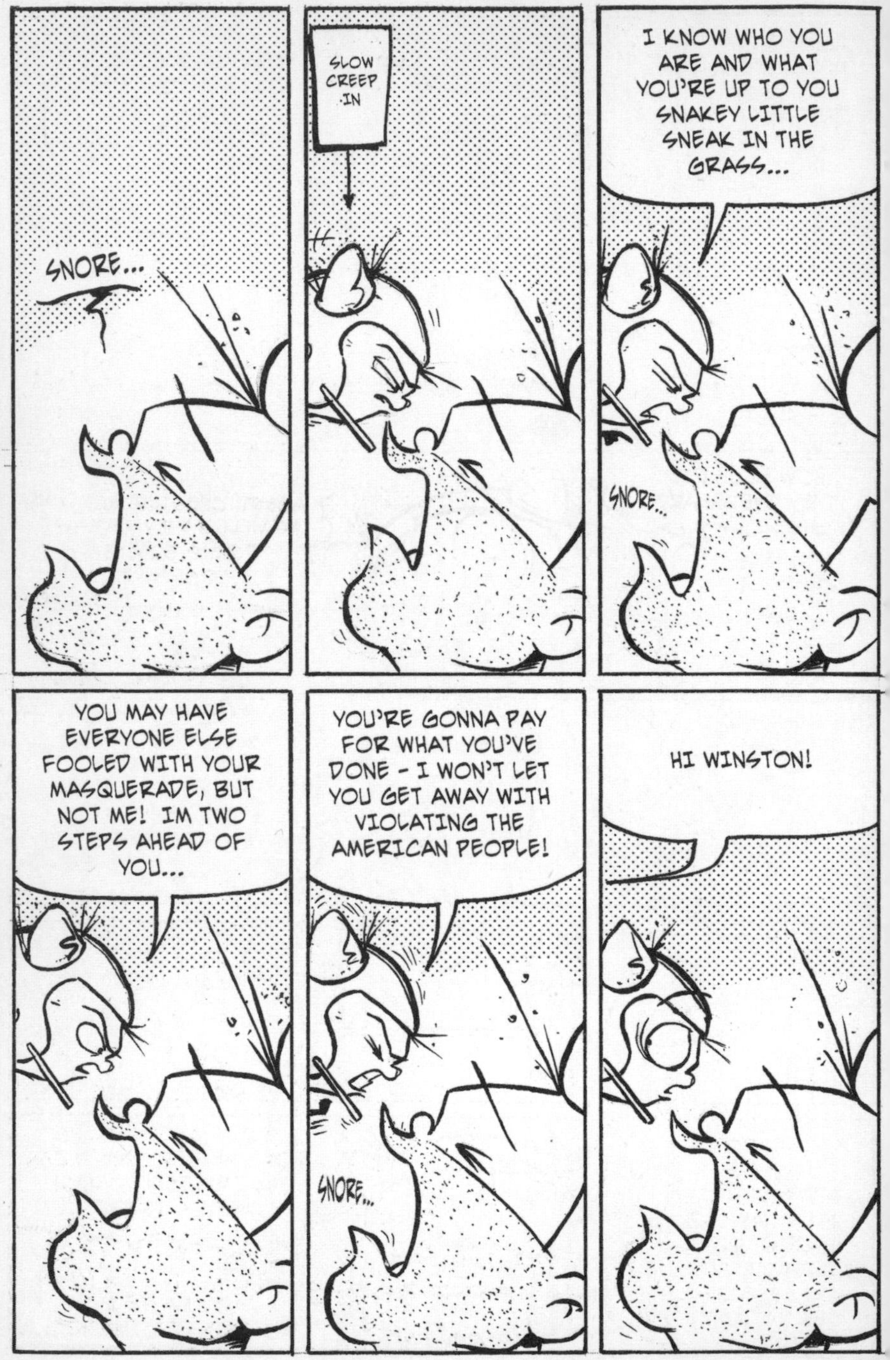
SNORE...
SLOW CREEP IN
I KNOW WHO YOU ARE AND WHAT YOU'RE UP TO YOU SNAKEY LITTLE SNEAK IN THE GRASS...
SNORE...
YOU MAY HAVE EVERYONE ELSE FOOLED WITH YOUR MASQUERADE, BUT NOT ME! IM TWO STEPS AHEAD OF YOU...
YOU'RE GONNA PAY FOR WHAT YOU'VE DONE - I WON'T LET YOU GET AWAY WITH VIOLATING THE AMERICAN PEOPLE!
SNORE...
HI WINSTON!

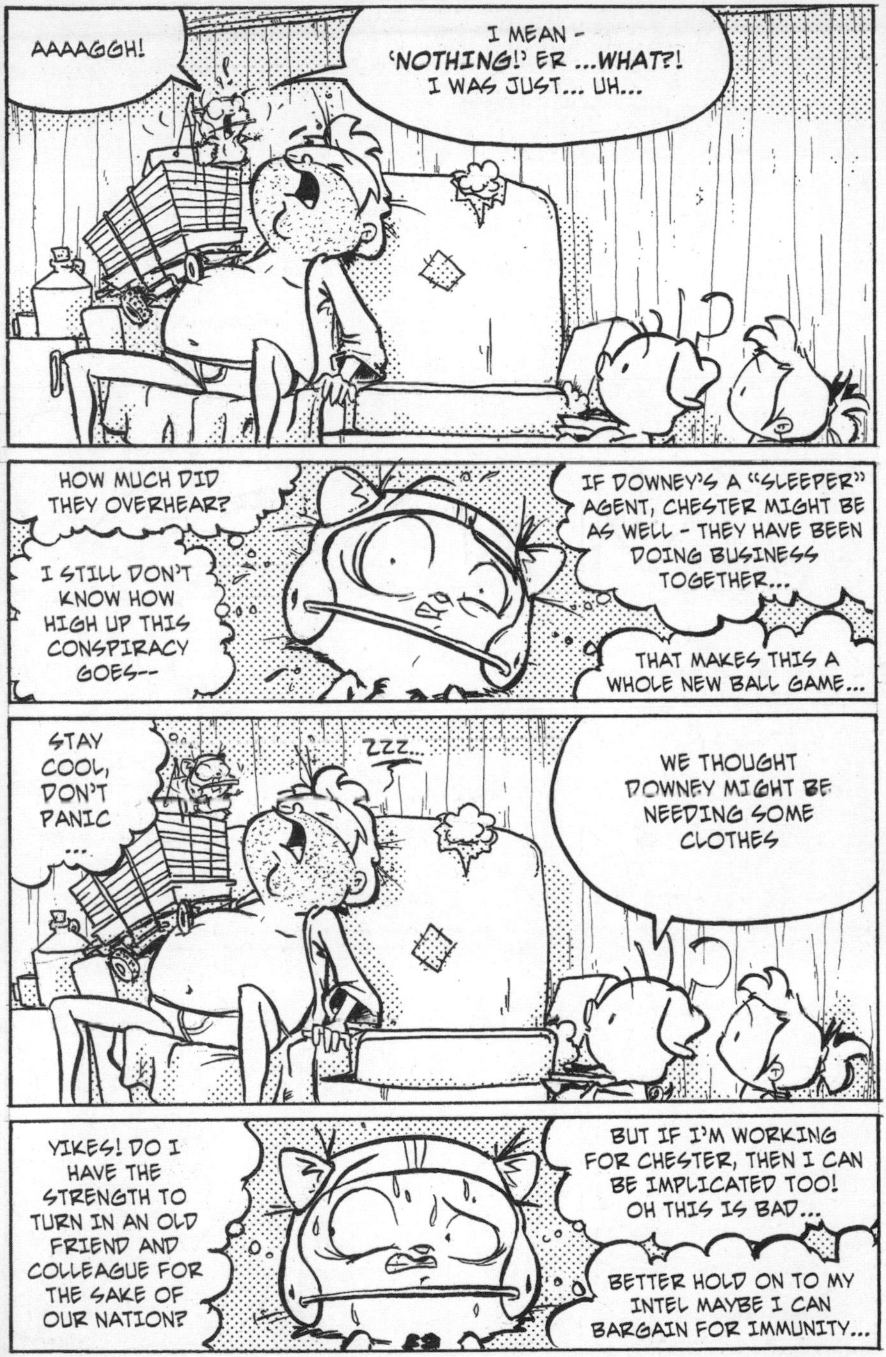
AAAAGGH!
I MEAN - 'NOTHING!' ER ...WHAT?! I WAS JUST... UH...
HOW MUCH DID THEY OVERHEAR?
I STILL DON'T KNOW HOW HIGH UP THIS CONSPIRACY GOES--
IF DOWNEY'S A "SLEEPER" AGENT, CHESTER MIGHT BE AS WELL - THEY HAVE BEEN DOING BUSINESS TOGETHER...
THAT MAKES THIS A WHOLE NEW BALL GAME...
STAY COOL, DON'T PANIC ...
ZZZ...
WE THOUGHT DOWNEY MIGHT BE NEEDING SOME CLOTHES
YIKES! DO I HAVE THE STRENGTH TO TURN IN AN OLD FRIEND AND COLLEAGUE FOR THE SAKE OF OUR NATION?
BUT IF I'M WORKING FOR CHESTER, THEN I CAN BE IMPLICATED TOO! OH THIS IS BAD...
BETTER HOLD ON TO MY INTEL MAYBE I CAN BARGAIN FOR IMMUNITY...

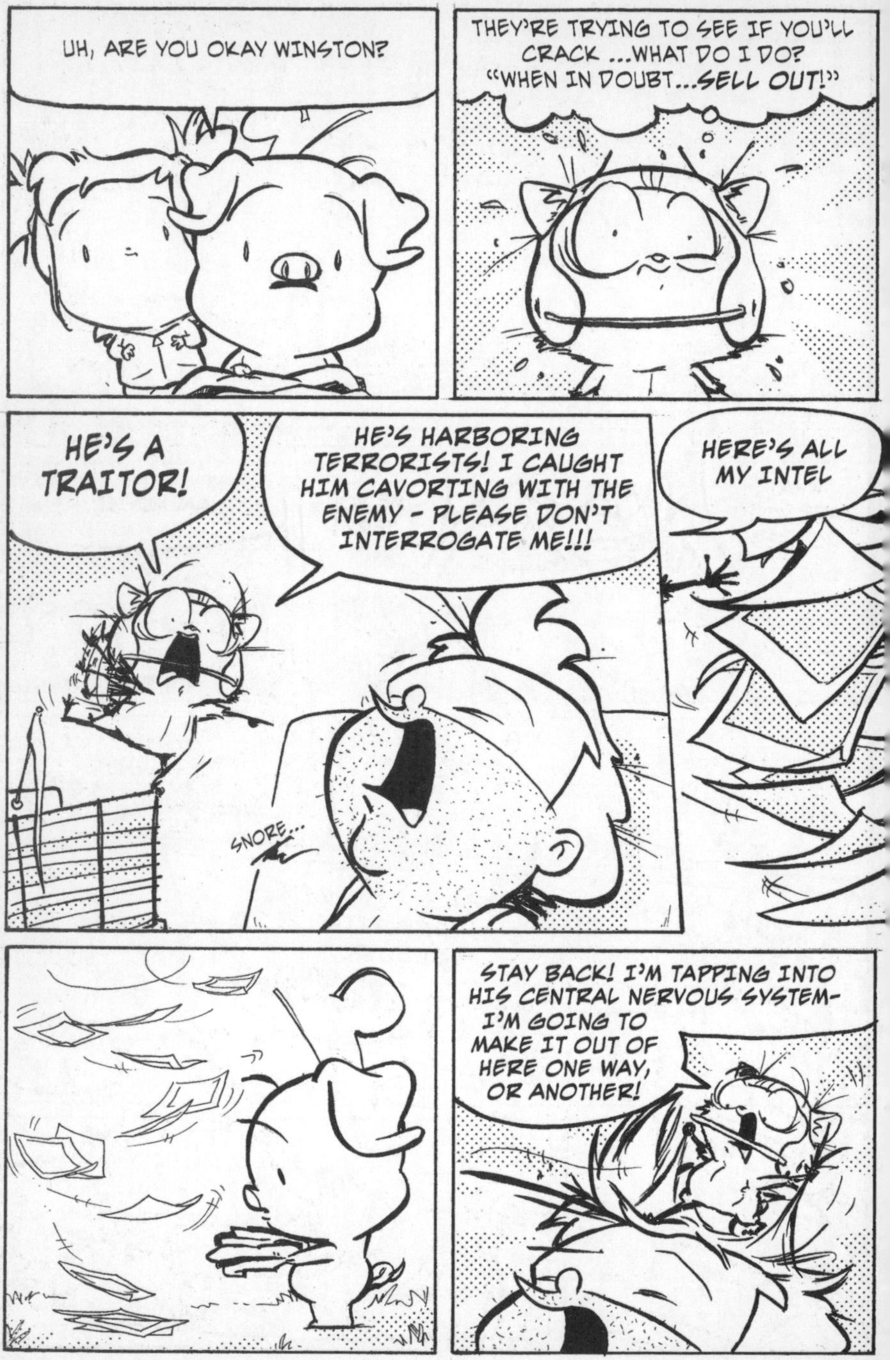
UH, ARE YOU OKAY WINSTON?
THEY'RE TRYING TO SEE IF YOU'LL CRACK ...WHAT DO I DO? "WHEN IN DOUBT...SELL OUT!"
HE'S A TRAITOR!
HE'S HARBORING TERRORISTS! I CAUGHT HIM CAVORTING WITH THE ENEMY - PLEASE DON'T INTERROGATE ME!!!
SNORE...
HERE'S ALL MY INTEL
STAY BACK! I'M TAPPING INTO HIS CENTRAL NERVOUS SYSTEM-
I'M GOING TO MAKE IT OUT OF HERE ONE WAY, OR ANOTHER!

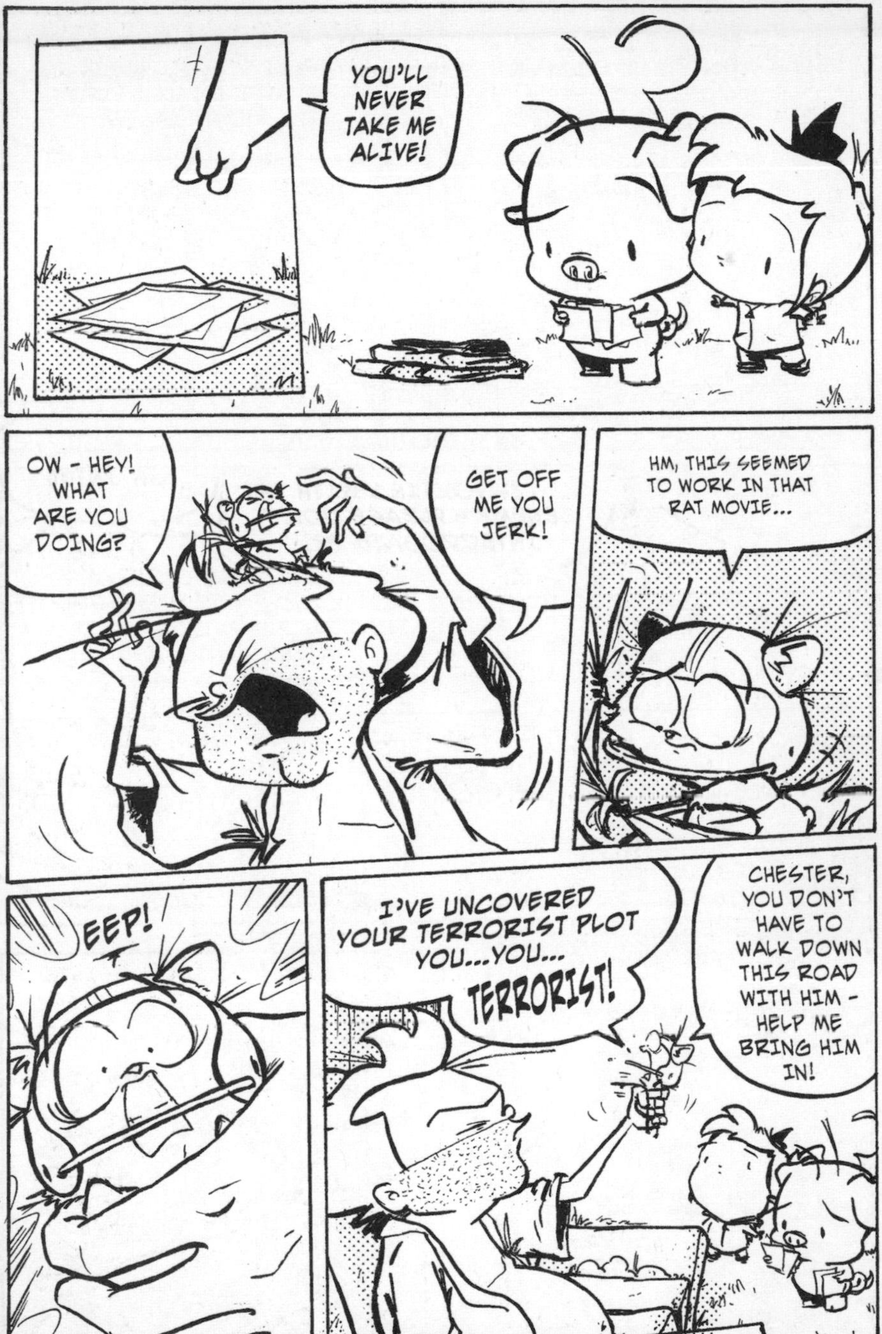
YOU'LL NEVER TAKE ME ALIVE!
OW - HEY! WHAT ARE YOU DOING?
GET OFF ME YOU JERK!
HM, THIS SEEMED TO WORK IN THAT RAT MOVIE...
EEP!
I'VE UNCOVERED YOUR TERRORIST PLOT YOU...YOU... TERRORIST!
CHESTER, YOU DON'T HAVE TO WALK DOWN THIS ROAD WITH HIM - HELP ME BRING HIM IN!

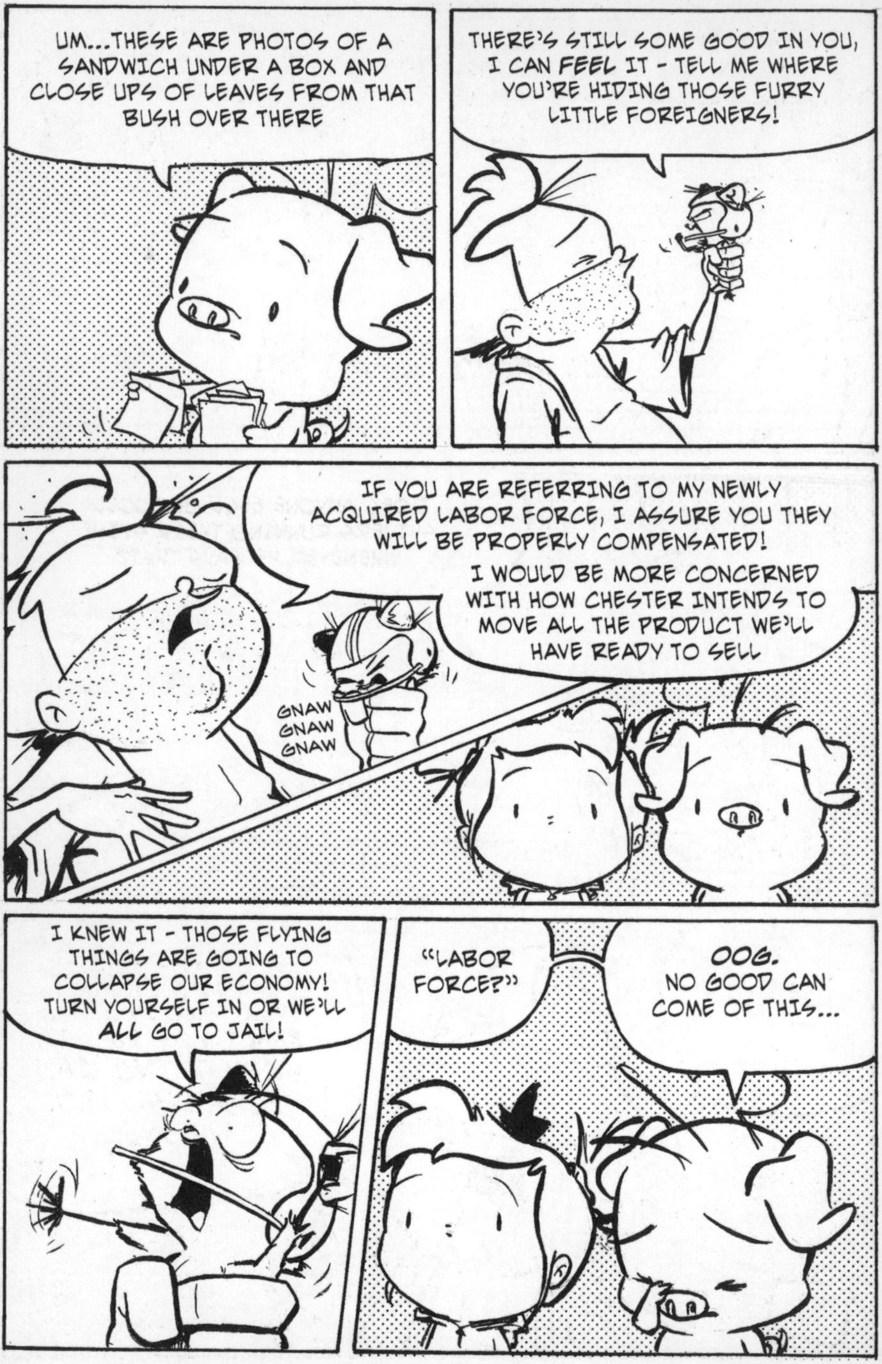
UM...THESE ARE PHOTOS OF A SANDWICH UNDER A BOX AND CLOSE UPS OF LEAVES FROM THAT BUSH OVER THERE
THERE'S STILL SOME GOOD IN YOU, I CAN FEEL IT - TELL ME WHERE YOU'RE HIDING THOSE FURRY LITTLE FOREIGNERS!
IF YOU ARE REFERRING TO MY NEWLY ACQUIRED LABOR FORCE, I ASSURE YOU THEY WILL BE PROPERLY COMPENSATED!
I WOULD BE MORE CONCERNED WITH HOW CHESTER INTENDS TO MOVE ALL THE PRODUCT WE'LL HAVE READY TO SELL
GNAW GNAW GNAW
I KNEW IT - THOSE FLYING THINGS ARE GOING TO COLLAPSE OUR ECONOMY! TURN YOURSELF IN OR WE'LL ALL GO TO JAIL!
"LABOR FORCE?"
OOG. NO GOOD CAN COME OF THIS...

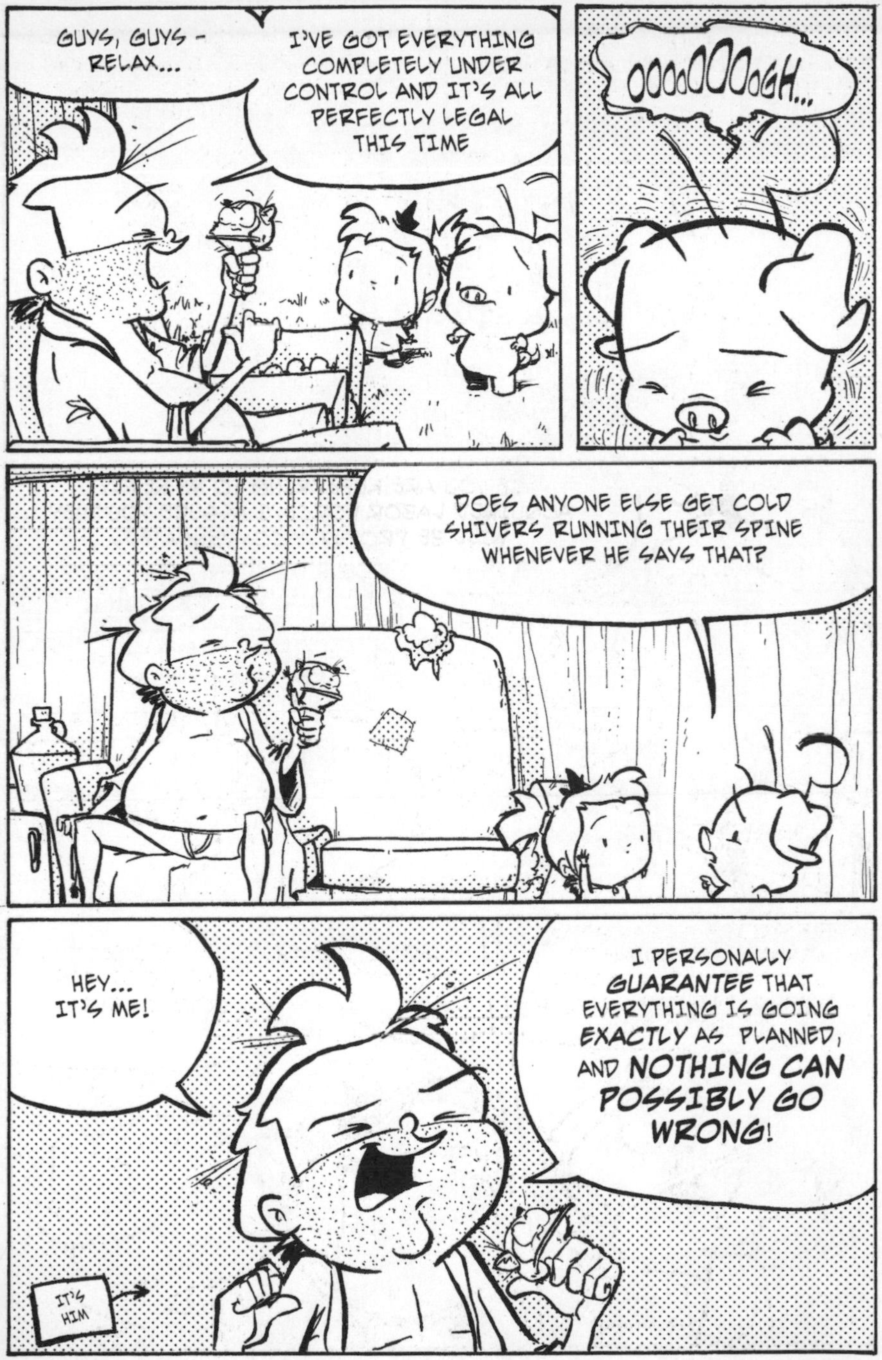
GUYS, GUYS - RELAX...
I'VE GOT EVERYTHING COMPLETELY UNDER CONTROL AND IT'S ALL PERFECTLY LEGAL THIS TIME
OOOoOOOoGH...
DOES ANYONE ELSE GET COLD SHIVERS RUNNING THEIR SPINE WHENEVER HE SAYS THAT?
HEY... IT'S ME!
I PERSONALLY GUARANTEE THAT EVERYTHING IS GOING EXACTLY AS PLANNED, AND NOTHING CAN POSSIBLY GO WRONG!
IT'S HIM

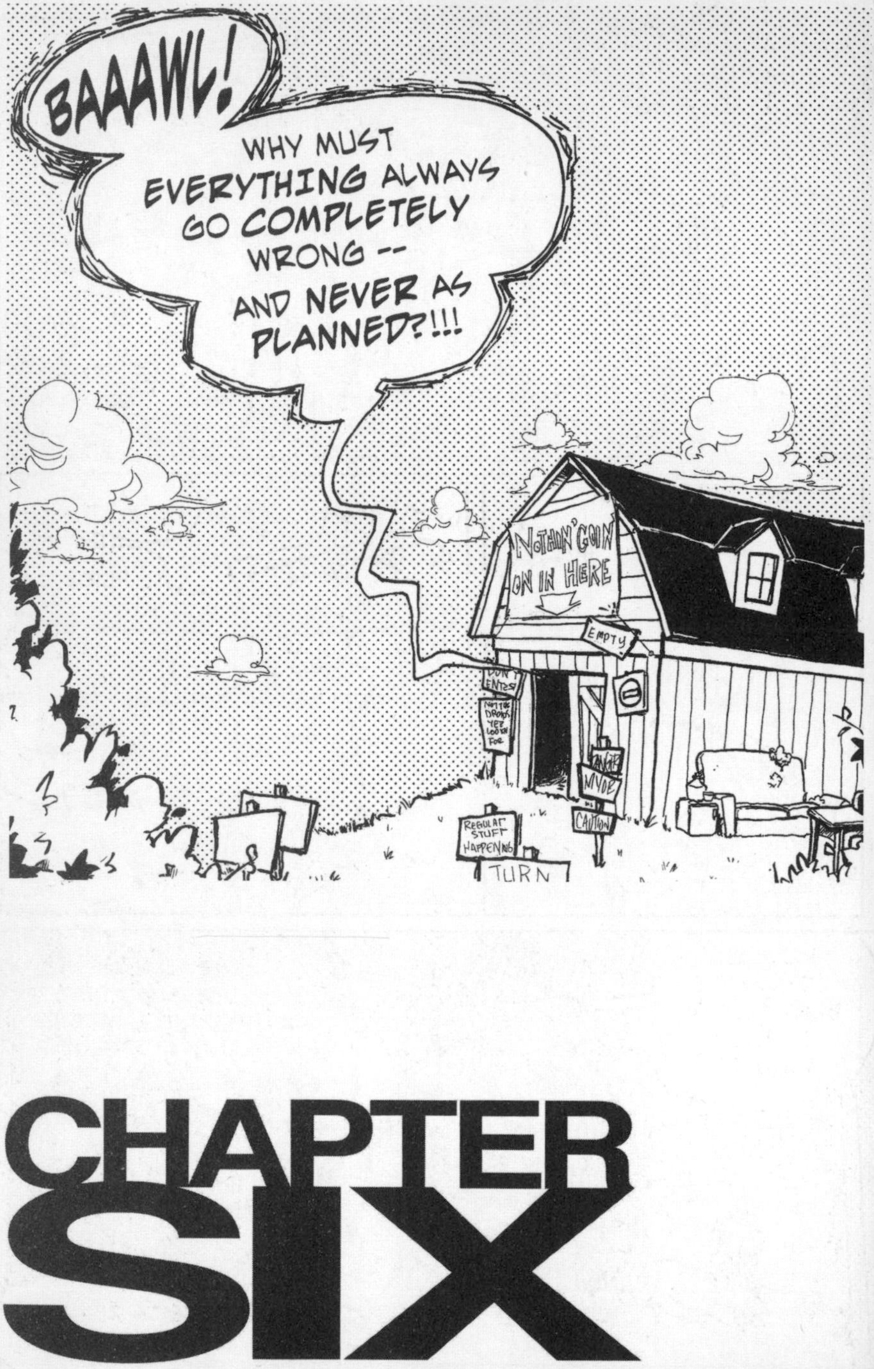
BAAAWL!
WHY MUST EVERYTHING ALWAYS GO COMPLETELY WRONG -- AND NEVER AS PLANNED?!!!
NOTHIN' GOIN ON IN HERE
EMPTY
CAUTION
REGULAR STUFF HAPPENING
TURN

CHAPTER SIX

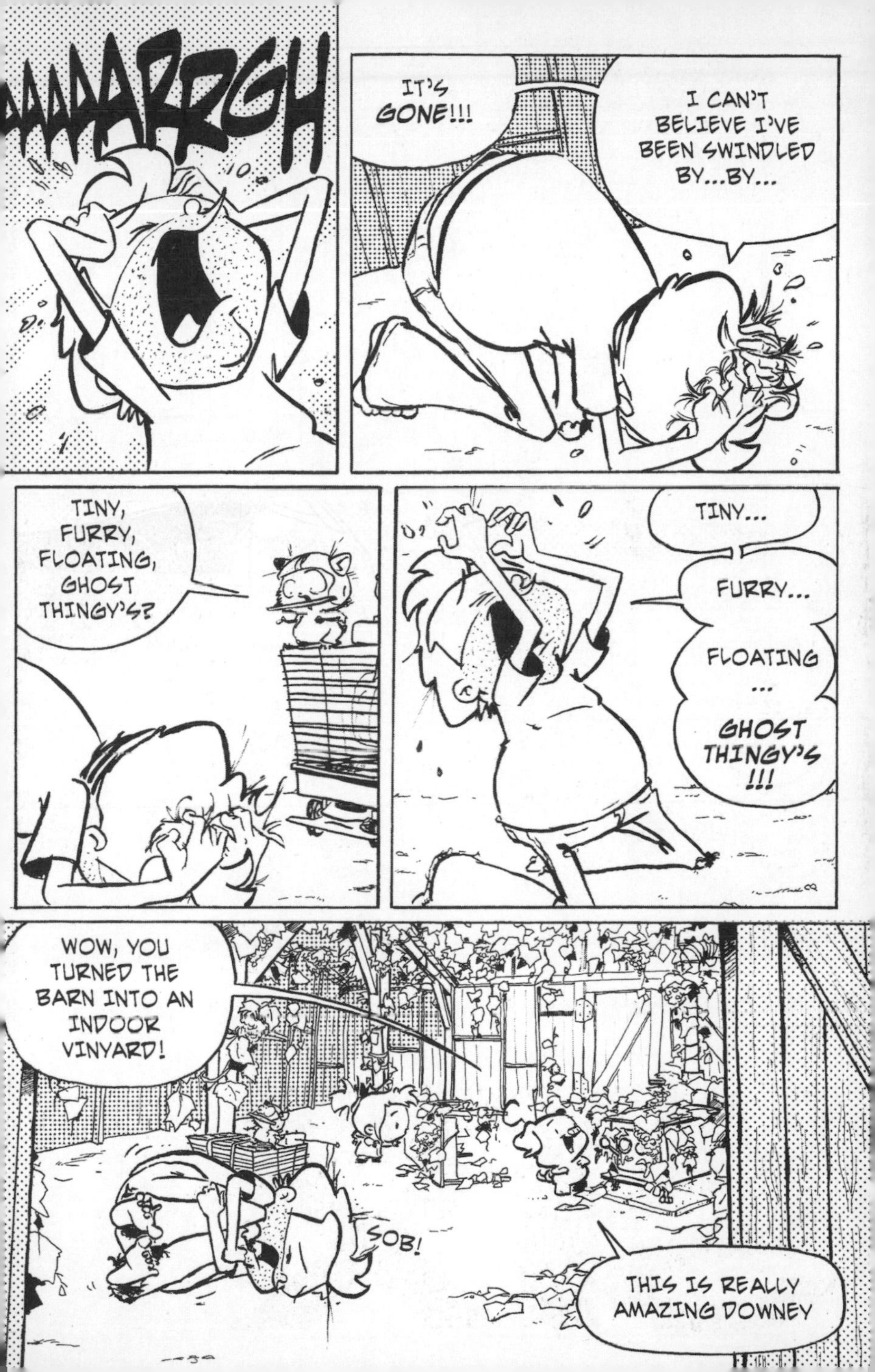
AAAAARRGH
IT'S GONE!!!
I CAN'T BELIEVE I'VE BEEN SWINDLED BY...BY...
TINY, FURRY, FLOATING, GHOST THINGY'S?
TINY...
FURRY...
FLOATING ...
GHOST THINGY'S !!!
WOW, YOU TURNED THE BARN INTO AN INDOOR VINYARD!
SOB!
THIS IS REALLY AMAZING DOWNEY

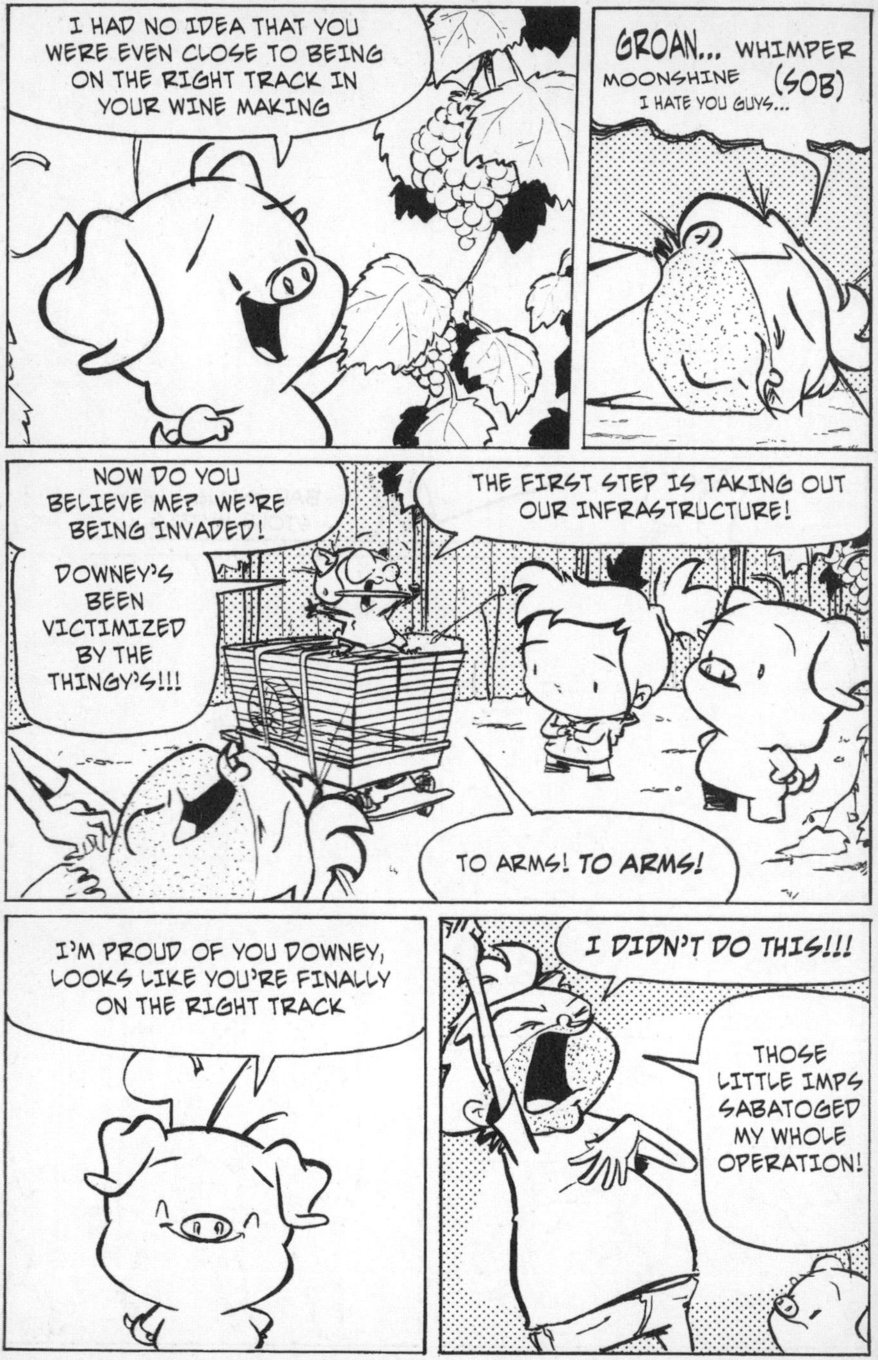
I HAD NO IDEA THAT YOU WERE EVEN CLOSE TO BEING ON THE RIGHT TRACK IN YOUR WINE MAKING
GROAN... WHIMPER
MOONSHINE
(SOB)
I HATE YOU GUYS...
NOW DO YOU BELIEVE ME? WE'RE BEING INVADED!
DOWNEY'S BEEN VICTIMIZED BY THE THINGY'S!!!
THE FIRST STEP IS TAKING OUT OUR INFRASTRUCTURE!
TO ARMS! TO ARMS!
I'M PROUD OF YOU DOWNEY, LOOKS LIKE YOU'RE FINALLY ON THE RIGHT TRACK
I DIDN'T DO THIS!!!
THOSE LITTLE IMPS SABATOGED MY WHOLE OPERATION!

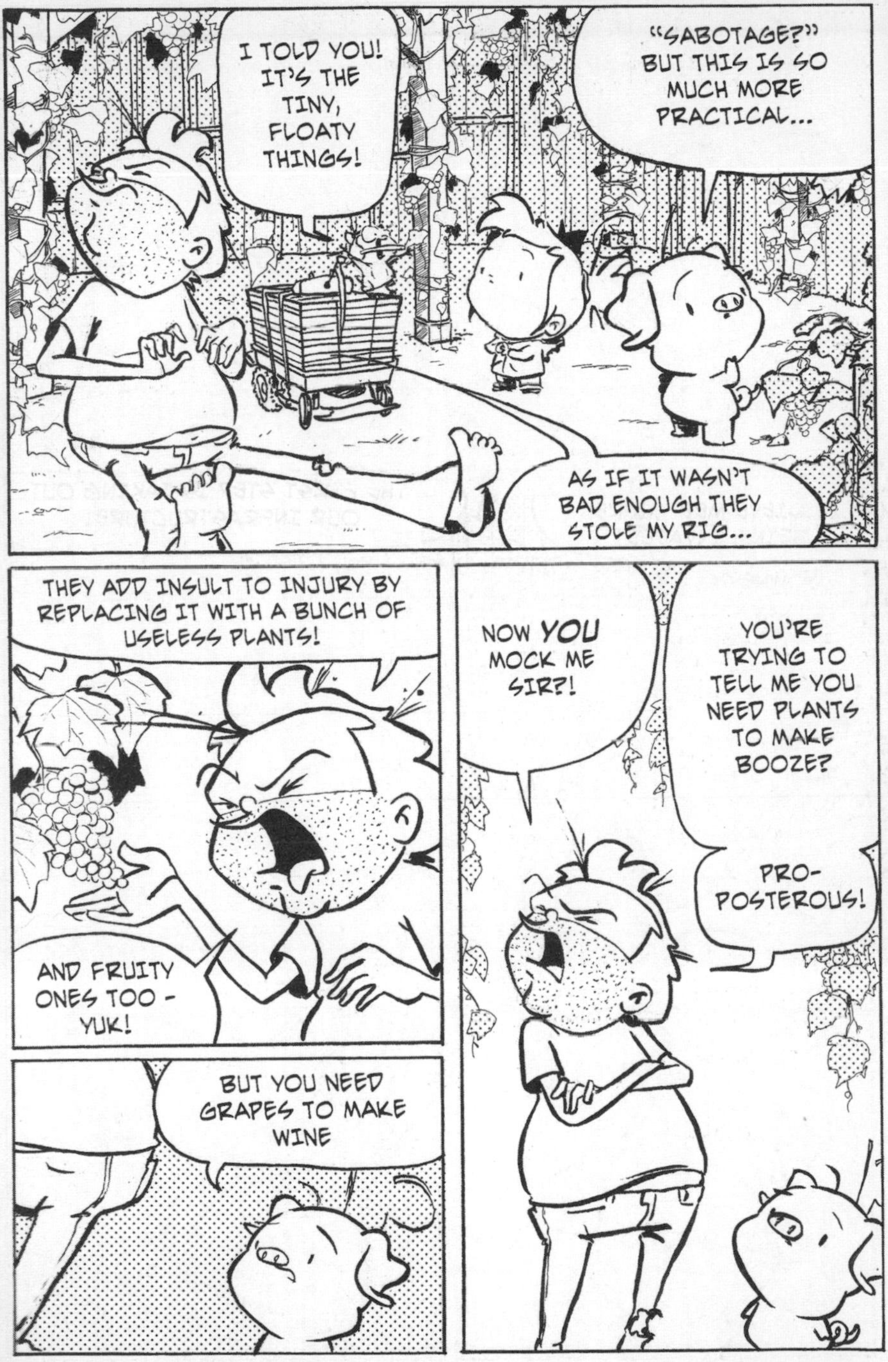
I TOLD YOU! IT'S THE TINY, FLOATY THINGS!
"SABOTAGE?" BUT THIS IS SO MUCH MORE PRACTICAL...
AS IF IT WASN'T BAD ENOUGH THEY STOLE MY RIG...
THEY ADD INSULT TO INJURY BY REPLACING IT WITH A BUNCH OF USELESS PLANTS!
AND FRUITY ONES TOO - YUK!
BUT YOU NEED GRAPES TO MAKE WINE
YOU'RE TRYING TO TELL ME YOU NEED PLANTS TO MAKE BOOZE?
PRO-POSTEROUS!
NOW YOU MOCK ME SIR?!

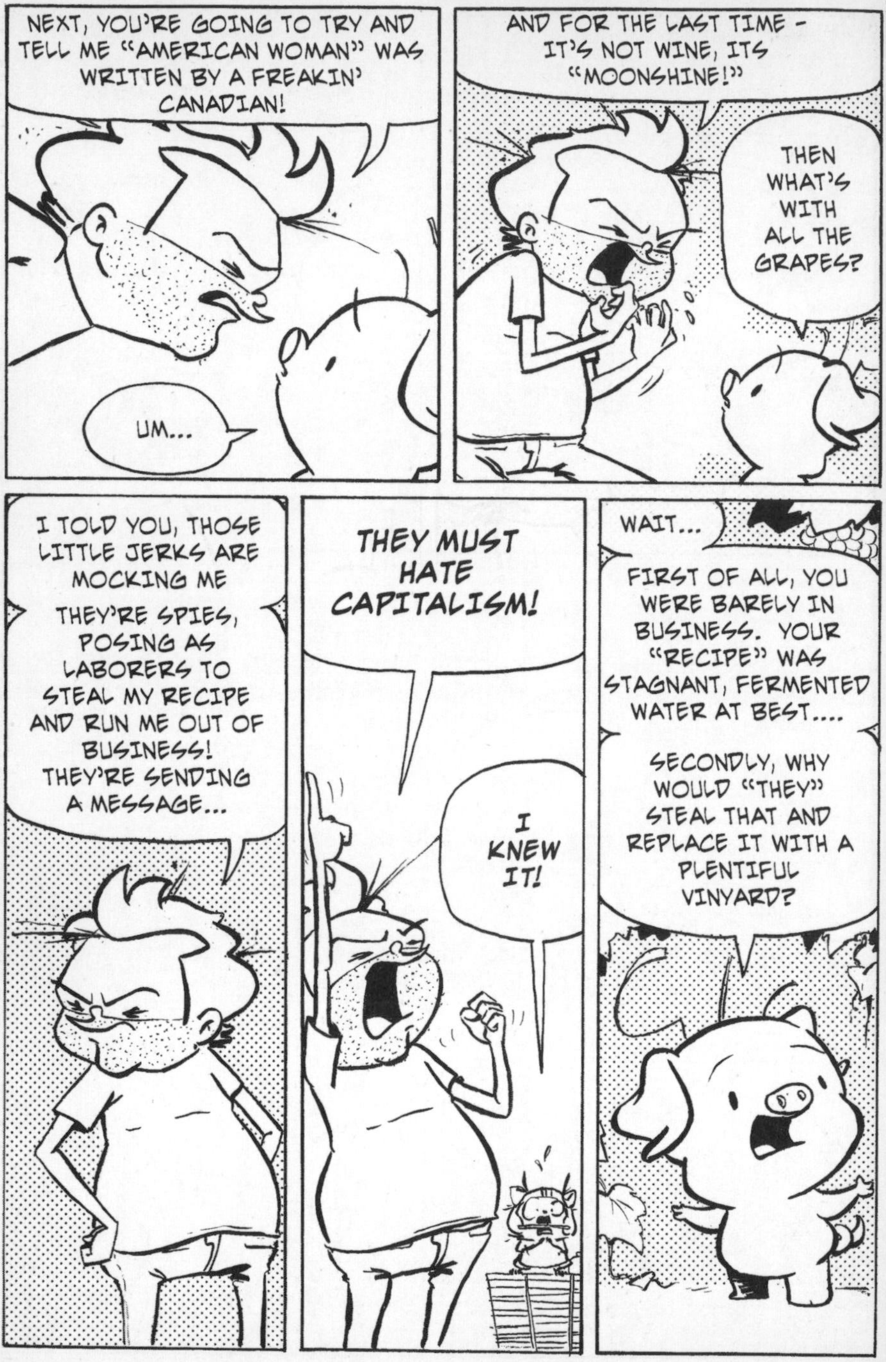
NEXT, YOU'RE GOING TO TRY AND TELL ME "AMERICAN WOMAN" WAS WRITTEN BY A FREAKIN' CANADIAN!
UM...
AND FOR THE LAST TIME - IT'S NOT WINE, ITS "MOONSHINE!"
THEN WHAT'S WITH ALL THE GRAPES?
I TOLD YOU, THOSE LITTLE JERKS ARE MOCKING ME
THEY'RE SPIES, POSING AS LABORERS TO STEAL MY RECIPE AND RUN ME OUT OF BUSINESS! THEY'RE SENDING A MESSAGE...
THEY MUST HATE CAPITALISM!
I KNEW IT!
WAIT...
FIRST OF ALL, YOU WERE BARELY IN BUSINESS. YOUR "RECIPE" WAS STAGNANT, FERMENTED WATER AT BEST....
SECONDLY, WHY WOULD "THEY" STEAL THAT AND REPLACE IT WITH A PLENTIFUL VINYARD?

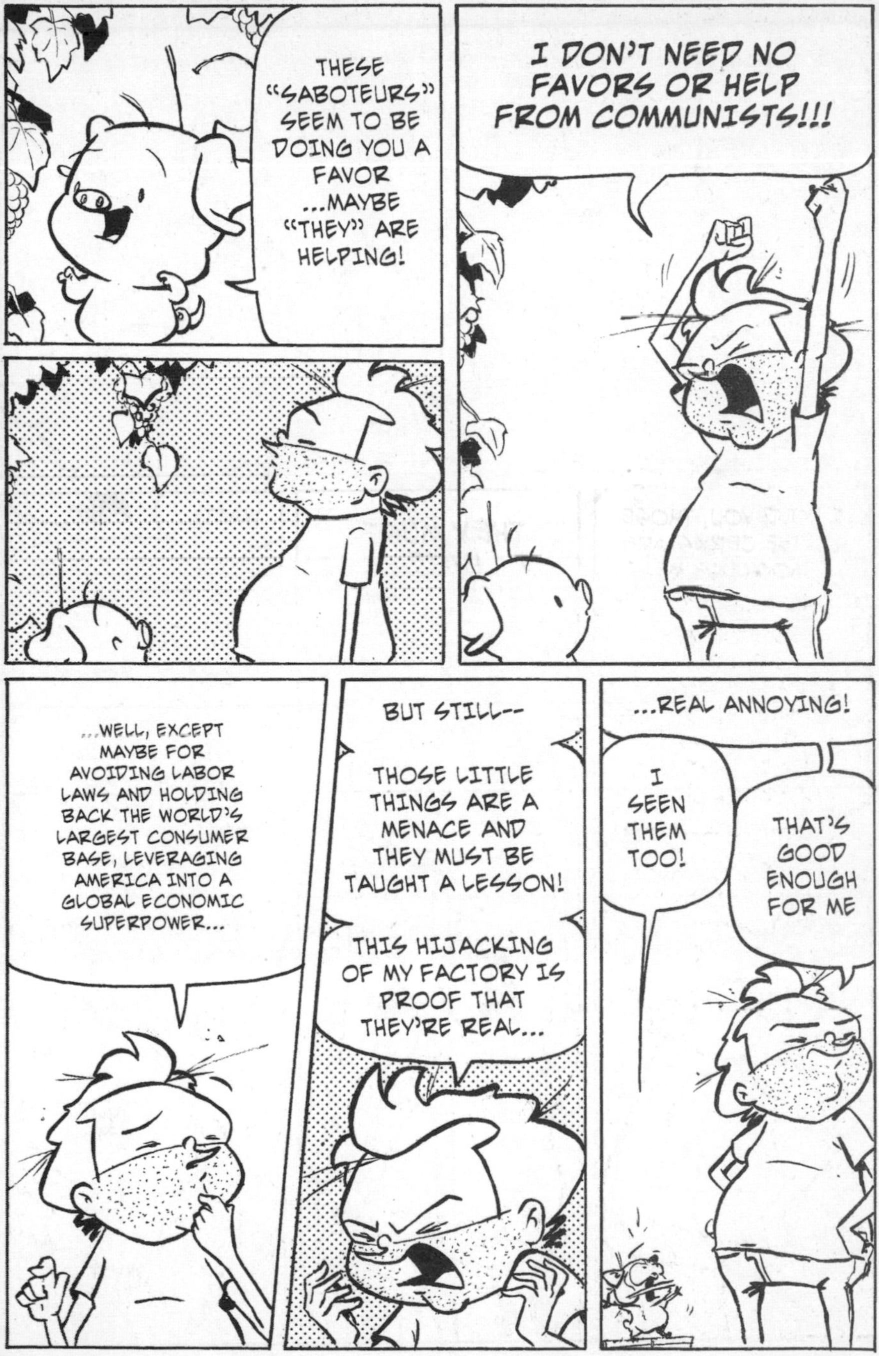
THESE "SABOTEURS" SEEM TO BE DOING YOU A FAVOR ...MAYBE "THEY" ARE HELPING!
I DON'T NEED NO FAVORS OR HELP FROM COMMUNISTS!!!
...WELL, EXCEPT MAYBE FOR AVOIDING LABOR LAWS AND HOLDING BACK THE WORLD'S LARGEST CONSUMER BASE, LEVERAGING AMERICA INTO A GLOBAL ECONOMIC SUPERPOWER...
BUT STILL--
THOSE LITTLE THINGS ARE A MENACE AND THEY MUST BE TAUGHT A LESSON!
THIS HIJACKING OF MY FACTORY IS PROOF THAT THEY'RE REAL...
...REAL ANNOYING!
I SEEN THEM TOO!
THAT'S GOOD ENOUGH FOR ME

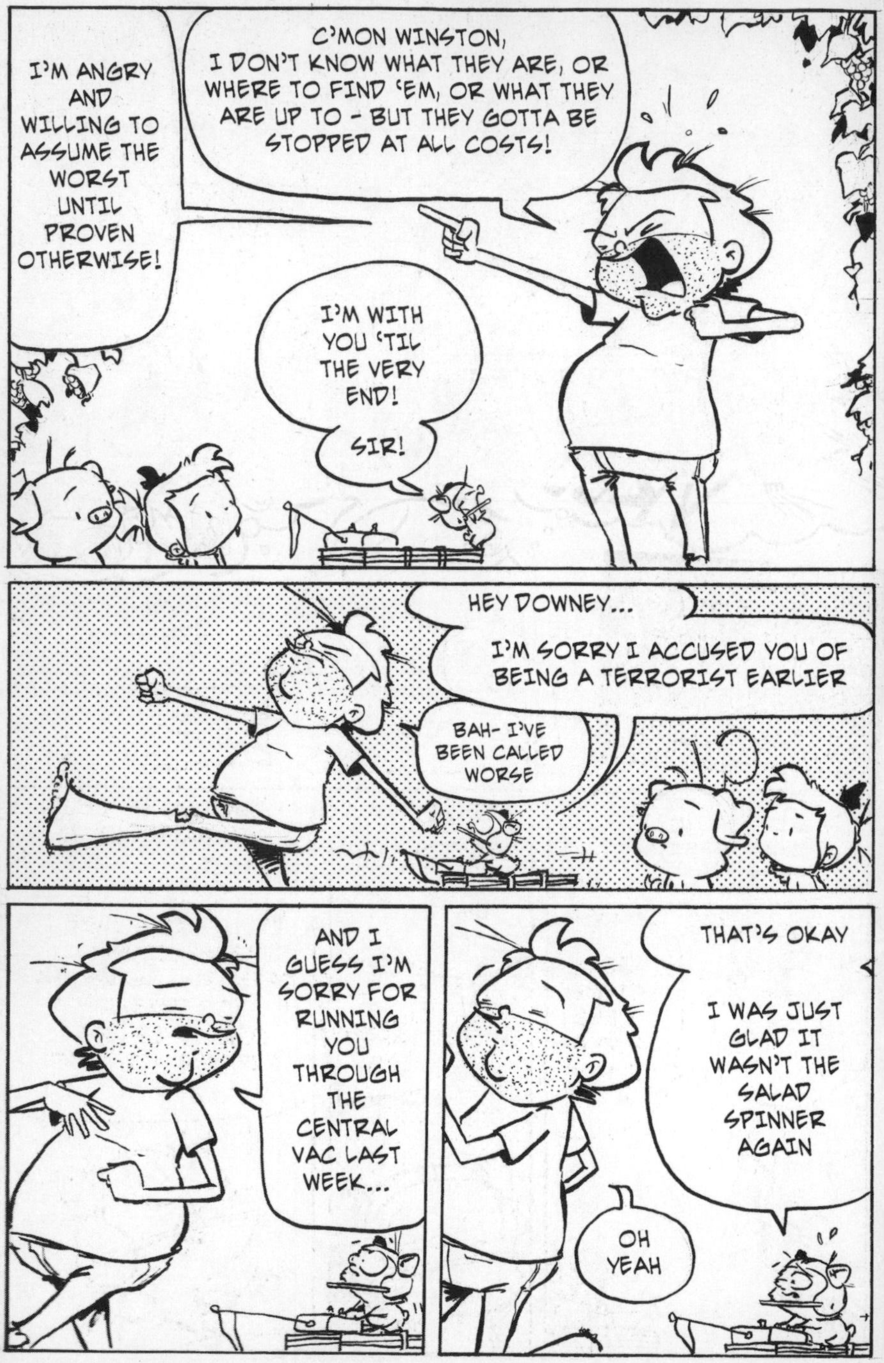
I'M ANGRY AND WILLING TO ASSUME THE WORST UNTIL PROVEN OTHERWISE!
C'MON WINSTON, I DON'T KNOW WHAT THEY ARE, OR WHERE TO FIND 'EM, OR WHAT THEY ARE UP TO - BUT THEY GOTTA BE STOPPED AT ALL COSTS!
I'M WITH YOU 'TIL THE VERY END!
SIR!
HEY DOWNEY...
I'M SORRY I ACCUSED YOU OF BEING A TERRORIST EARLIER
BAH- I'VE BEEN CALLED WORSE
AND I GUESS I'M SORRY FOR RUNNING YOU THROUGH THE CENTRAL VAC LAST WEEK...
THAT'S OKAY
I WAS JUST GLAD IT WASN'T THE SALAD SPINNER AGAIN
OH YEAH

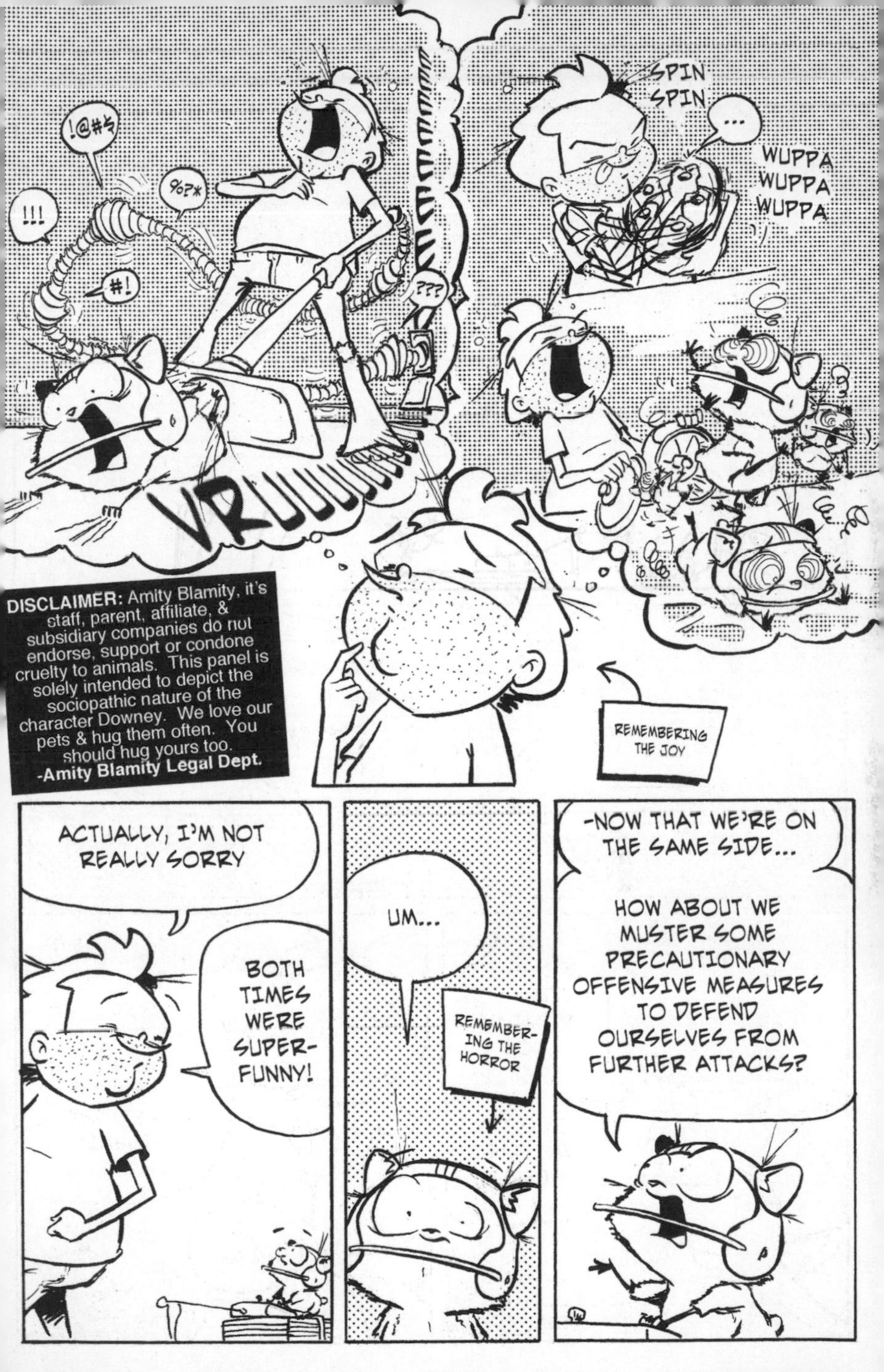
!!!
%?*
#!
???
SPIN
SPIN
...
WUPPA
WUPPA
WUPPA
DISCLAIMER: Amity Blamity, it's staff, parent, affiliate, & subsidiary companies do not endorse, support or condone cruelty to animals. This panel is solely intended to depict the sociopathic nature of the character Downey. We love our pets & hug them often. You should hug yours too.
-Amity Blamity Legal Dept.
REMEMBERING THE JOY
ACTUALLY, I'M NOT REALLY SORRY
BOTH TIMES WERE SUPER-FUNNY!
UM...
REMEMBER-ING THE HORROR
-NOW THAT WE'RE ON THE SAME SIDE...
HOW ABOUT WE MUSTER SOME PRECAUTIONARY OFFENSIVE MEASURES TO DEFEND OURSELVES FROM FURTHER ATTACKS?

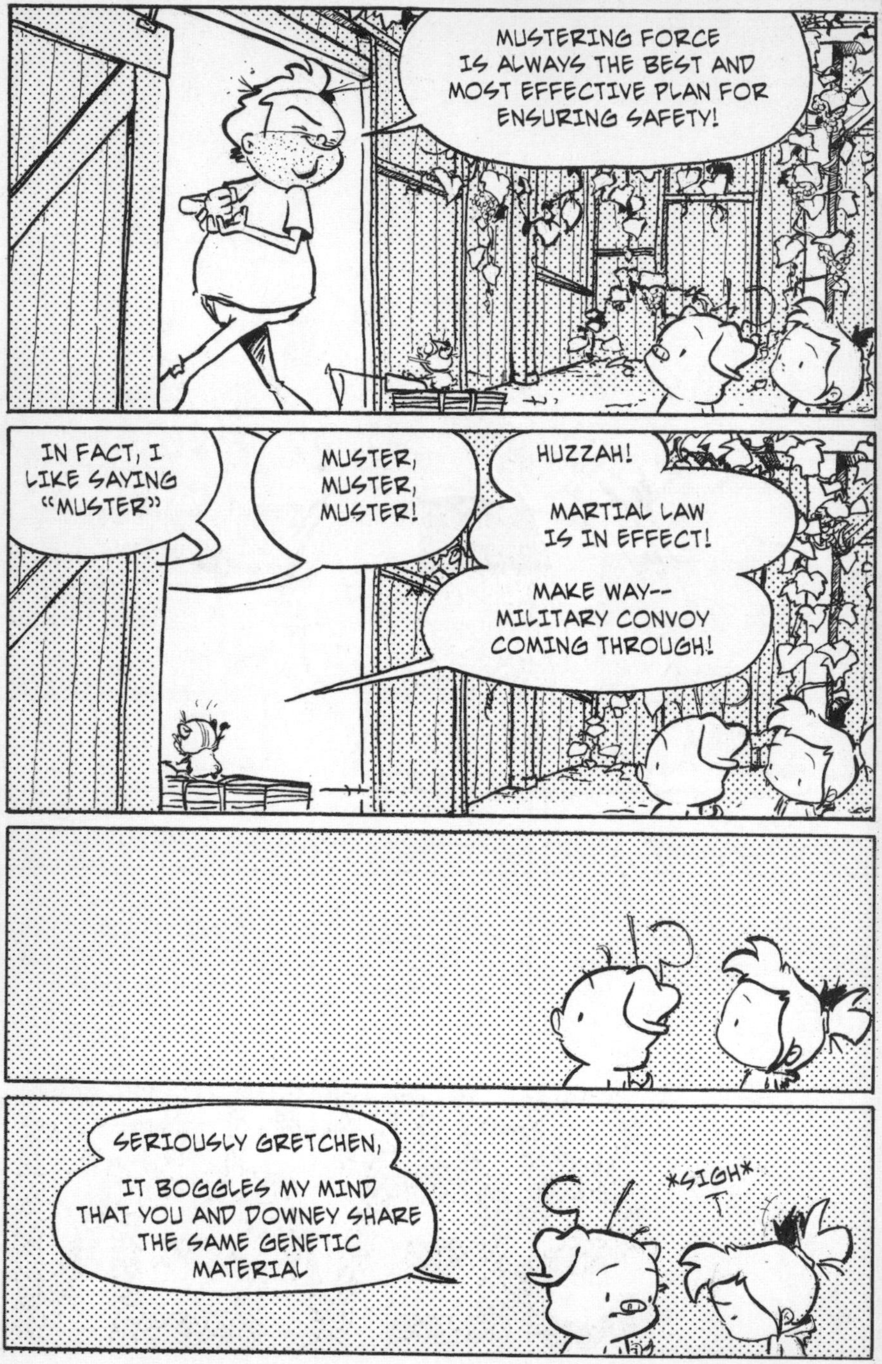
MUSTERING FORCE IS ALWAYS THE BEST AND MOST EFFECTIVE PLAN FOR ENSURING SAFETY!
IN FACT, I LIKE SAYING "MUSTER"
MUSTER, MUSTER, MUSTER!
HUZZAH!
MARTIAL LAW IS IN EFFECT!
MAKE WAY-- MILITARY CONVOY COMING THROUGH!
SERIOUSLY GRETCHEN,
IT BOGGLES MY MIND THAT YOU AND DOWNEY SHARE THE SAME GENETIC MATERIAL
SIGH

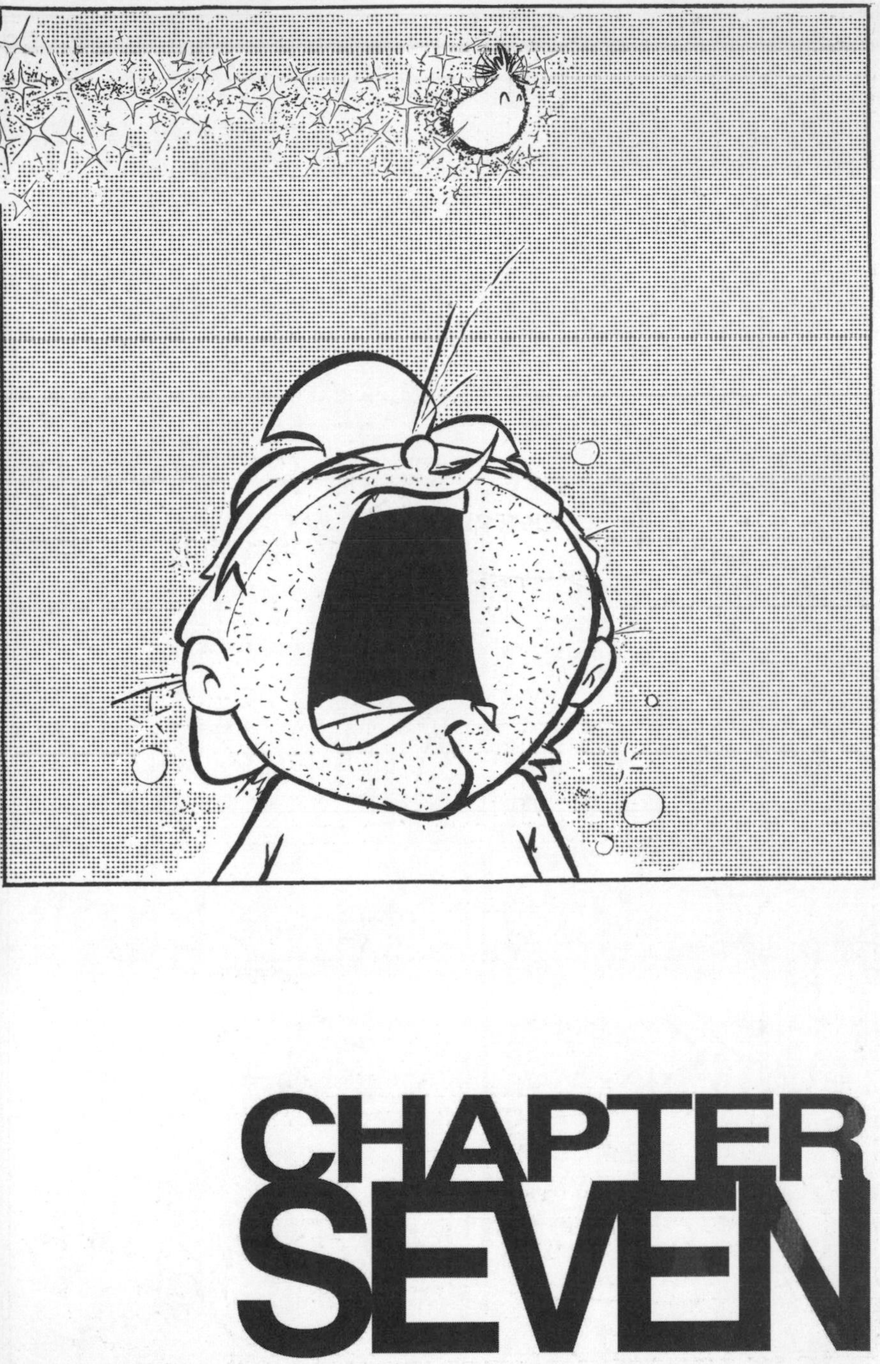

CHAPTER SEVEN

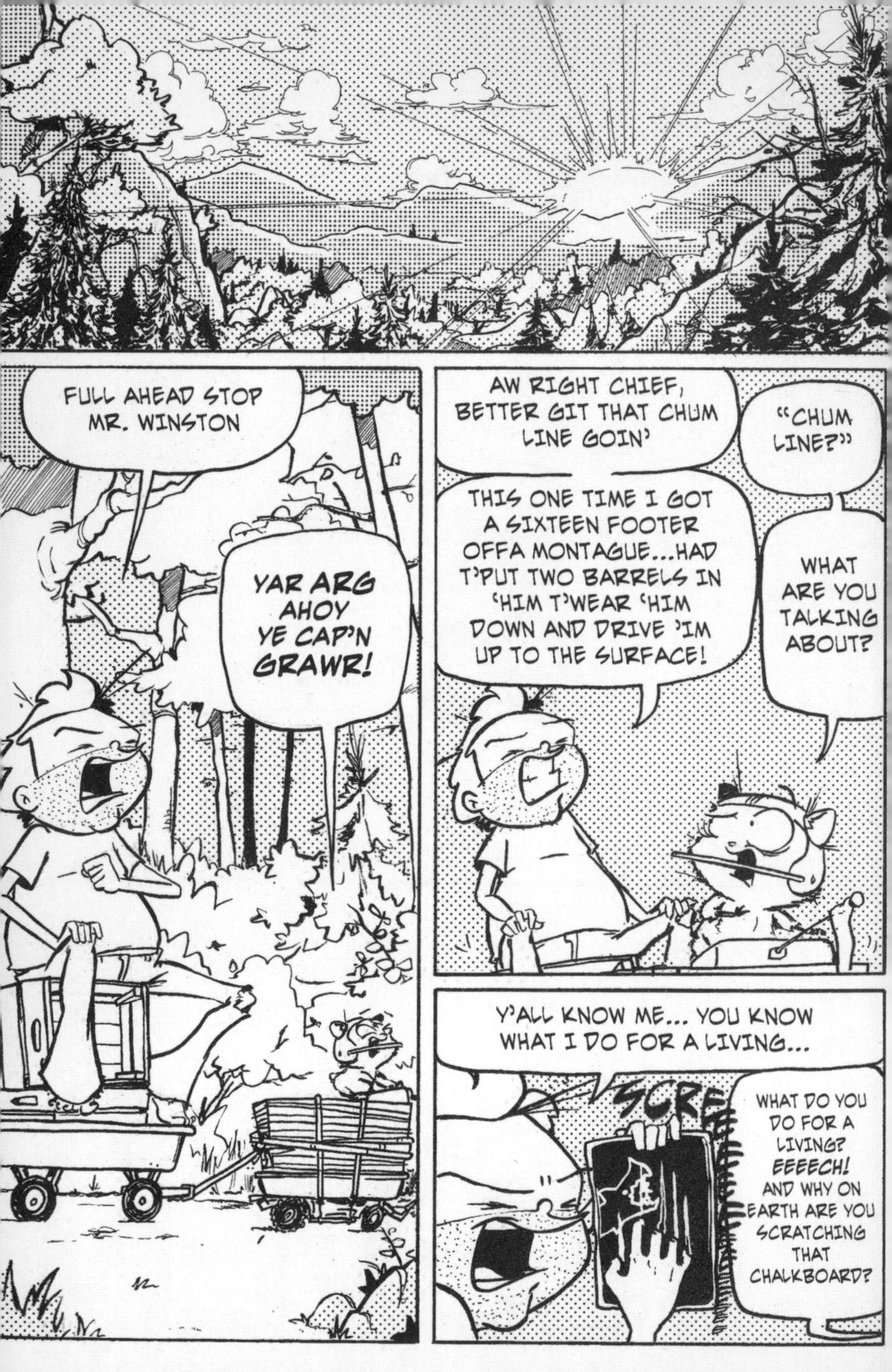
FULL AHEAD STOP MR. WINSTON
YAR ARG AHOY YE CAP'N GRAWR!
AW RIGHT CHIEF, BETTER GIT THAT CHUM LINE GOIN'
"CHUM LINE?"
THIS ONE TIME I GOT A SIXTEEN FOOTER OFFA MONTAGUE...HAD T'PUT TWO BARRELS IN 'HIM T'WEAR 'HIM DOWN AND DRIVE 'IM UP TO THE SURFACE!
WHAT ARE YOU TALKING ABOUT?
Y'ALL KNOW ME... YOU KNOW WHAT I DO FOR A LIVING...
SCRE
WHAT DO YOU DO FOR A LIVING? EEEECH! AND WHY ON EARTH ARE YOU SCRATCHING THAT CHALKBOARD?

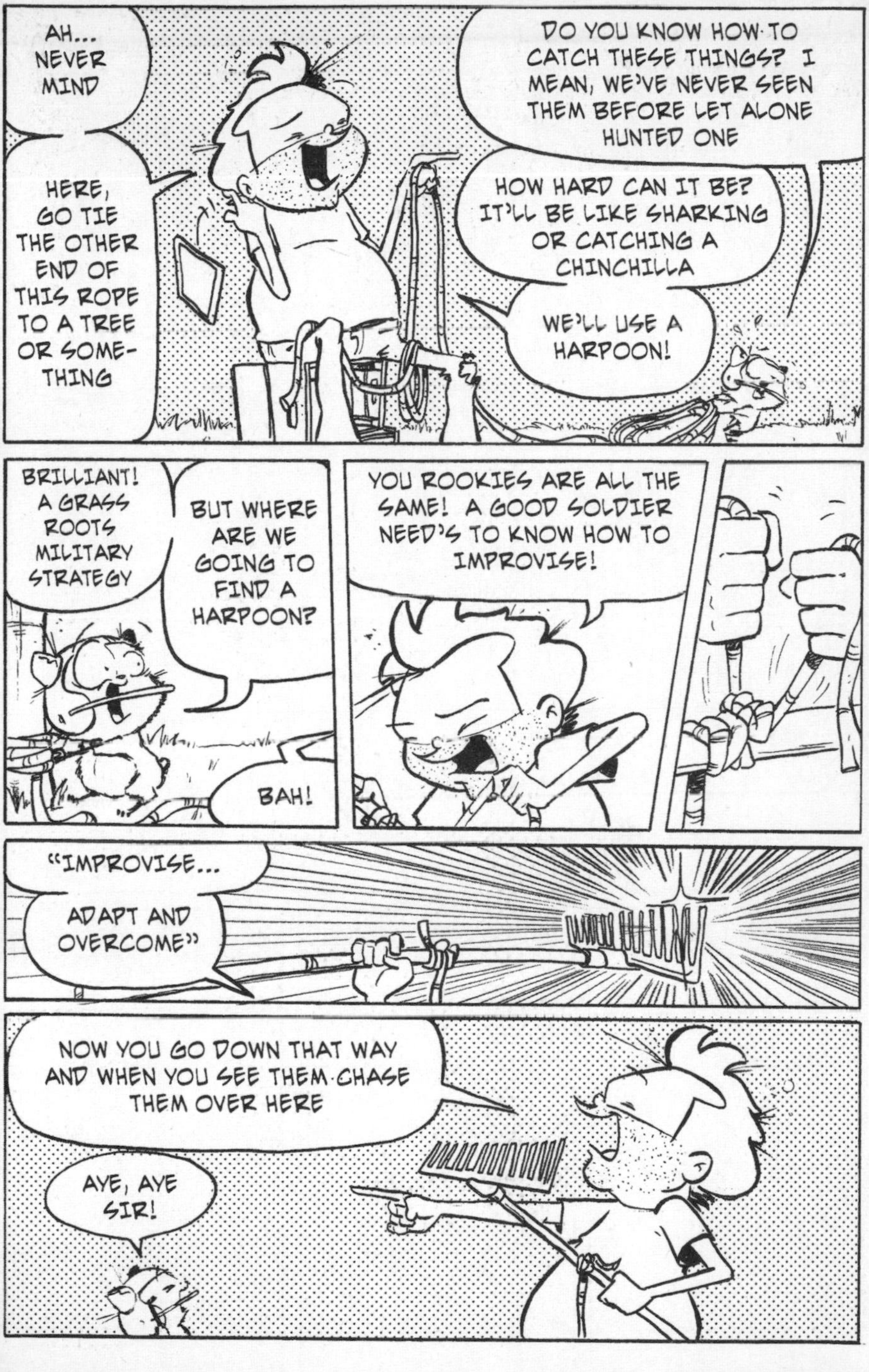
AH... NEVER MIND
HERE, GO TIE THE OTHER END OF THIS ROPE TO A TREE OR SOME-THING
DO YOU KNOW HOW TO CATCH THESE THINGS? I MEAN, WE'VE NEVER SEEN THEM BEFORE LET ALONE HUNTED ONE
HOW HARD CAN IT BE? IT'LL BE LIKE SHARKING OR CATCHING A CHINCHILLA
WE'LL USE A HARPOON!
BRILLIANT! A GRASS ROOTS MILITARY STRATEGY
BUT WHERE ARE WE GOING TO FIND A HARPOON?
BAH!
YOU ROOKIES ARE ALL THE SAME! A GOOD SOLDIER NEED'S TO KNOW HOW TO IMPROVISE!
"IMPROVISE...
ADAPT AND OVERCOME"
NOW YOU GO DOWN THAT WAY AND WHEN YOU SEE THEM CHASE THEM OVER HERE
AYE, AYE SIR!

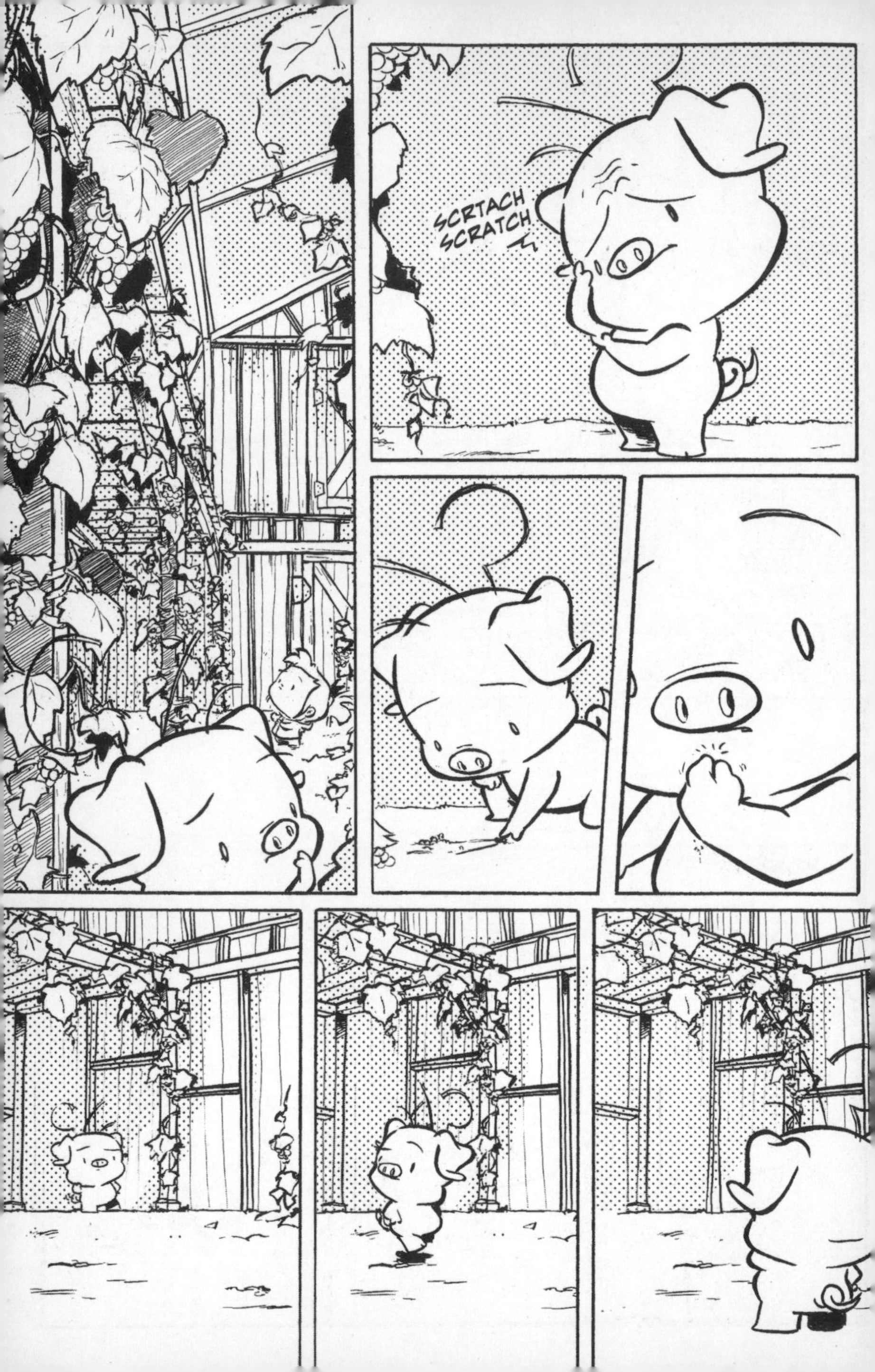
SCRTACH
SCRATCH

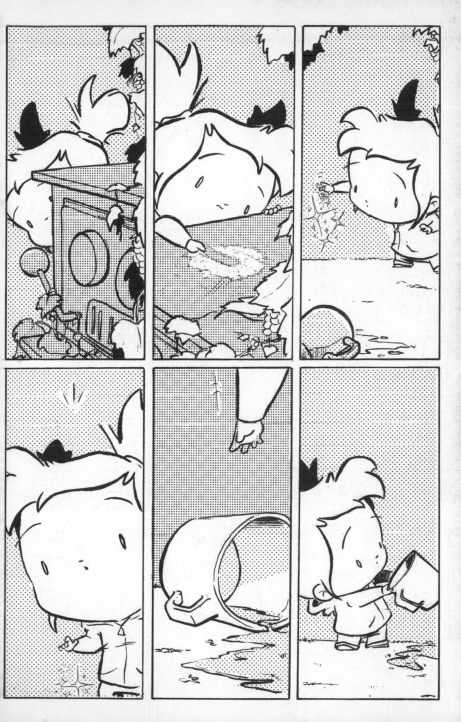

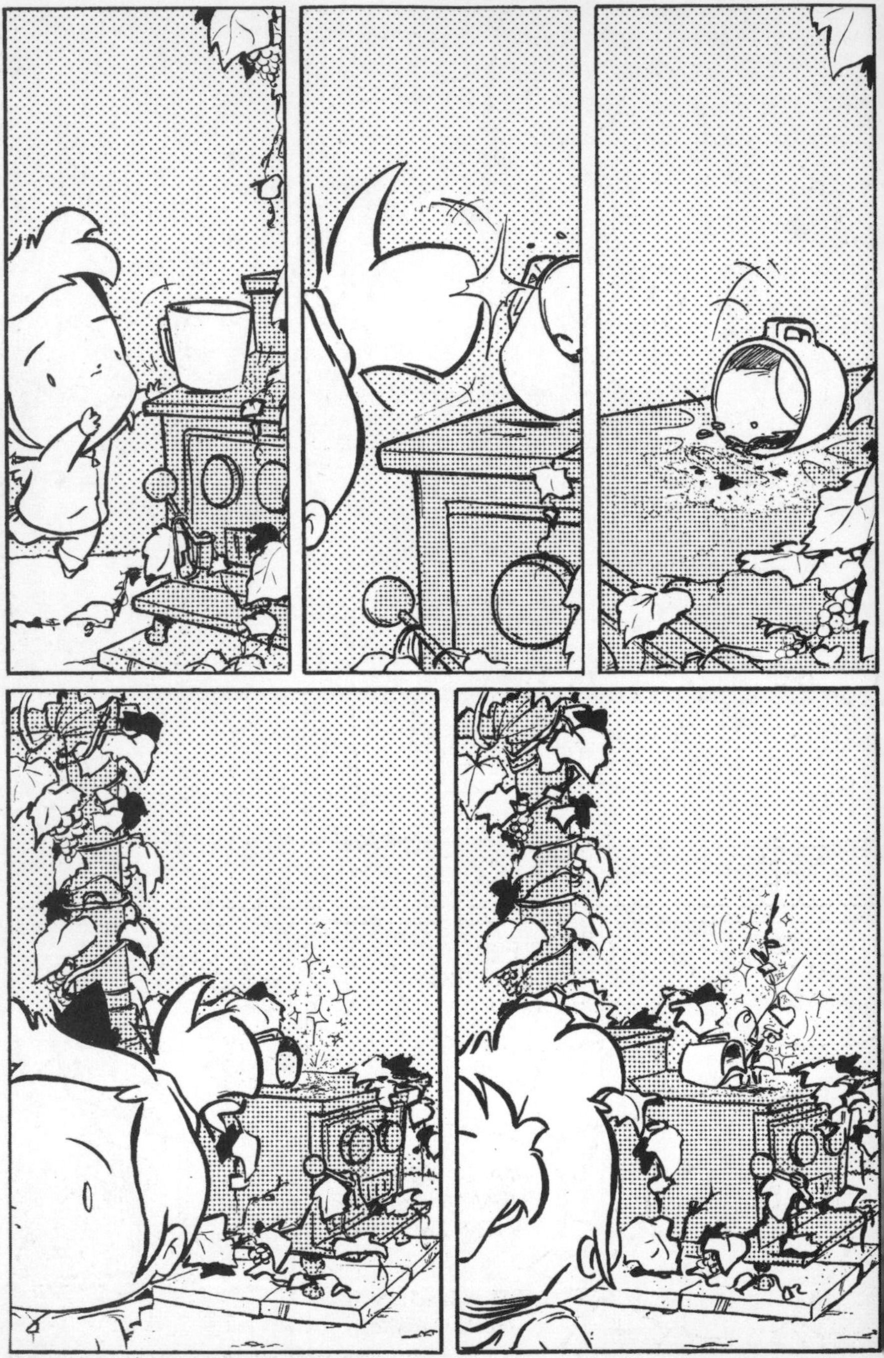

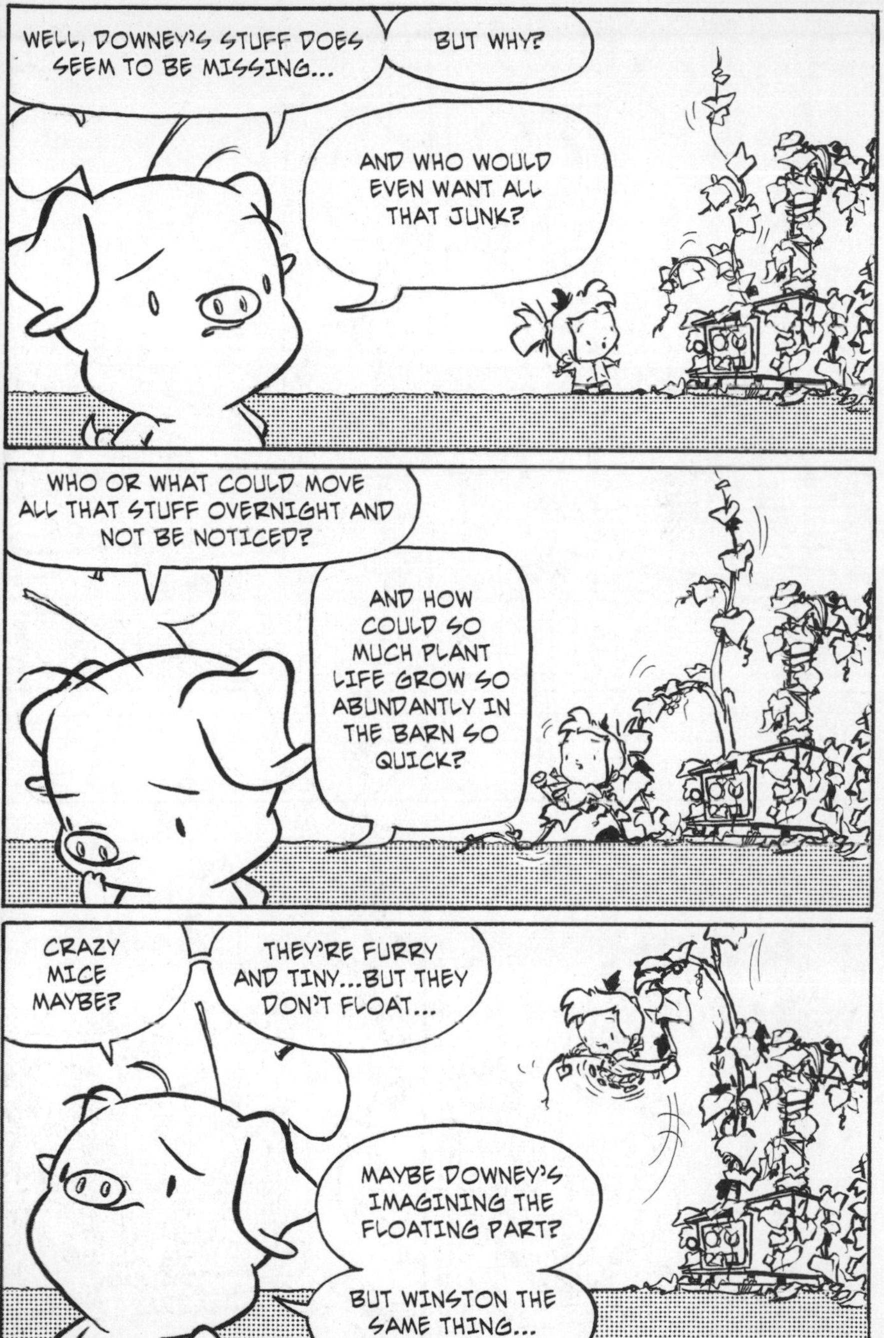
WELL, DOWNEY'S STUFF DOES SEEM TO BE MISSING...
BUT WHY?
AND WHO WOULD EVEN WANT ALL THAT JUNK?
WHO OR WHAT COULD MOVE ALL THAT STUFF OVERNIGHT AND NOT BE NOTICED?
AND HOW COULD SO MUCH PLANT LIFE GROW SO ABUNDANTLY IN THE BARN SO QUICK?
CRAZY MICE MAYBE?
THEY'RE FURRY AND TINY...BUT THEY DON'T FLOAT...
MAYBE DOWNEY'S IMAGINING THE FLOATING PART?
BUT WINSTON THE SAME THING...

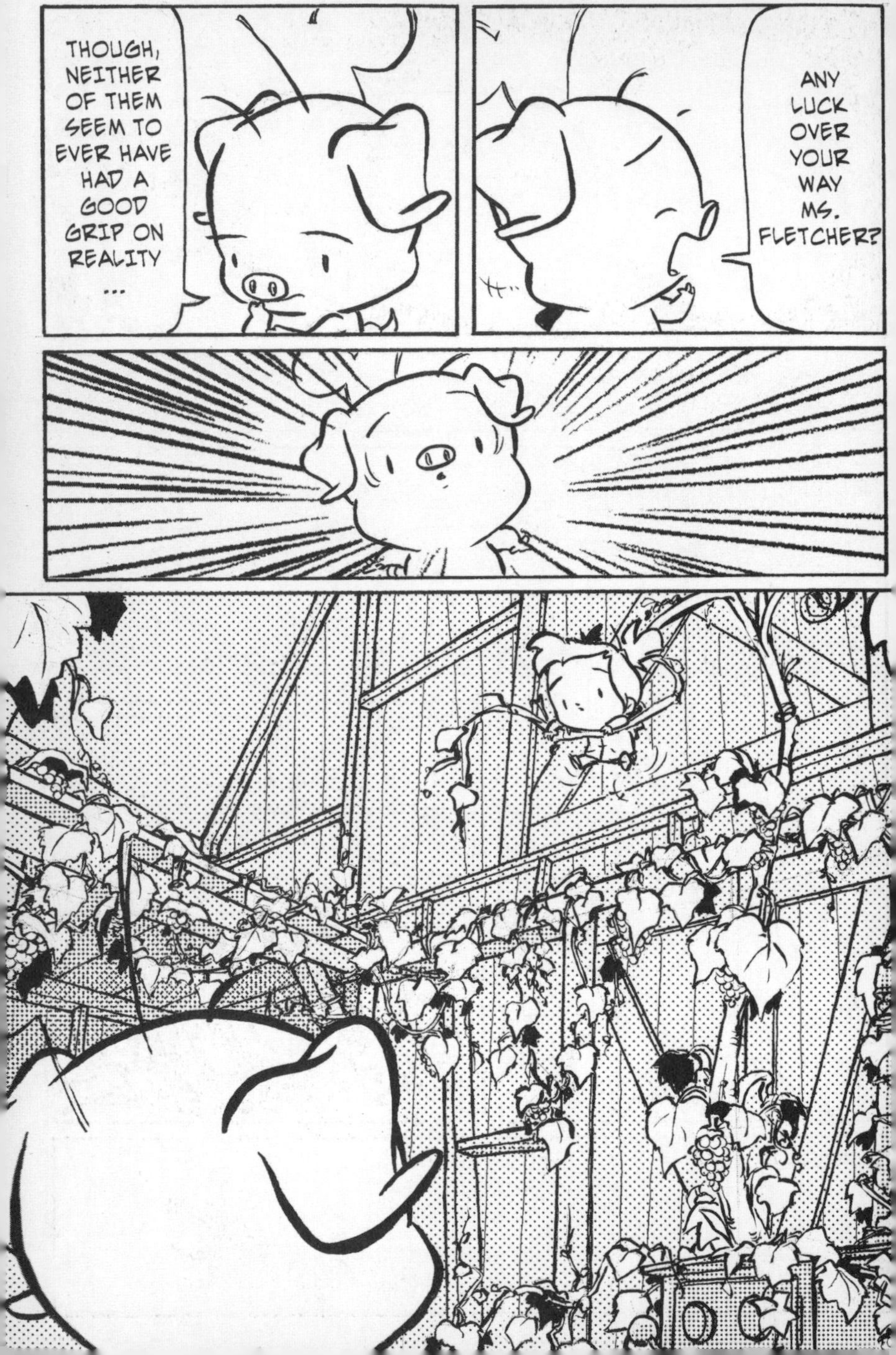
THOUGH, NEITHER OF THEM SEEM TO EVER HAVE HAD A GOOD GRIP ON REALITY ...
ANY LUCK OVER YOUR WAY MS. FLETCHER?

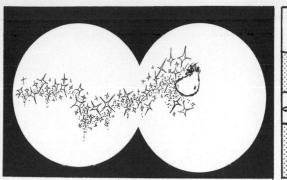

BINGO

"..FAREWELL AND ADIEU TO YOU FINE SPANISH LADIES..."

THONGGG...

NOW WINSTON!

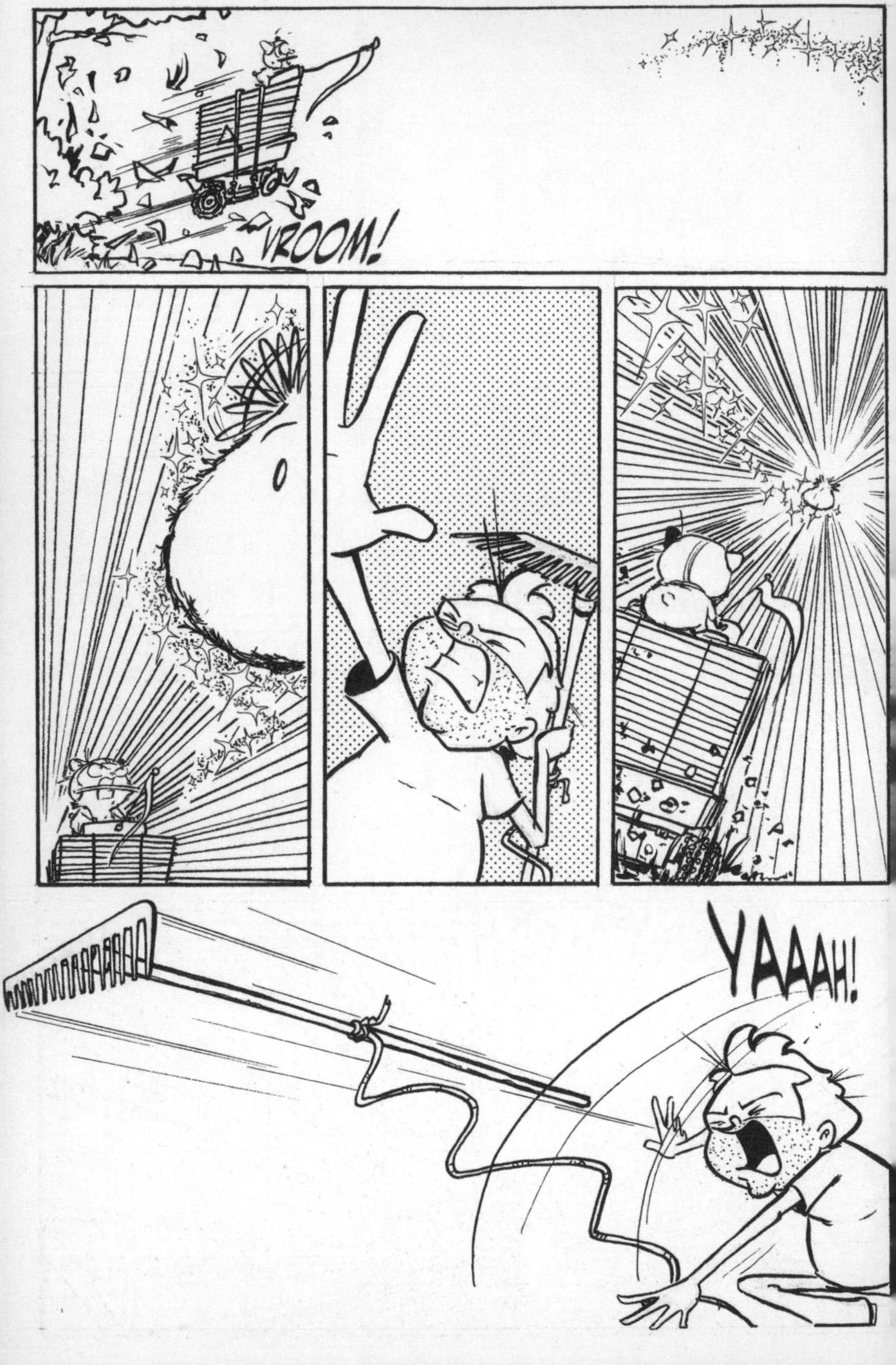
VROOM!
YAAAH!

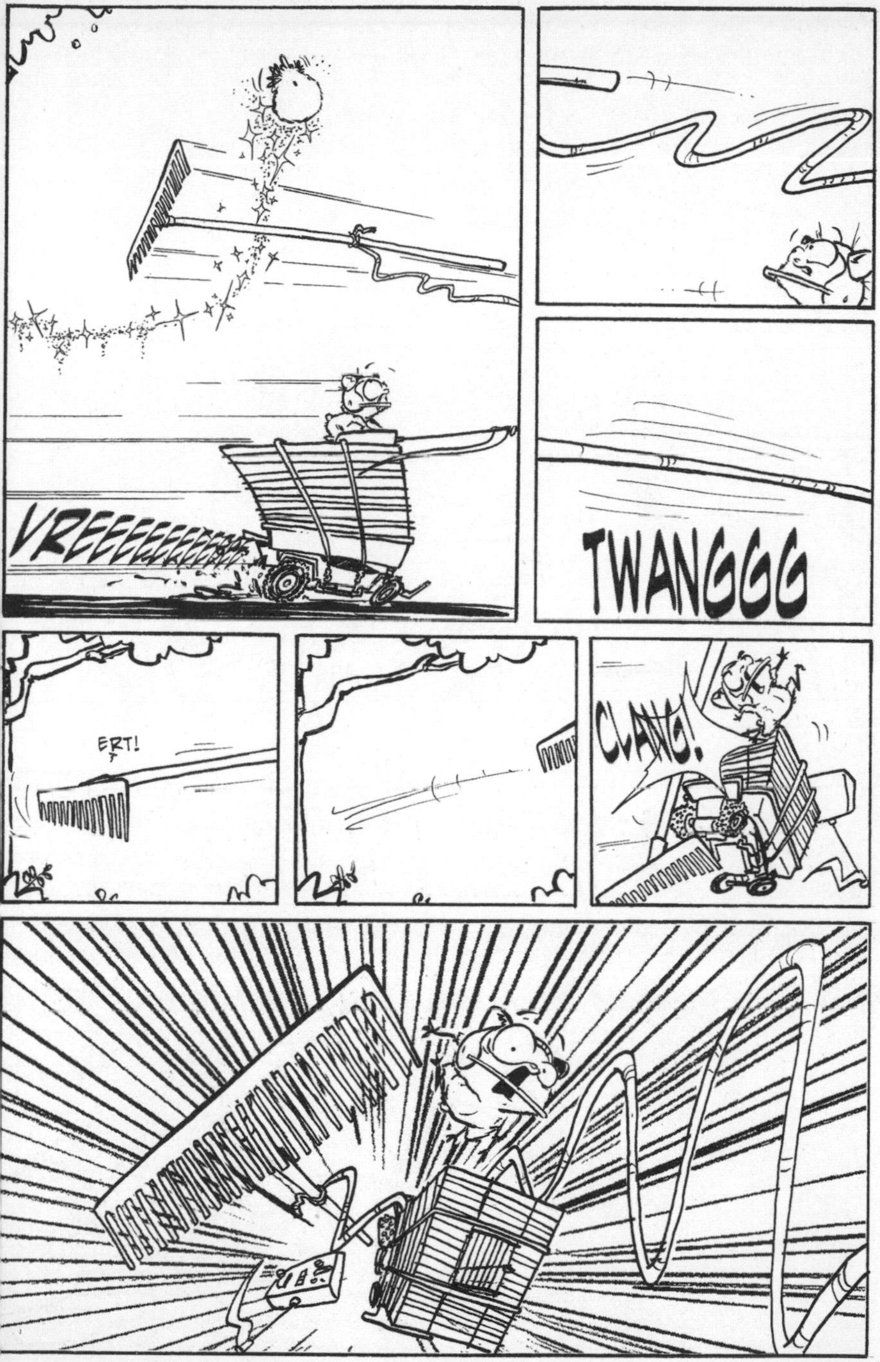
VREEEEEEEEEEE
TWANGGG
ERT!
CLANG!

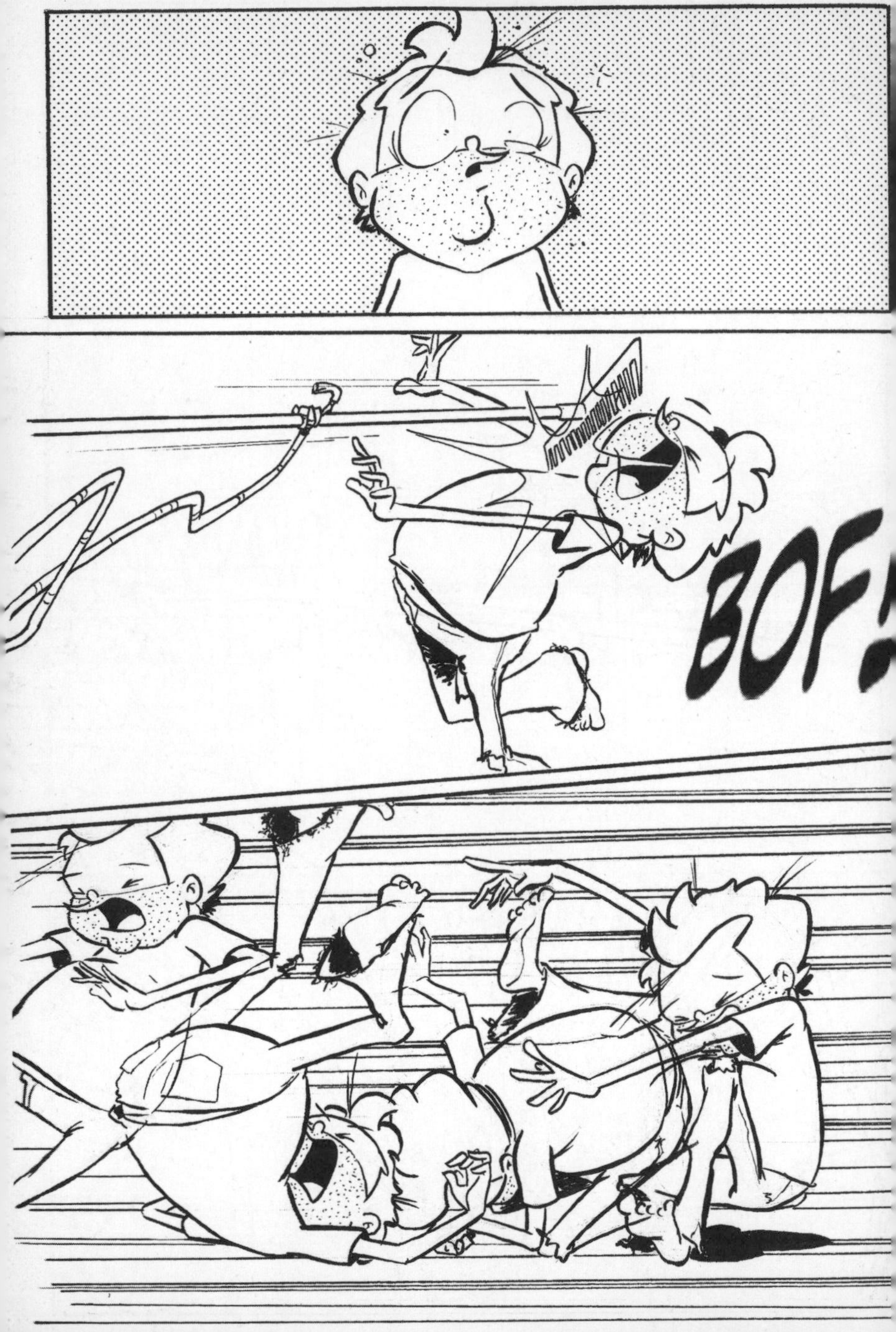
BOF!

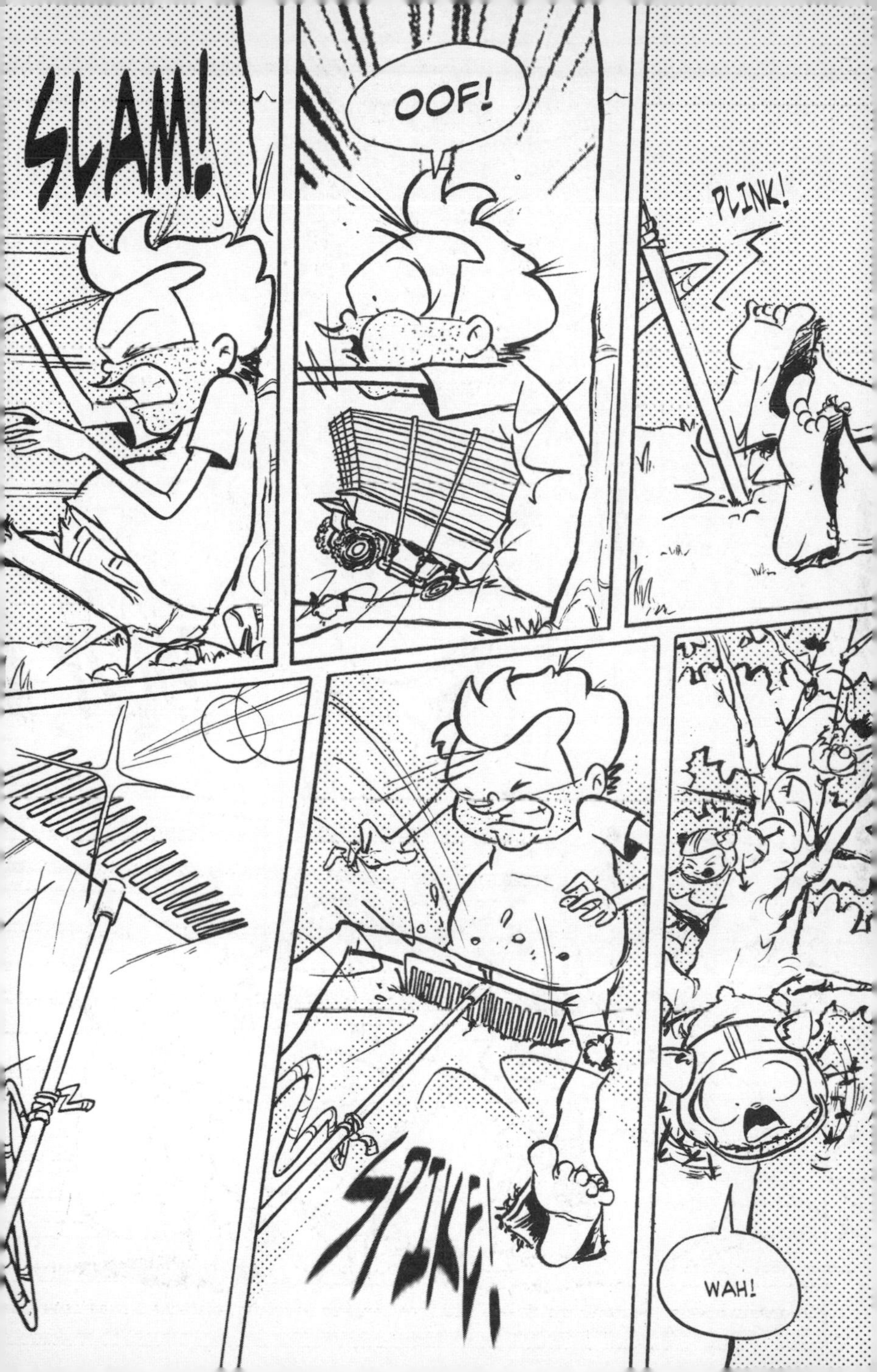
SLAM!
OOF!
PLINK!
SPIKE!
WAH!

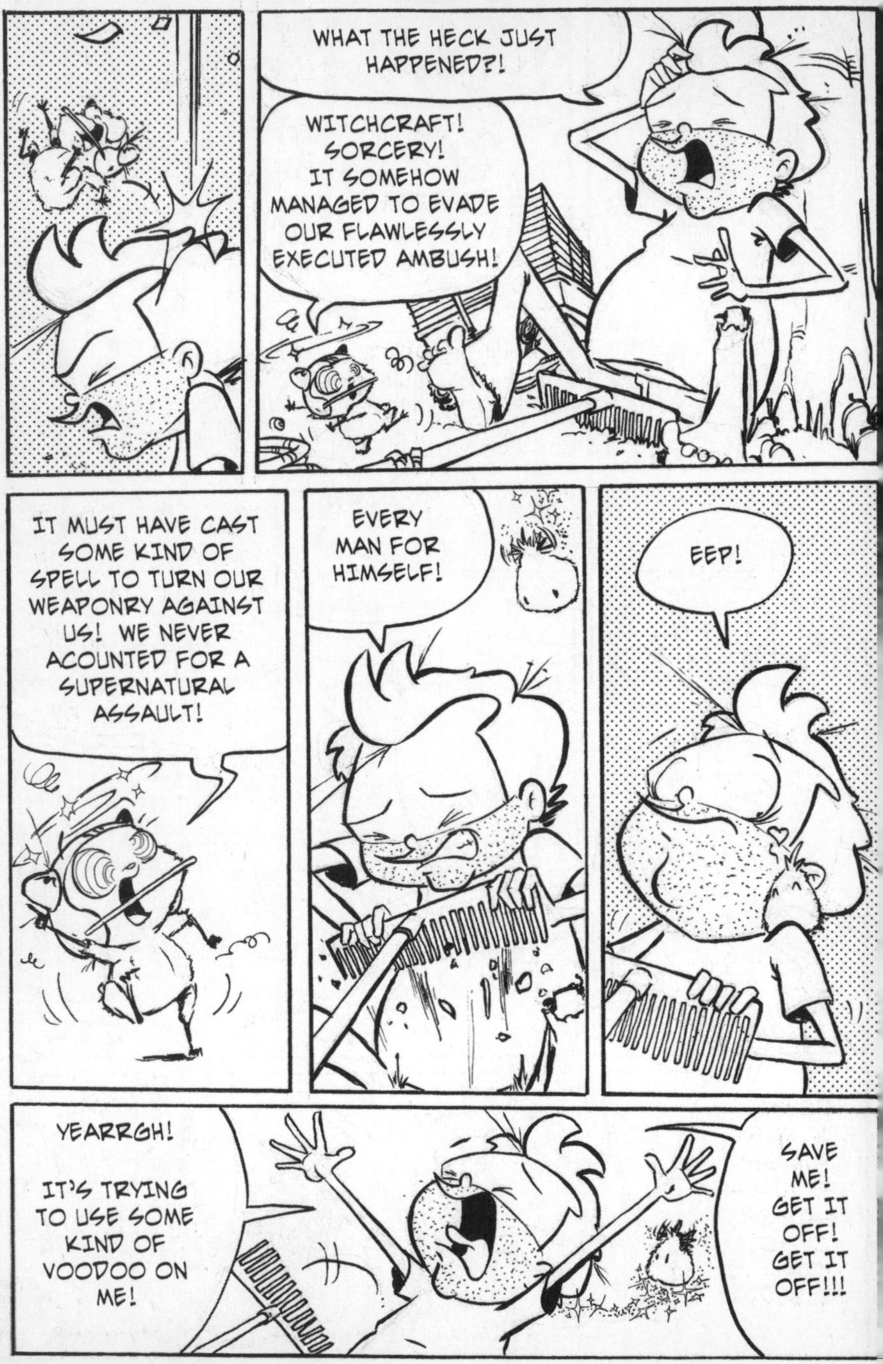
WHAT THE HECK JUST HAPPENED?!
WITCHCRAFT! SORCERY! IT SOMEHOW MANAGED TO EVADE OUR FLAWLESSLY EXECUTED AMBUSH!
IT MUST HAVE CAST SOME KIND OF SPELL TO TURN OUR WEAPONRY AGAINST US! WE NEVER ACOUNTED FOR A SUPERNATURAL ASSAULT!
EVERY MAN FOR HIMSELF!
EEP!
YEARRGH!
IT'S TRYING TO USE SOME KIND OF VOODOO ON ME!
SAVE ME! GET IT OFF! GET IT OFF!!!

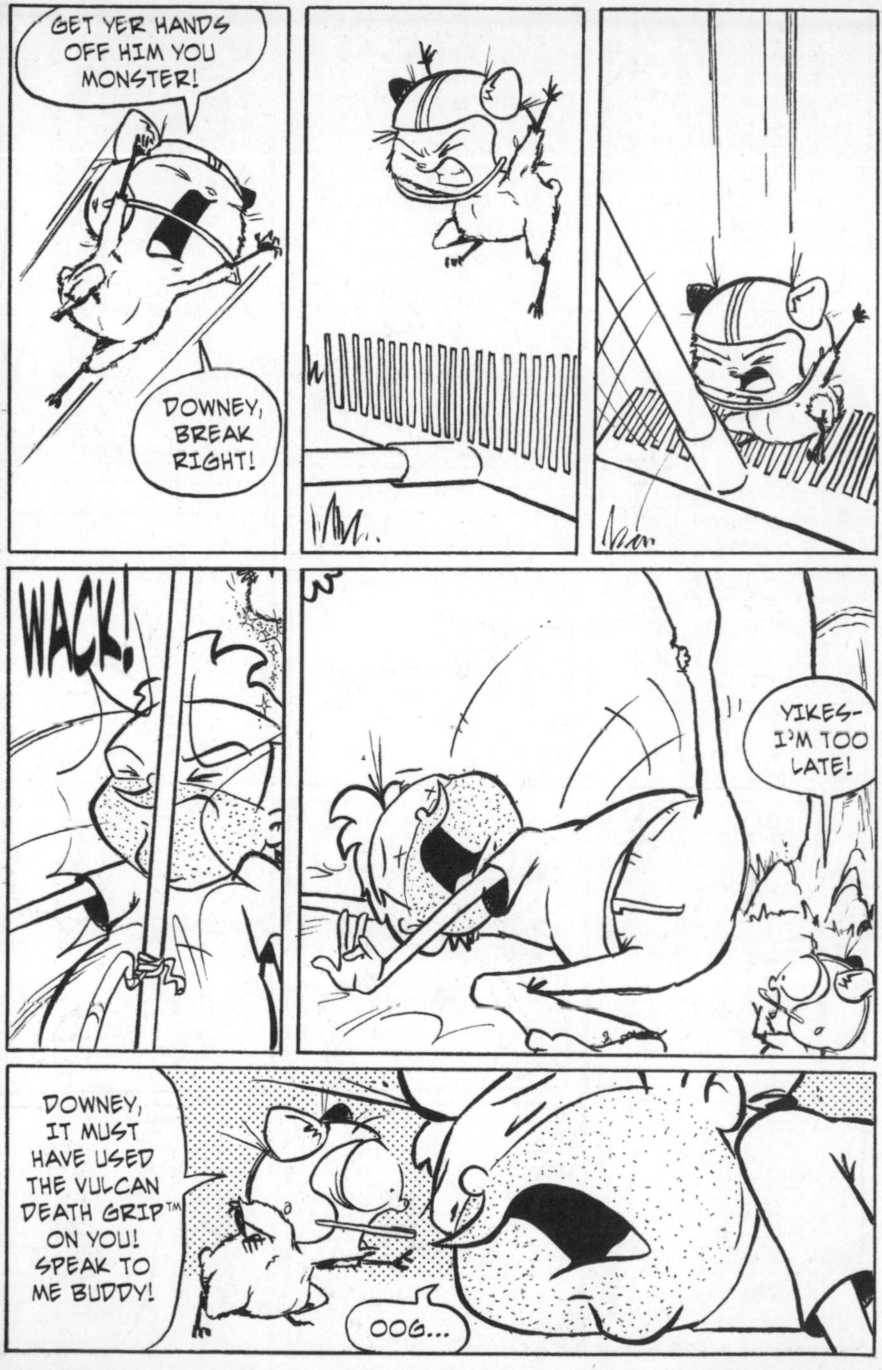
GET YER HANDS OFF HIM YOU MONSTER!
DOWNEY, BREAK RIGHT!
WACK!
YIKES- I'M TOO LATE!
DOWNEY, IT MUST HAVE USED THE VULCAN DEATH GRIP™ ON YOU! SPEAK TO ME BUDDY!
OOG...

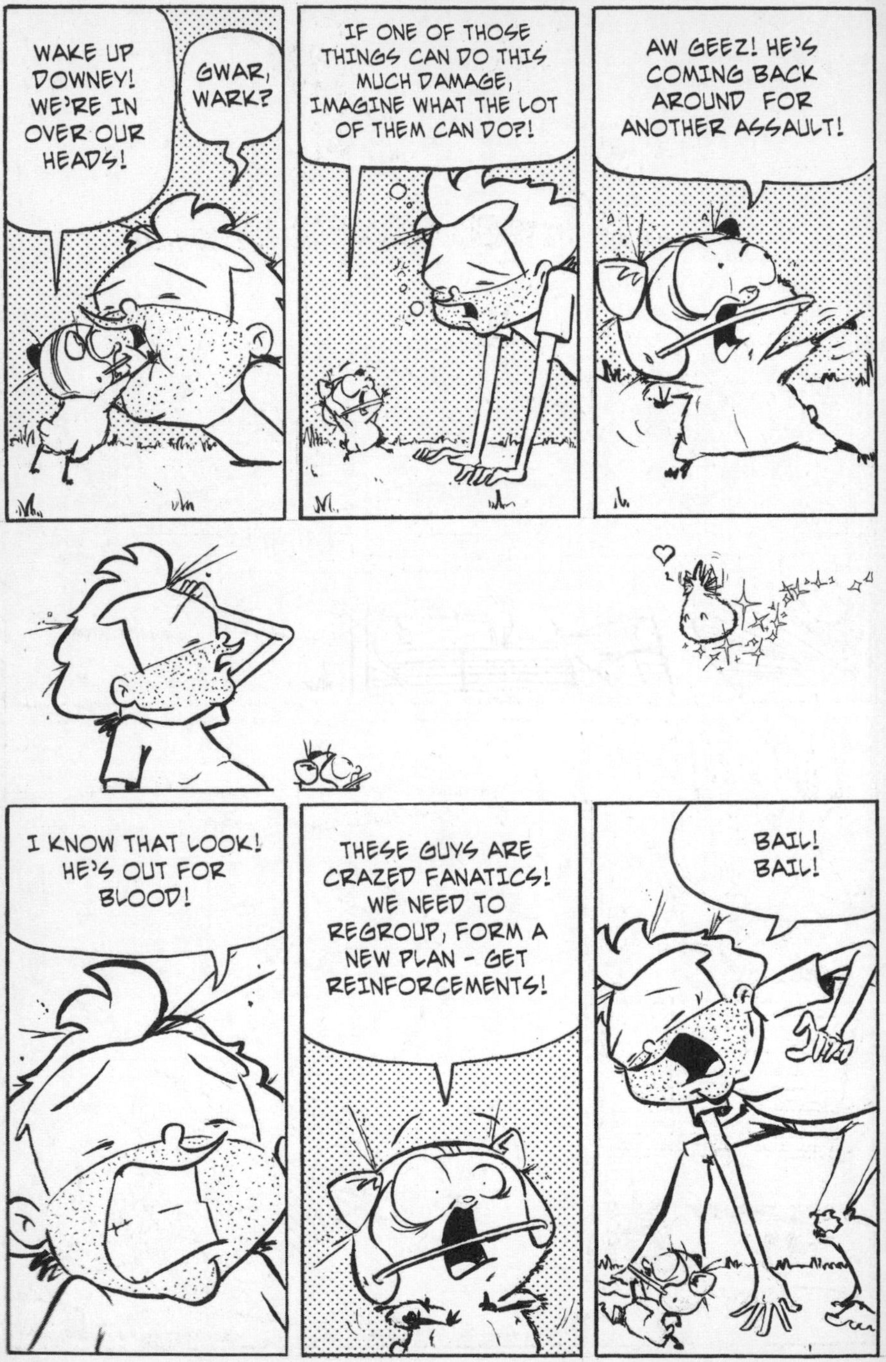
WAKE UP DOWNEY! WE'RE IN OVER OUR HEADS!
GWAR, WARK?
IF ONE OF THOSE THINGS CAN DO THIS MUCH DAMAGE, IMAGINE WHAT THE LOT OF THEM CAN DO?!
AW GEEZ! HE'S COMING BACK AROUND FOR ANOTHER ASSAULT!
I KNOW THAT LOOK! HE'S OUT FOR BLOOD!
THESE GUYS ARE CRAZED FANATICS! WE NEED TO REGROUP, FORM A NEW PLAN - GET REINFORCEMENTS!
BAIL! BAIL!

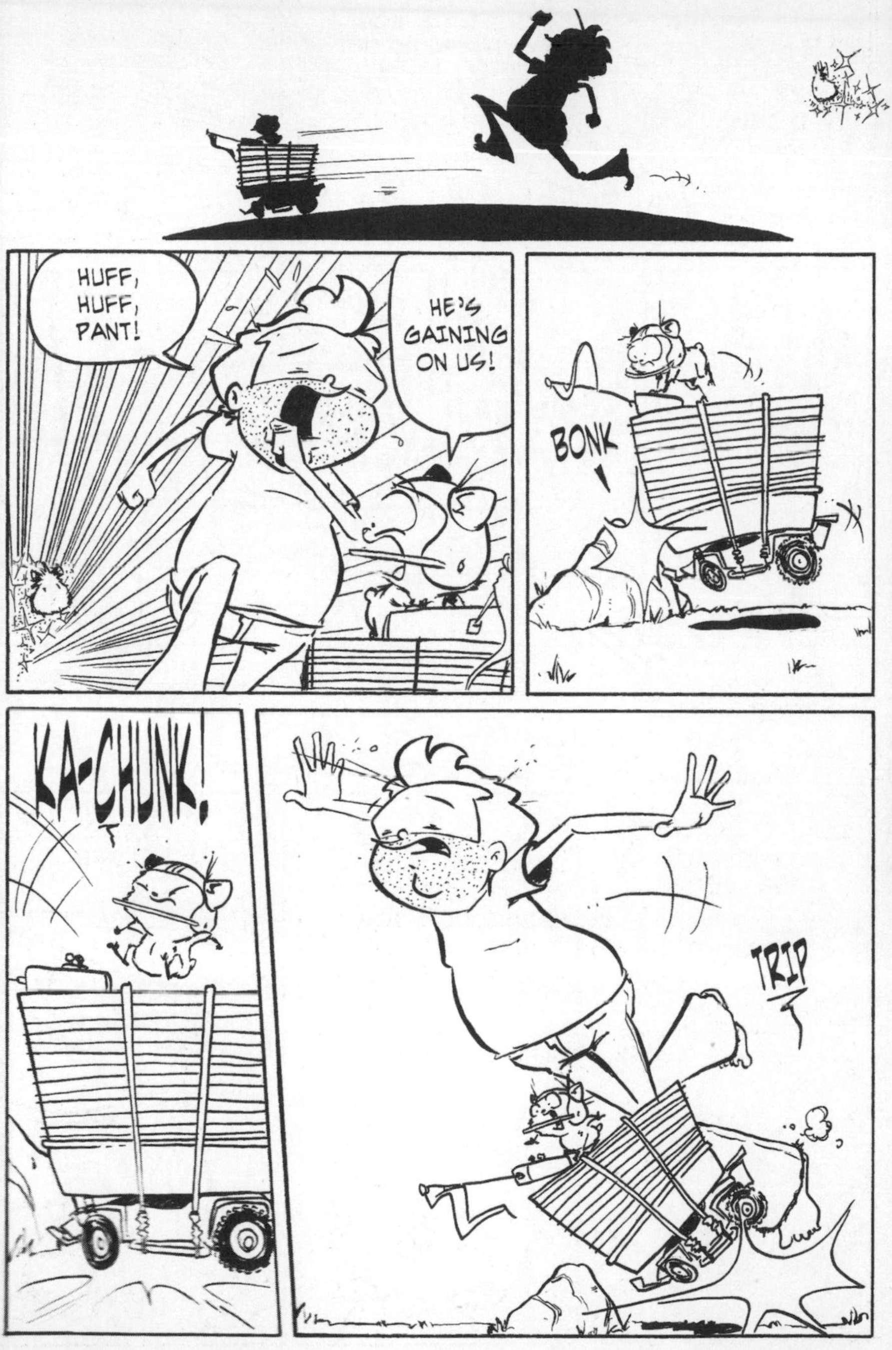
HUFF, HUFF, PANT!
HE'S GAINING ON US!
BONK
KA-CHUNK!
TRIP

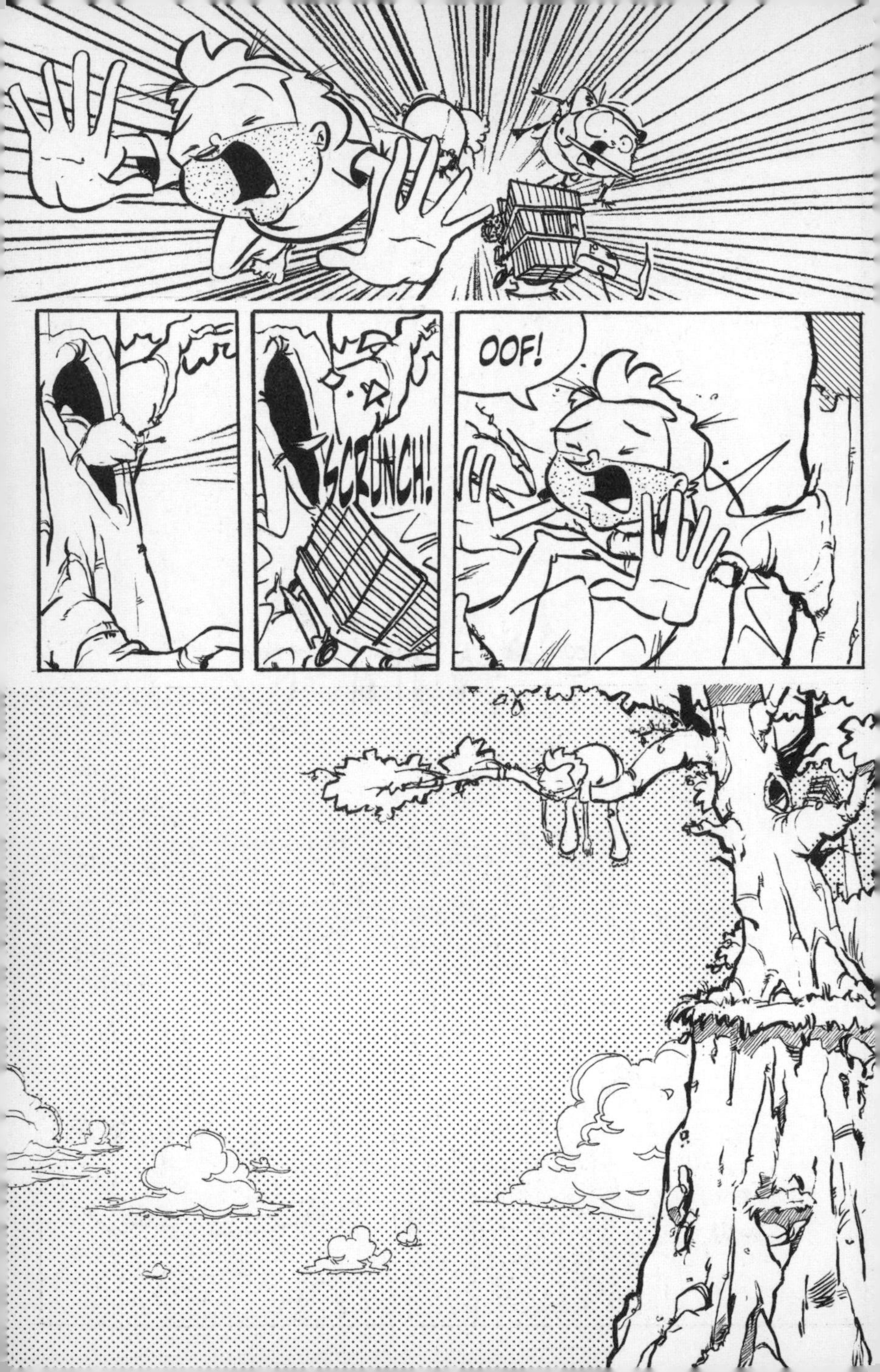
SCRUNCH!
OOF!

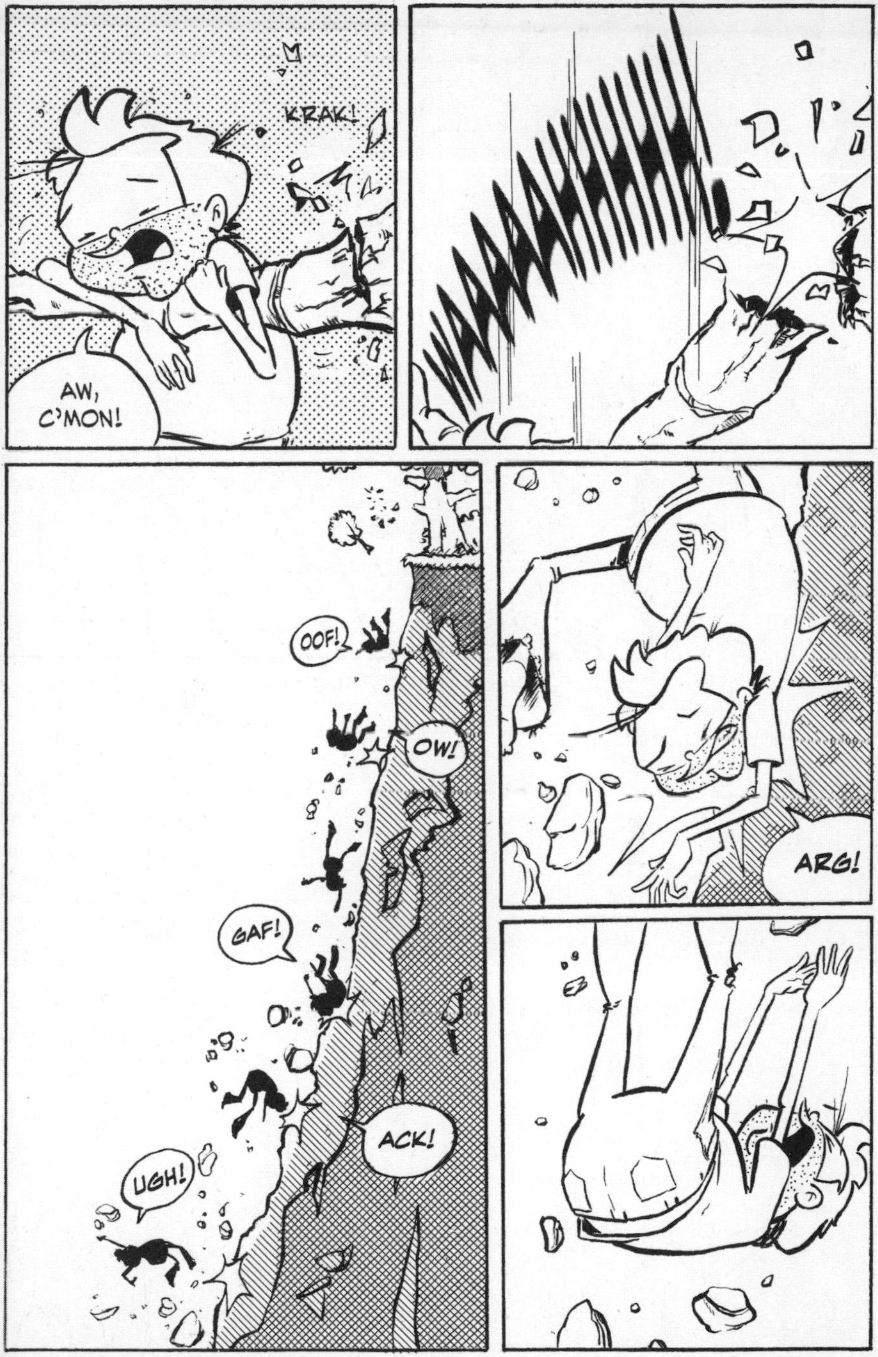
KRAK!
AW, C'MON!
WAAAAHHHHH!
OOF!
OW!
GAF!
ACK!
UGH!
ARG!

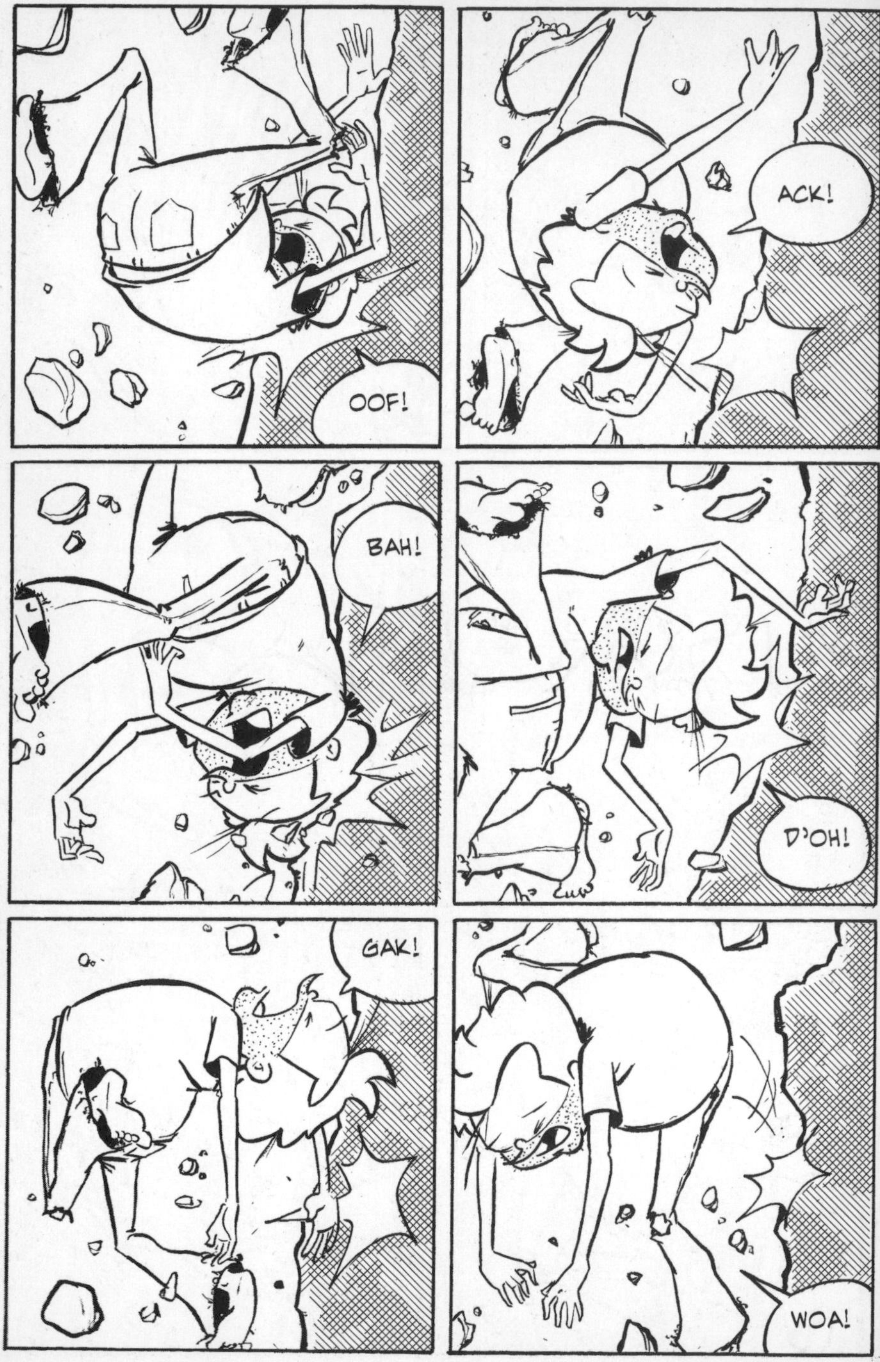
OOF!
ACK!
BAH!
D'OH!
GAK!
WOA!

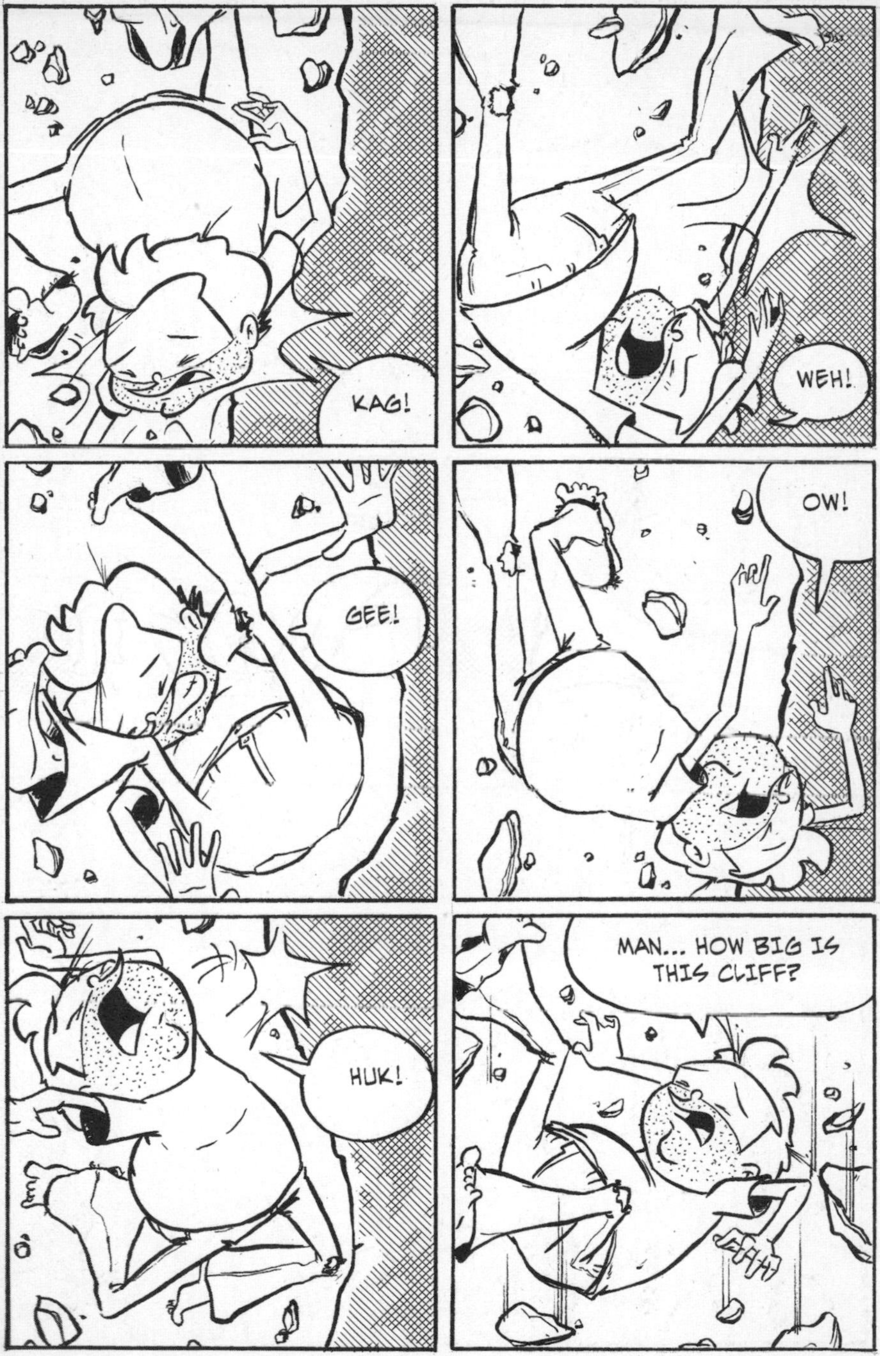
KAG!
WEH!
GEE!
OW!
HUK!
MAN... HOW BIG IS THIS CLIFF?

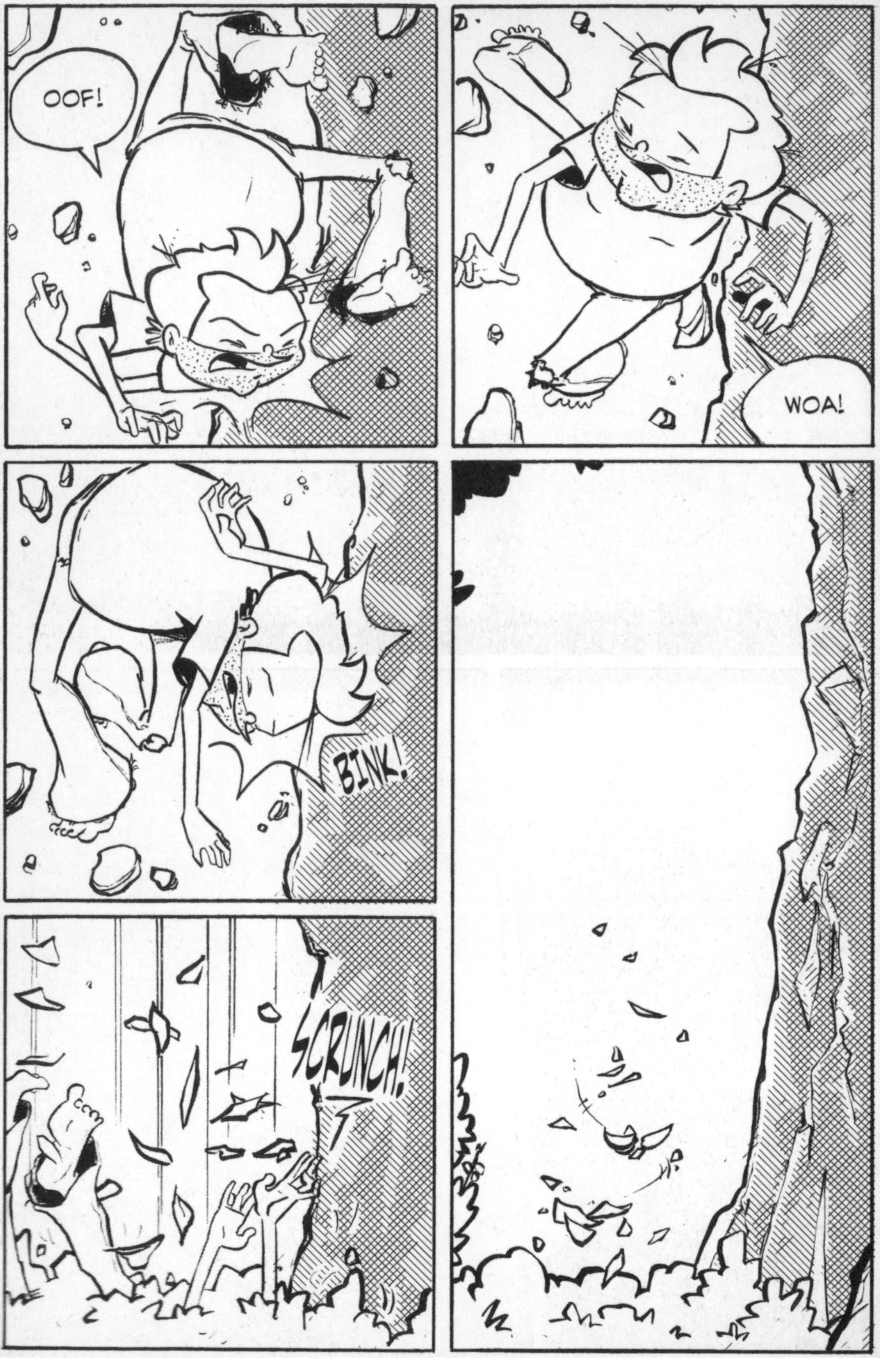
OOF!
WOA!
BINK!
SCRUNCH!

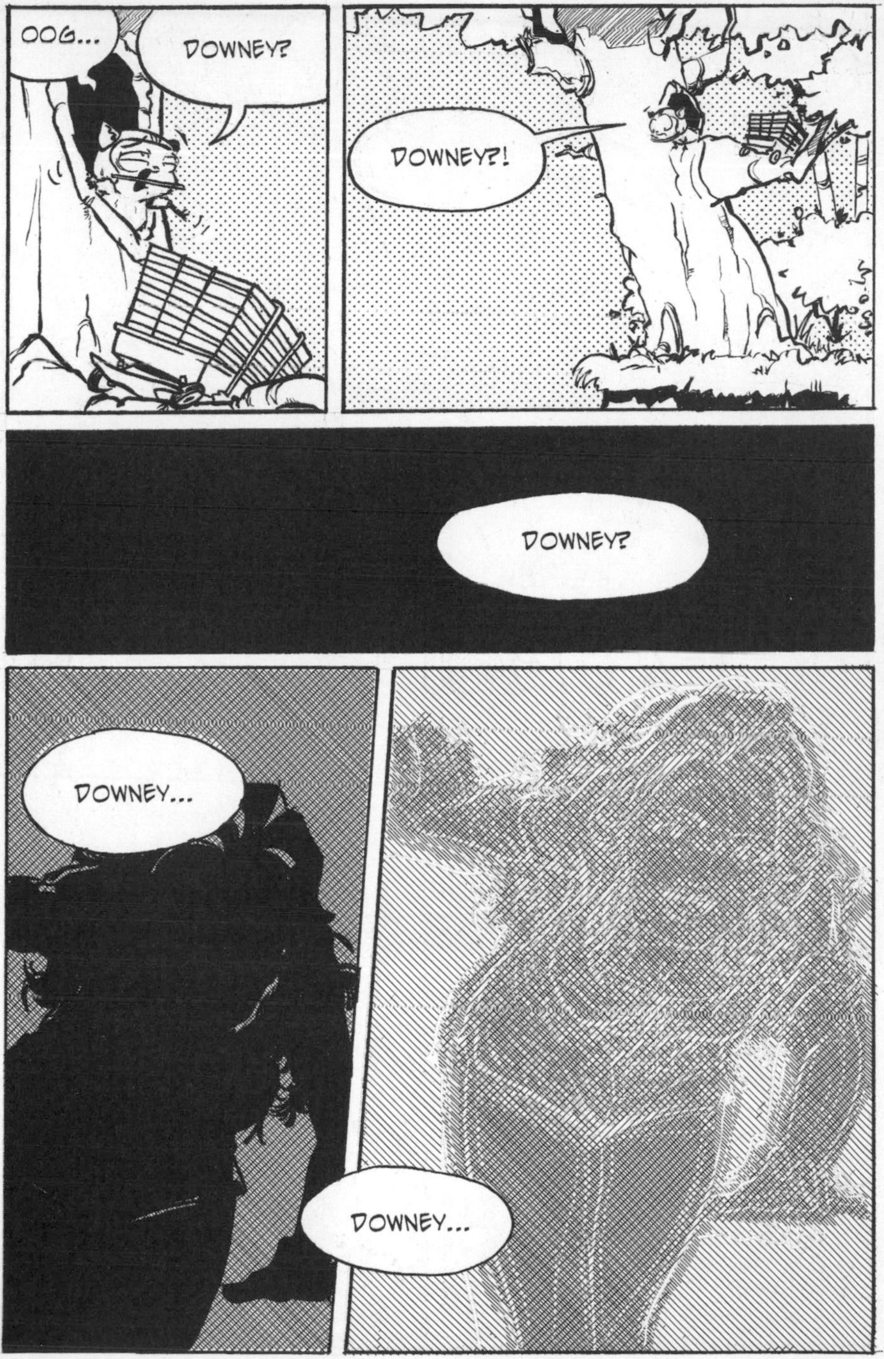
OOG...
DOWNEY?
DOWNEY?!
DOWNEY?
DOWNEY...
DOWNEY...

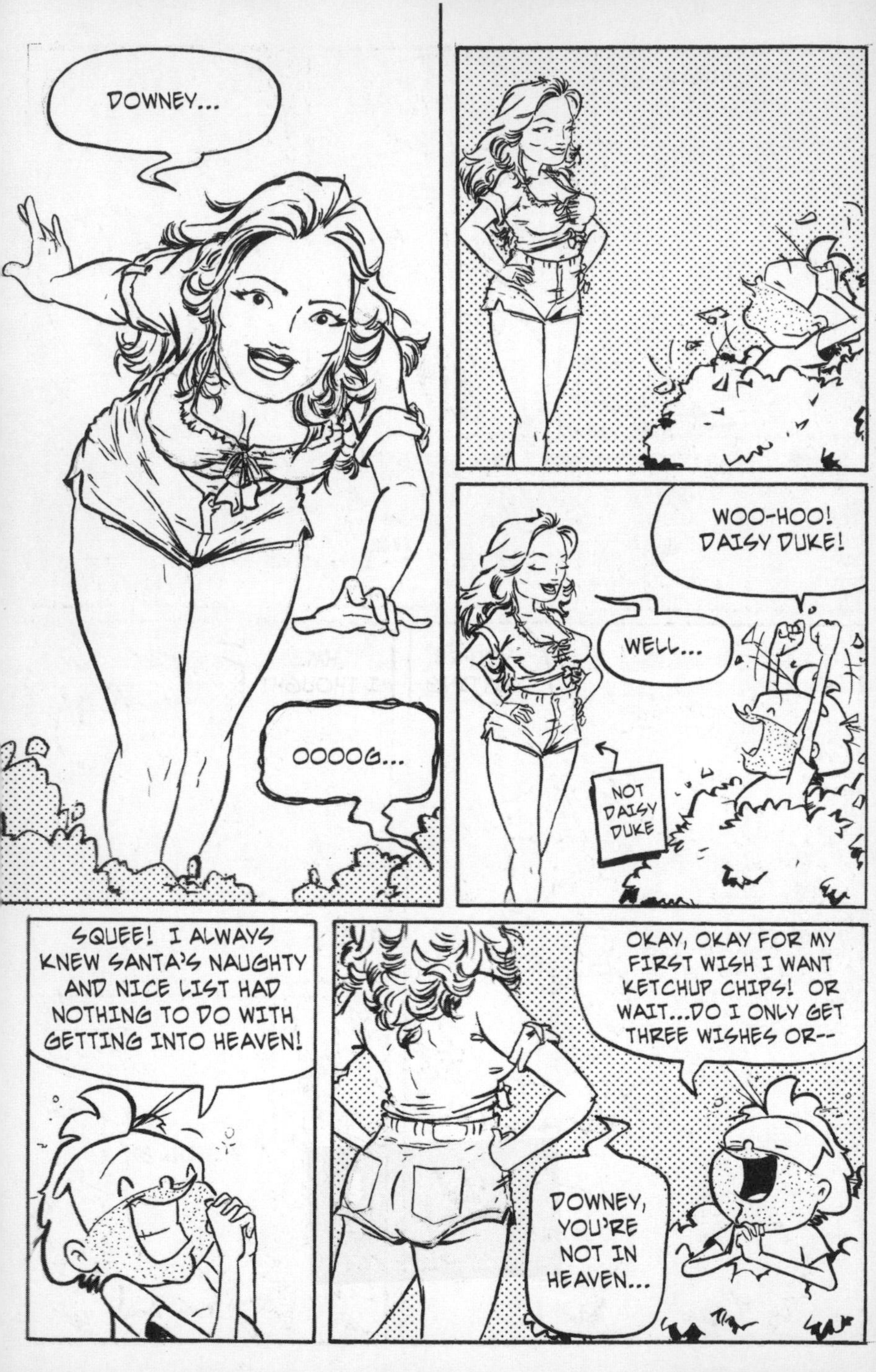
DOWNEY...
OOOOG...
WOO-HOO! DAISY DUKE!
WELL...
NOT DAISY DUKE
SQUEE! I ALWAYS KNEW SANTA'S NAUGHTY AND NICE LIST HAD NOTHING TO DO WITH GETTING INTO HEAVEN!
OKAY, OKAY FOR MY FIRST WISH I WANT KETCHUP CHIPS! OR WAIT...DO I ONLY GET THREE WISHES OR--
DOWNEY, YOU'RE NOT IN HEAVEN...

I HAVE SOMETHING TO TELL YOU...

OKAY!

*SLOW MOTION PANEL

YOU'RE SITTING IN A THORN BUSH

HUH?

HM. I THOUGHT THAT TINGLY SENSATION WAS JUST --

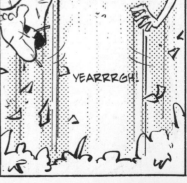

YEARRRGH!

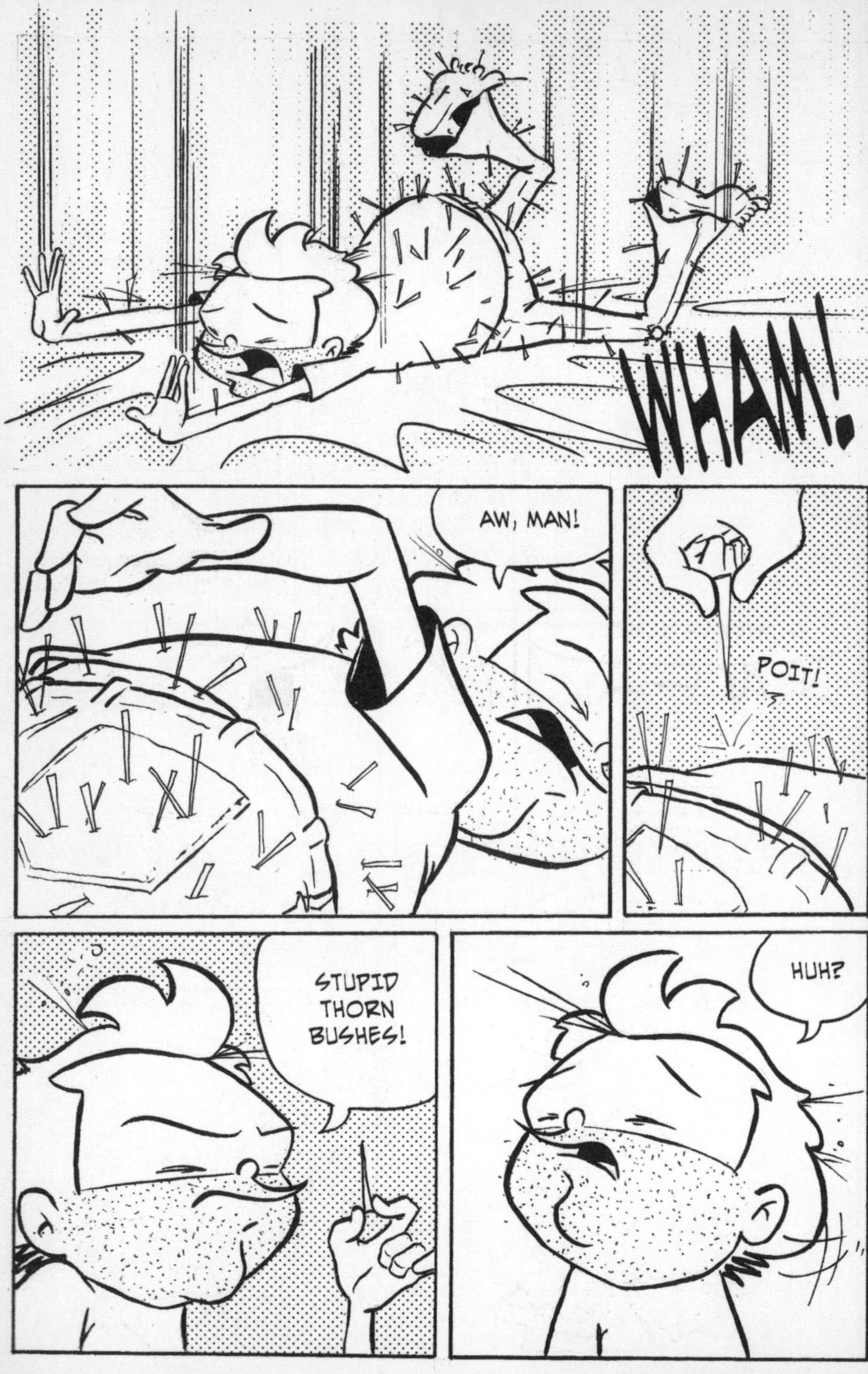
WHAM!
AW, MAN!
POIT!
STUPID THORN BUSHES!
HUH?

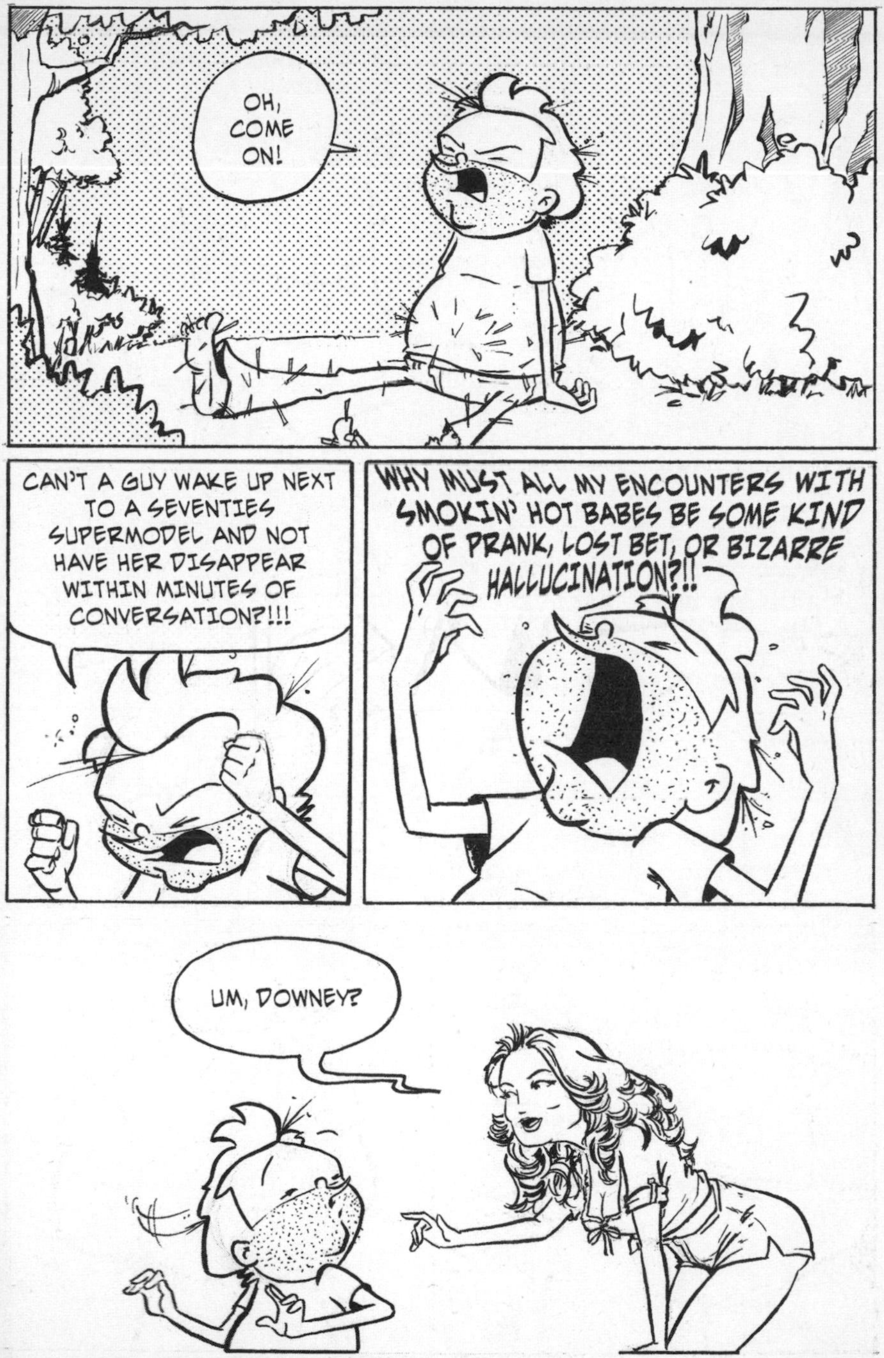
OH, COME ON!
CAN'T A GUY WAKE UP NEXT TO A SEVENTIES SUPERMODEL AND NOT HAVE HER DISAPPEAR WITHIN MINUTES OF CONVERSATION?!!!
WHY MUST ALL MY ENCOUNTERS WITH SMOKIN' HOT BABES BE SOME KIND OF PRANK, LOST BET, OR BIZARRE HALLUCINATION?!!
UM, DOWNEY?

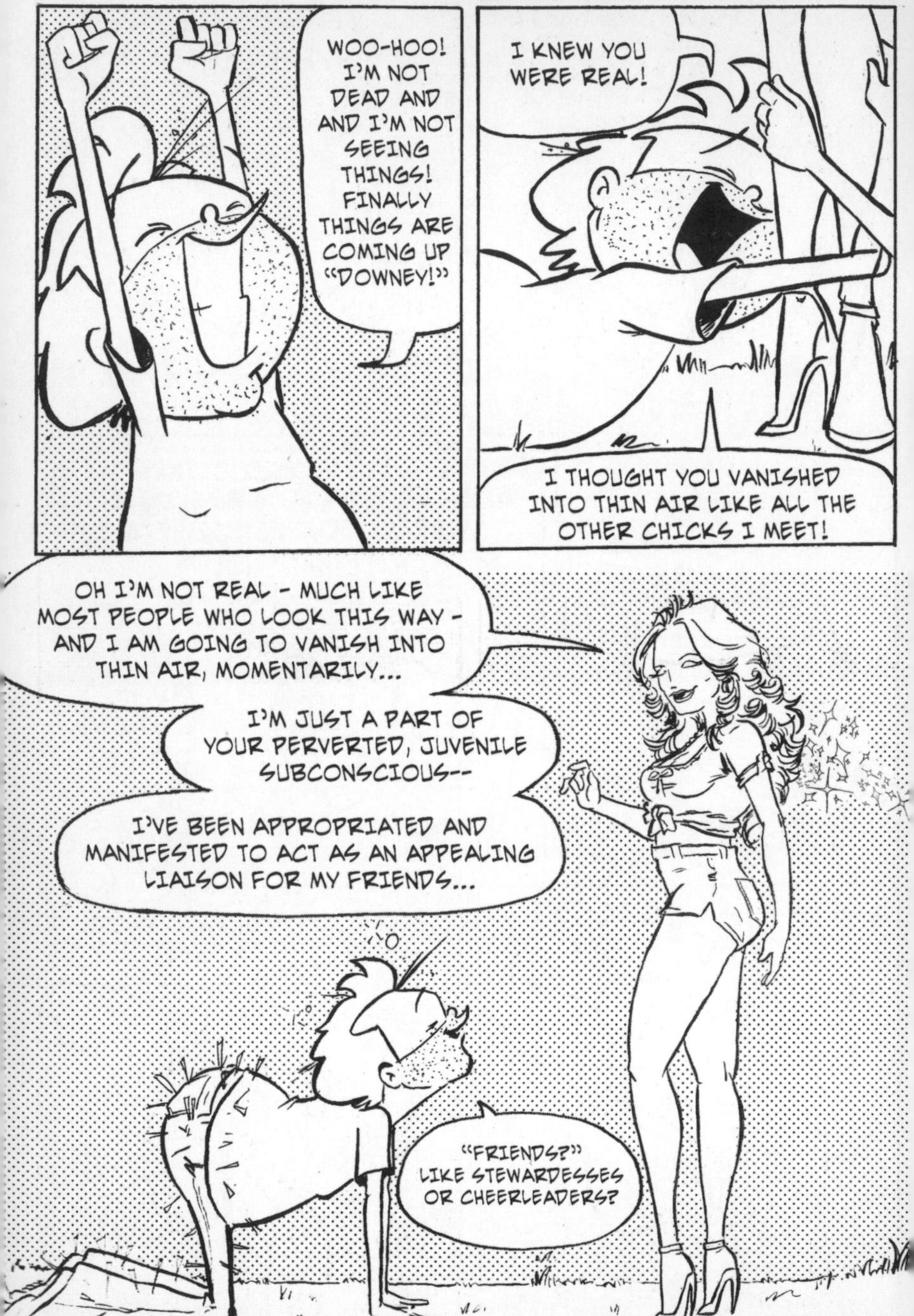
WOO-HOO! I'M NOT DEAD AND AND I'M NOT SEEING THINGS! FINALLY THINGS ARE COMING UP "DOWNEY!"
I KNEW YOU WERE REAL!
I THOUGHT YOU VANISHED INTO THIN AIR LIKE ALL THE OTHER CHICKS I MEET!
OH I'M NOT REAL - MUCH LIKE MOST PEOPLE WHO LOOK THIS WAY - AND I AM GOING TO VANISH INTO THIN AIR, MOMENTARILY...
I'M JUST A PART OF YOUR PERVERTED, JUVENILE SUBCONSCIOUS--
I'VE BEEN APPROPRIATED AND MANIFESTED TO ACT AS AN APPEALING LIAISON FOR MY FRIENDS...
"FRIENDS?" LIKE STEWARDESSES OR CHEERLEADERS?

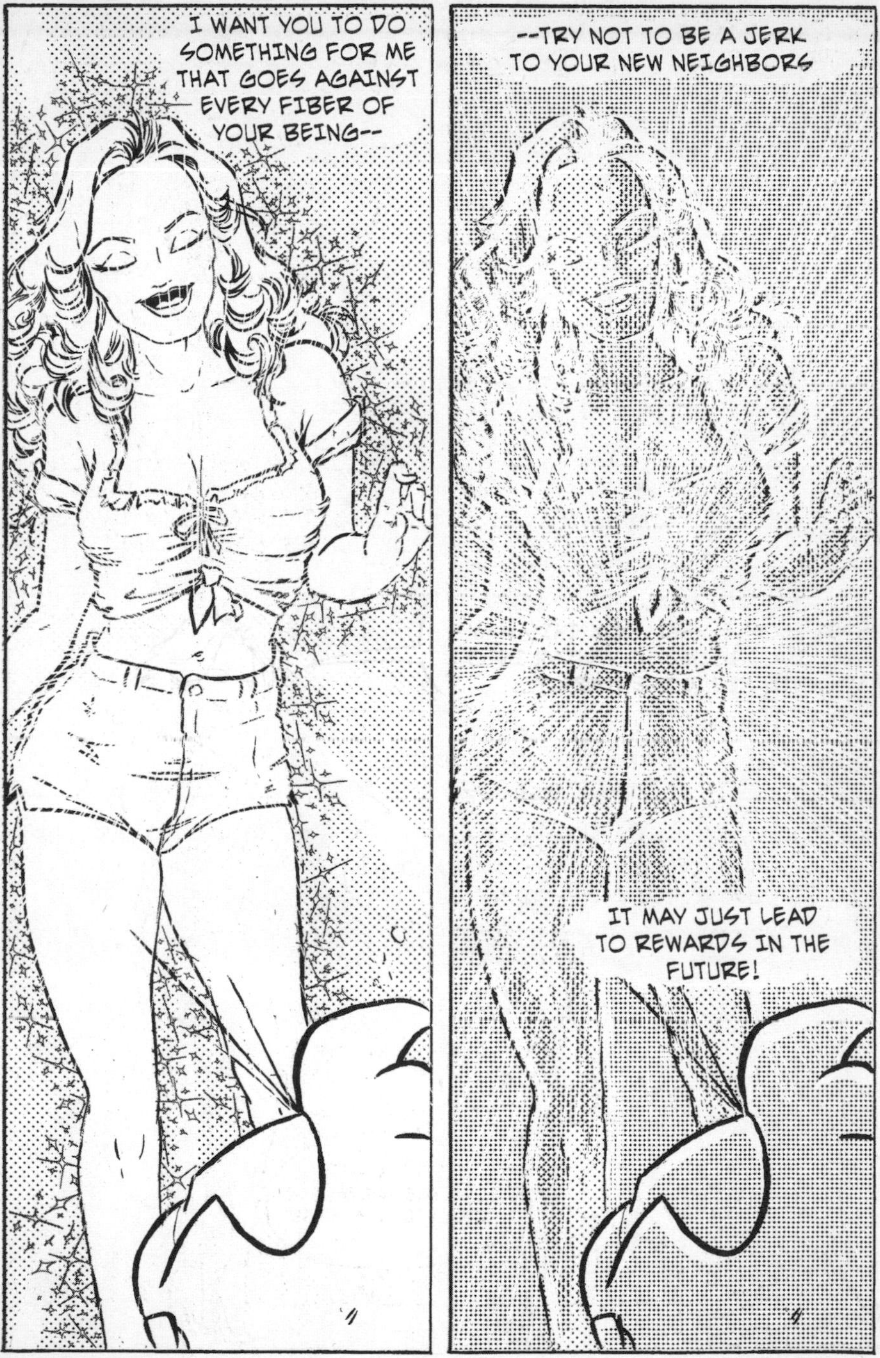
I WANT YOU TO DO SOMETHING FOR ME THAT GOES AGAINST EVERY FIBER OF YOUR BEING--
--TRY NOT TO BE A JERK TO YOUR NEW NEIGHBORS
IT MAY JUST LEAD TO REWARDS IN THE FUTURE!

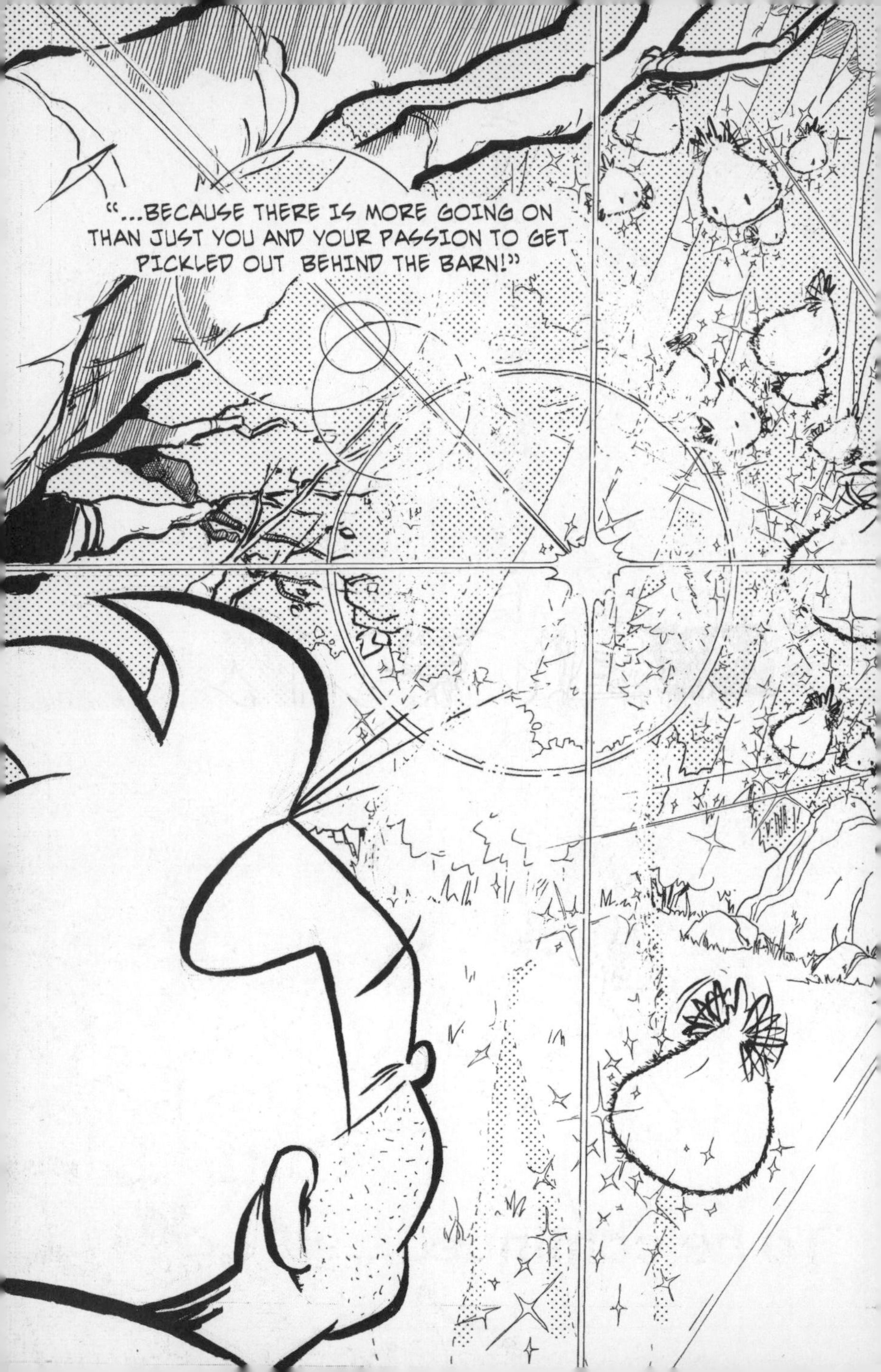
"...BECAUSE THERE IS MORE GOING ON THAN JUST YOU AND YOUR PASSION TO GET PICKLED OUT BEHIND THE BARN!"

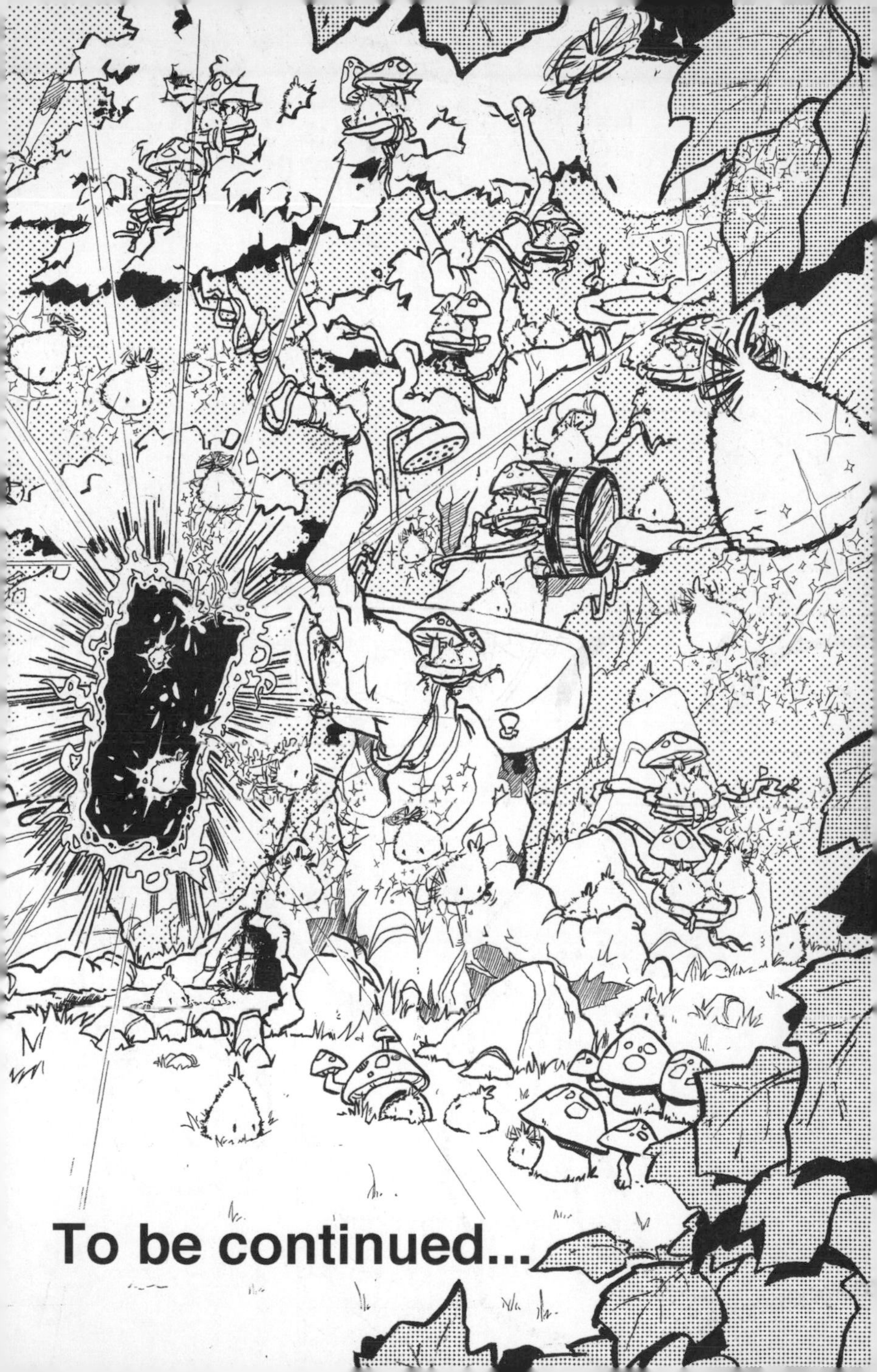
To be continued...

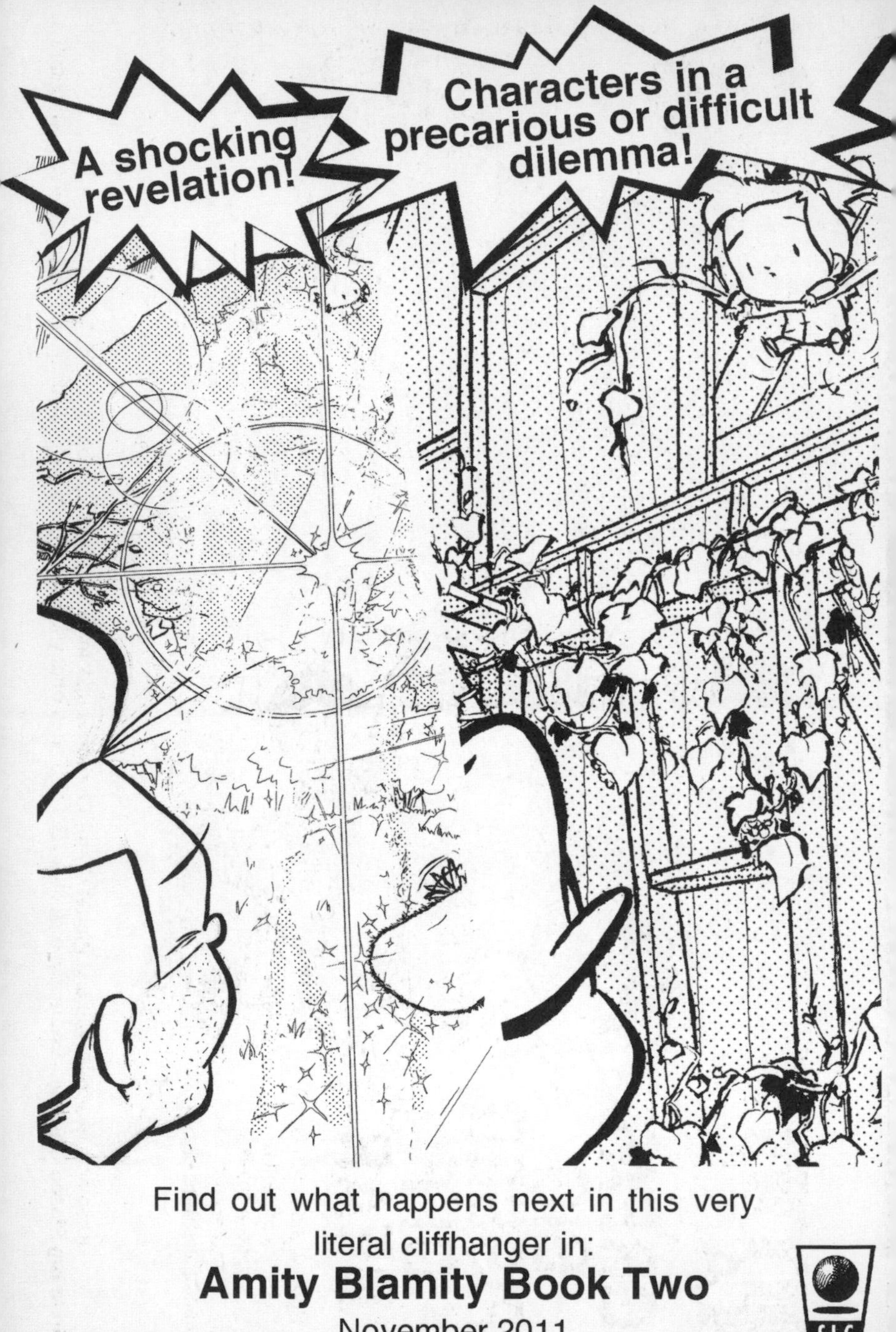
A shocking revelation!
Characters in a precarious or difficult dilemma!

Find out what happens next in this very literal cliffhanger in:

Amity Blamity Book Two

November 2011

Great Big Pissed Off Bear is copyright 2010 Planet Doom Studios.

amity BLAMITY

MEETS:

GREAT
BIG
PISSED
OFF
BEAR

Special Guest Pin-Up
by the brilliant &
super-talented
Matt Wendt
mattroplex.blogspot.com

Keep an eye out for Matt and **Planet Doom Studios** at upcoming comic conventions near you to get your copy of **Great Big Pissed Off Bear**. Get ready to laugh as GBPOB does what you wish you could do to all the stupid people across America!

Author Portrait by Curtis Carey
curtisandtara.blogspot.com

Mike White

Mike White is from Canada. He now lives in San Francisco. He draws comics while the cats are sleeping. This is his first book.

Special Thanks:
Shinyoung Park, Dan Vado, Mom, Dad, Lisa Eastlack, Rachel Keeler, Mr. & Mrs. Keeler, Erin Stein, Emily Brenner, Greg Hyland, J. Torres, Franz De Leon, Chris Butcher, Jim Zubkovich, Ray Long, Matt Wendt, Curtis & Tara, Jonathan Chan, Vincent Kukua, Jana Cook, Marcus Lee, Comic Geek Speak, Indie Spinner Rack, Comic Relief, Mission Comics & Art, Kevin Colabuono, Berkeley Breathed, Bill Watterson, Jeff Smith, Kevin Smith, Scott Mosier, Robert Rodriguez, South Park Studios, Skywalker Ranch, everyone who shared a kind/encouraging word to me along the way, and most especially: Thank YOU, for picking up this book.

Amity Blamity Book One

Creator, Writer, Artist:
Mike White
amityblamity.blogspot.com
twitter.com/mikewhitecomics

Cover design:
Lisa Eastlack
lisa.eastlack@gmail.com

Publisher & Editor:
Dan Vado

SLG Publishing
P.O. Box 26427
San Jose, CA 95159
www.slgcomic.com

Amity Blamity is TM & © Mike White. All rights reserved. No portion of this publication may be reproduced without the permission of Mike White and SLG Publishing, except for purposes of review.